Russia and European Human-Rights Law

Law in Eastern Europe

General Editor

William B. Simons

VOLUME 64

The titles published in this series are listed at *brill.com/laee*

Russia and European Human-Rights Law

The Rise of the Civilizational Argument

Edited by

Lauri Mälksoo

BRILL
NIJHOFF

LEIDEN | BOSTON

Library of Congress Control Number: 2014953395

ISSN 0075-823X
ISBN 978-90-04-20330-3 (hardback)
ISBN 978-90-04-20331-0 (e-book)

This book is printed on acid-free paper.

TABLE OF CONTENTS

Preface

Lauri Mälksoo

I would like to thank the publisher Brill Nijhoff and Professor William B. Simons for suggesting publication of the symposium "Russia and European Human-Rights Law: Progress, Tensions and Perspectives" in a separate book. The symposium was first published as a Special Issue: 37(2-3) *Review of Central and East European Law* (2012). In this *Law in Eastern Europe* volume, the materials of the *RCEEL* Special Issue have been reprinted without amendments. However, with the kind permission of the publisher and the editors, we have here also added to the materials of the symposium a slightly revised version of my article entitled "The Human Rights Concept of the Russian Orthodox Church and Its Patriarch Kirill I: A Critical Appraisal", first published in W. Benedek, F. Benoit-Rohmer, W. Karl, and M. Nowak (eds.), *European Yearbook on Human Rights* (Neuer Wissenschaftlicher Verlag, Vienna, 2013), 403-416.

Moreover, we again would like to acknowledge that research for this volume has been supported by generous grants from the European Research Council, and since 2014, also from the Estonian Research Council.

The main purpose of this new introduction is to update the narrative and to indicate what have been some newest and further developments in the field of human rights in Russia.

If anything, the last one and one-half years have proved the topicality of research on Russia and human-rights law because, in the opinion of many analysts in the media, Russia's official response to the European discourse of human rights—especially to Western criticisms towards Russia—has become more determined, principled and tougher. In some instance, this has resulted in concrete legislative changes. For example, Dorothea Schönfeld's suggestion that the EU should support Russia's genuine civil society rather than count on progress based on the interaction with the government would not work so well these days since Russian NGOs, by a recent legislative initiative, would be labeled as 'foreign agents' when accepting donations from abroad.

In recent years, Moscow's rhetorical reliance on the 'civilizational' argument—*i.e.*, the point that Russia is a different civilization from the West and, therefore, does not need to fully accept Western interpretations of human rights—has been further elaborated and strengthened. This tendency was the main reason underlying our decision also to include in this book project the discussion on Patriarch Kirill I's views on human rights; they amount to nothing less than a direct and quite well thought-through affront to the 'Western' liberal concept of human rights.

Lauri Mälksoo, ed.
Russia and European Human-Rights Law: The Rise of the Civilizational Argument vii-xii

Why does Russia seem to have specific problems in the Council of Europe's human rights protection system? The historically well-established debate on Russia's complex love-hate relationship with Europe continues to be combined with debates on the universality and cultural relativism of human rights. Olesia Zakharova, a sociologist and philosopher from Irkutsk State University, has observed how—in Russia and the West—internal debates on human rights continue to be shaped quite differently. She argues that, in the West, the language of the debates on human rights is, as a rule, rational and "legal" whereas instead in Russia, the language of public officials tends to be based on notions of morality and "justice".[1] Alexander Kovalev, a prominent international-law professor at the Diplomatic Academy in Moscow, has come to the conclusion that the 2006 Orthodox Declaration on Human Rights (discussed in this book in the chapter on Patriarch Kirill I's views) "not only reflects the views of the Church but, also, of a principled position of Russia".[2] At the same time, Professor Kovalev himself supports in principle the universality of human rights.[3]

The discovery that Russia might be a unique Eurasian civilization and that this would have legitimate implications on its understanding of human rights has not been made somewhere at the ideological margins of the Russian society but by individuals at the very heart of the power. For instance, in his recent article celebrating the XX year anniversary of the Russian Constitution, Valerii Zor'kin, Chairman of the Constitutional Court of the Russian Federation, raised a call to study further the historical-civilizational particularities of Russia that would inevitably shape its constitutional interpretations and practices.[4] Zor'kin's overall position on Europe and its human rights protection system is a major ideological balancing act: on the one hand, Zor'kin seems to be in favor of Russia staying in the Strasbourg system while, on the other, he seems to demand that Russia be given as wide a margin of appreciation as possible.[5]

The Chairperson of the State *Duma*'s foreign relations committee, Alexei Pushkov, holds the view that the liberal revolution in the West has entered its "destructive phase"[6] whereas Patriarch Kirill I considers the increasing legalization

1 Olesia Zakharova, "Na raznykh iazykakh", *Nezavisimaia Gazeta* (25 March 2013), available at <http://www.ng.ru/ideas/2013-03-25/9_values.html>. Unless otherwise noted, all translations from the Russian into English in this chapter are by the present author.

2 Aleksandr Kovalev, *Mezhdunarodnaia zashchita prav cheloveka* (Statut, Moscow, 2013), 86.

3 *Ibid.*, 22-23.

4 Valerii Zor'kin, "Konstitutsionnyi vektor Rossii", *Rossiiskaia Gazeta* (19 November 2013), available at <http://www.rg.ru/2013/11/19/posizia.html>.

5 Valerii Zor'kin, *Konstitutsionno-pravovoe razvitie Rossii* (Norma, Moscow, 2011), 414-440.

6 Konstantin Volkov, "Liberal'naia revoliutsiia na Zapade pereshla v razrushitel'nuiu fazu", *Izvestiia* (21 December 2013), available at <http://izvestia.ru/news/562933>.

of same-sex marriages in the West to be an "apocalyptic symptom".[7] These are the *gosudarstvenniki* in the Russian political-legal system for whom state sovereignty is the supreme principle and who, as a consequence, reject the "exaggerated" individualist interpretations of human rights. In particular, LGBT rights seem to have become a symbol in Russia of what has gone wrong with Western concepts of human rights. Historically, this is not all too surprising in a country where homosexual acts ("*pederastiia*") were criminalized until only twenty-five years ago.

Dissatisfaction with the West has triggered proposals for constitutional change in Russia. For example, State *Duma* deputy Evgenii Fedorov from the governing "United Russia" fraction recently has suggested that the Russian constitutional law and practice have been moved out of balance in favor of international (and European human-rights) law and that the Constitutional Court Act should be amended to establish the supremacy of the domestic-constitutional interpretation of human-rights law.[8] However, some opposition politicians see this as the Kremlin's antagonistic response to the Russian government's defeats in the Strasbourg system and increasing rejection of the ultimate compulsory nature of the Court's jurisprudence.[9]

The same deputy, Fedorov, also has suggested amending the Russian Constitution to strike out the prohibition of state ideology from the current version.[10] Other Russian activist analysts have suggested that Russia should write altogether a new, Orthodox constitution—partly because the Russian state as such is at least as important a value as human rights and, also, because the current constitution places too much emphasis on human rights.[11] Given that Russia—since the Soviet period—has a history of "symmetric ideological responses" to the West, the State *Duma* in late 2012 started to review surveys on human rights situation in the US and the EU, prepared by the Commissioner of Human Rights at the Russian Ministry for Foreign Affairs, Konstantin Dolgov.[12]

7 "Patriarkh Kirill: Legalizatsiia odnopolykh brakov – apokalipticheskii simptom", *Grani.ru* (22 July 2013), available at <http://grani.ru/Politics/Russia/m.217100.html>.

8 Elena Teslova, "Resheniia ESPCh perestanut byt' obiazatel'nymi dlia rossiiskikh sudov", *Izvestiia* (24 December 2013), available at <http://izvestia.ru/news/563034>.

9 *Ibid.*

10 Elena Malai, "V Gosdume khotiat iskliuchit' punkt konstitutsii o zaprete gosideologii", *Izvestiia* (29 November 2013), available at <http://izvestia.ru/news/561554>. See, also, <http://www.ng.ru/news/450884.html>.

11 Stepan Sulakshin, "Konstitutsiiu Rossii nado meniat' radikal'no", *Nezavisimaia Gazeta* (6 December 2013), available at <http://www.ng.ru/ideas/2013-12-06/5_constitution.html>. See, also, the editorial "Rolevye igry s konstitutsiei", *Nezavisimaia Gazeta* (27 November 2013), available at <http://www.ng.ru/editorial/2013-11-27/2_red.html>.

12 Elena Chernenko, "Nekto ne mozhet byt' obraztsom demokratii. Upolnomochennyi MID RF po pravam cheloveka o problemakh s demokratiei v SShA", *Kommersant* (29 October 2012), available at <http://www.kommersant.ru/doc/2055389>; Sofiia Samokhina *et al.*, "MID zachital Amerike ee poprannye prava", *Kommersant* (23 October 2012), available

Of course, considering that nothing concrete so far came out of another deputy's (Mr. Torshin) suggested amendments, discussed in the 2012 *Review of Central and East European Law* (RCEEL) Special Issue, it is also possible that "tough" statements—which take rhetorical distance from the European discourse of human rights and its criticism on Russia—are a particular Russian way of letting off political steam. Perhaps such statements and proposals are not even meant to lead to any concrete legislative changes but, rather, to make the situation more digestible to wide segments of the Russian population which believe that "order" in the country is more important value than "human rights". According to a 2013 survey of the Levada Center, the percentage of the Russians who think that "order" is more important than "human rights" (in itself a peculiar question to ask) has increased to 55.[13]

In terms of the state practice, the following tendencies have been noteworthy over the past two years. In the conclusion to the *RCEEL* Special Issue, I had alluded—by way of general background of international legal developments—to Russia's forthcoming accession to WTO which, indeed, happened in August 2012. However, this has not meant that the EU and Russia have stopped discussing the permissibility of protectionist measures; in a recent survey, German exporters specifically singled out restrictions to trade in the Russian Federation.[14] In terms of state compliance, parallels between international trade law and European human-rights law are suggesting themselves.

Most significantly in the context of European human-rights law, on 6 December 2013, Russia's Constitutional Court finally gave its response in the *Markin* case which contains both conciliatory tones and, at the same time, sets new limits *vis-à-vis* the ECtHR.[15] In substantive terms, the Constitutional Court accepted the conclusions of the ECtHR in *Markin*; yet, it also determined that, in the future, it will itself decide on how such judgments issued in Strasbourg—and colliding with St. Petersburg's own previous rulings—would be implemented in

at <http://www.kommersant.ru/doc/2050786>; Iurii Paniev, "MID RF vzialsia za prava cheloveka v Evrosoiuze", *Nezavisimaia Gazeta* (6 December 2012), available at <http://www.ng.ru/world/2012-12-06/7_prava.html>; and Elena Chernenko, "Rossiia sravnit demokratiiu s obraztsami", *Kommersant* (14 May 2012), available at <http://www.kommersant.ru/doc/1933351>.

13 Levada Tsentr, "Vse bol'she rossiian schitaet, chto poriadok v strane vazhnee prav cheloveka", *Grani.ru* (25 September 2013), available at <http://grani.ru/Politics/Russia/m.219352.html>. Over the prior five years, the percentage had increased from 51% to 55% of the adult population.

14 *Going International. Erfahrungen und Perspektiven der deutschen Wirtschaft im Auslandsgeschäft*, Deutscher Industrie- und Handelskammertag (DIHK) 2013-2014, available at <http://www.dihk.de/themenfelder/international/aussenwirtschaftspolitik-recht/umfragen-und-zahlen/going-international>.

15 Postanovlenie Konstitutsionnoga Suda Rossiiskoi Federatsii (6 December 2013), No.27-P/2013, available at <http://www.ksrf.ru/ru/Decision/Pages/default.aspx>.

Russia.[16] Good news for Russian-European cooperation in human-rights law is that Anatolii Kovler, the former Russian-elected judge in the ECtHR, recently has joined the Russian Constitutional Court as a counselor. Most likely, he will provide the Russian Constitutional Court with "insider information" on how the ECtHR functions and thinks and, at least, inform the Constitutional Court justices in St. Petersburg about potential collisions with Strasbourg. Whether or not to follow this advice 'directly from Europe' remains something which Chief Justice Zor'kin and his colleagues at the Constitutional Court will have to decide.

In another case, this time involving the Supreme Court of the Russian Federation, policy analysts have already lamented Russia's first case of dismissal of a Strasbourg judgment.[17] In reality, it was not a clear case of non-compliance but, simply, an example of how Moscow and Strasbourg increasingly think and act differently on human-rights violations. The case concerns Alexei Pichugin, the imprisoned former security chief of the company Yukos. In fall 2012, the ECtHR found that in the criminal case against Pichugin, the Russian government had committed a number of violations of the ECHR, including failure to hold a public hearing and to offer sufficient opportunities to Pichugin to challenge incriminatory testimony.[18] One year later, in 2013, the Russian Supreme Court upheld the life sentence of Pichugin, refusing to amend the sentence.[19] This amounted to the awkward situation where—after a negative judgment of the ECtHR—Russia would pay compensation for serious violations of criminal procedure norms and standards but refuse to touch the very sentence that came about partly as a consequence of those violations of criminal procedure law. In this way, Russia's highest courts have started to test the limits of political patience in the Strasbourg system.

However, altogether, it is noteworthy that individual complaints from the Russian Federation have slightly decreased over the last two years although experts

16 Anna Pushkarskaia, 'Konstitutsionnyi sud uravnial sebia s evropeiskim", *Kommersant* (7 December 2013), <http://kommersant.ru/doc/2363210>. See, also, "KS budet samostoiatel'no reshat' vopros o primenimosti postanovlenii ESPCh", *Rossiiskaia Gazeta* (6 December 2013), available at <http://rg.ru/2013/12/06/ks-anons.html>.

17 Andrei Malgin, "Putin's Law", *Project Syndicate* (17 December 2013), available at <http://www.project-syndicate.org/commentary/andrei-malgin-on-russia-s-increasing-rejection-of-its-international-legal-commitments>.

18 *Pichugin v. Russia* (Judgment of 23 October 2012; final on 18 March 2013), Application No.38623/03.

19 "Russia Defies European Court over Former Yukos Exec Pichugin", *RFE/RL* (23 October 2013), available at <http://www.rferl.org/content/pichugin-russia-supreme-court/25146195.html>. The Court's judgment is: Postanovlenie Prezidiuma Verkhovnogo Suda RF (23 October 2013) No.141-P13S, "O vozobnovlenii proizvodstva po ugolovnomu delu vvidu novykh obstoiatel'stva" (not officially published according to the "Consultant Plus" database note on this decision), available at <http://base.consultant.ru/cons/cgi/online.cgi?req=doc;base=ARB;n=365719>.

are not yet sure why this has come about.[20] One reason might be that Russian lawyers have started to understand that the jurisdiction of the ECtHR will not be established easily and have stopped bombing Strasbourg with applications "just in case".

To sum up: concerning main developments in human rights and Russia, civilizational rhetoric is increasingly used among the Russian political elite as a shield against human-rights criticisms from the "liberal West". The doctrine of Russia's civilizational uniqueness—in front of our very eyes—is evolving into Russia's own official idiosyncratic "margin of appreciation doctrine" *vis-à-vis* the Council of Europe and the European Court of Human Rights. Considering Russia's history and geography—in some ways—this makes sense. However, what makes sense for Europe which once created the Council of Europe and its human rights protection system? Who will 'civilize' whom? The unwillingness to deal with this fundamental question may lead to the conclusion that the Emperor has no clothes. Compared to its Cold-War era predecessor, the ECtHR has possibly become an inter-civilizational phenomenon. This comes with costs. The coming years will tell whether the Russian Federation's participation in the ECtHR will lead to a significant ideological and juridical break among the key actors or, perhaps unexpectedly, still to a wider convergence from "Lisbon to Vladivostok".

Tartu,
January 2014

20 Aleksandra Samarina, "Rossiiane stali rezhe zhalovat'sia Evrope", *Nezavisimaia Gazeta* (6 February 2013), available at <http://www.ng.ru/politics/2013-02-06/2_strasbourg.html>.

Foreword

Angelika Nussberger

Every collective work presenting research results can be seen as an offer of dialogue. It might be a one-sided dialogue with readers tacitly approving of or rejecting the author's views, or it might be an initiative for exchange calling upon readers to react. This volume in the series *Law in Eastern Europe*, "Russia and European Human-Rights Law: The Rise of the Civilizational Argument", edited by *Lauri Mälksoo*, goes far beyond this basic form of scientific dialogue. It mirrors an intense exchange of views among researchers coming from different academic backgrounds and reflecting on current developments in Russia from various points of view. Developments in human-rights law in Russia can be assessed from inside as well as from outside—from neighbouring countries as well as from those farther away. Achievements and difficulties can be discussed from the legal point of view but, also, from philosophical, sociological and historical perspectives. This collection integrates all these approaches, asks uneasy questions and gives controversial answers, puts forward theses and antitheses, confronts the inside and the outside view on Russia and warns readers 'not to miss the forest for the trees'. However, the young researchers who have taken part in this project share one common point of departure: the belief that human rights do matter. They must not be misunderstood as constantly repeated lip-service but must be effectively implemented—even if this necessitates structural changes.

The controversy about Russia's 'European identity' can be seen as a red thread throughout Russian history. Russia is a part of Europe and at the same time distances itself from Europe; it is, as *Petr Preclik* has nicely put it, "tiptoeing on the edge of the European system" (*Preclik*, 34). This never-ending cultural debate culminates in the present-day controversy about the role which human rights play and the role which they should play in Russia both in the political sphere and in the everyday life of citizens. It may be said that the present discussion reflects old stereotypes—the dichotomy between the views of 'Westerners' who are not only open to ideas from Western Europe but, also, who criticize Russia for lagging behind modernity, and 'Slavophiles', who consider Russia's uniqueness and differences as true values. Whoever takes a stand in the human-rights debate also takes a stand in the debate on Russia's mission in the world.

Human rights are laid down in many different documents and legal texts. The European Convention, however, matters most, as the European Court of Human Rights has the competence to take legally binding decisions on human-rights violations in all the member states of the Council of Europe. This volume, therefore, rightly focuses on implementation in Russia of decisions of the European

Lauri Mälksoo, ed.
Russia and European Human-Rights Law: The Rise of the Civilizational Argument 1-3

Court of Human Rights, especially in areas that are controversial and culturally highly sensitive such as freedom of the media and freedom of religion.

The Russian Federation acceded to the European Convention on Human Rights in 1998. A little more than a decade later, the complaints of its citizens amounted to almost one-third of all complaints brought before the Court out of the 47 member countries, and hundreds of human-rights violations are found each year. Nevertheless, *Dorothea Schönfeld* holds in her chapter "Tilting at Windmills?" that European organizations are only "partly successful" in Russia. So she asks: "What are the reasons for the constant rejection of European ideas and proposals by the Russian authorities and Russian society?" It is tempting to find answers in cultural traditions, in the fact that "the unity of the Russian people and a collective Russian spirit are considered to be more important than individual self-fulfillment" (*Schönfeld*, 133). Yet, it is also rightly stated that "history is never linear and easy to grasp; rather, it is a row of achievements, regressions, eruptions and unexpected events" (*Schönfeld*, 128).

This aspect is put forward by the Russian contributor *Vladislav Starzhenetskii*, stressing "the general picture of developments that have been achieved and current activity that is so much work-in-progress" (*Starzhenetskii*, 207). In his view, there is no profound gap between European and Russian values. He sees human-rights problems in Chechnia, violations of freedom of expression, religion, assembly and association as "a matter of balancing different conflicting values and the proportionality of measures taken to protect public interests" (*Starzhenetskii*, 211). Preconditions for implementing human rights are different due to the size of the country, its population, its neighbours and its history: "It is a country with one of the most dramatic histories in the twentieth century, with almost irreconcilable contradictions, which it is still trying to overcome" (*Starzhenetskii*, 211). Despite all the controversial high-profile cases, he remains optimistic about the influence of the European Court of Human Rights: "The good news is that judgments of the ECtHR serve as an effective inducement for Russia to reconsider its policy and regulations in problematic spheres of human-rights compliance" (*Starzhenetskii*, 212)

Petr Preclik interprets the discussion about implementation of human rights in Russia as a specific example of the "constitutive paradox of both international law and the human-rights movement, *i.e.*, neither international law nor human rights can ever be really universal; however, any concession from the universality claim would be mortal to the concepts as such" (*Preclik*, 33). In his view, Russia uses human-rights discourse in a process of 'self-determination' in order to demonstrate that it is ahead of Western-led globalization, determining its own fate, not a mere slave to it or to Western demands.

The persistence of different perceptions is confirmed by findings in specific areas of human-rights law such as freedom of religion and freedom of the press:

"Differences in the operation of systems in relation to freedom of religion—extrapolated to a general level—form a large part of this awkwardness" (*Hallinan*, 203). *Dara Hallinan* therefore speaks in his analysis of "Orthodox pluralism" of an "awkward friction" between Russia and the Council of Europe (*Hallinan, ibid.*). This friction is, however, not only a European problem but, also, part of the inter-civilizational dialogue on human rights. Therefore, *Lauri Mälksoo's* chapter in this volume on the human-rights concept of the Russian Orthodox Church is an important contribution to the debate on the cultural bias of human rights and their universality or relativity.

The tone of some of the analyses presented in the book is thus somewhat critical and pessimistic. But even if optimistic views might not outweigh the more sceptical approaches, the Volume, in its entirety, reflects the complexity of the subject and a broad 'margin of appreciation' in assessing the *status quo*.

If implementation of human rights in Russia is seen as a new facet of Russia's old inner conflict between 'East' and 'West', it is clear that whatever answer is given will be a provisional one. From this perspective, the optimistic view—seeing Russia on the road towards faithful adherence to human rights—would not contradict the pessimistic view of an insurmountable gap between Western individualistic human-rights philosophy and Russian collectivist approaches. Both visions would just catch a momentary view of a continuing oscillation between two extremes. The relationship between Russia and European human-rights law, thus, remains an open question that calls for further discussion and further development.

The European Convention on Human Rights is not only a 'living instrument' but, also, is the motor of dynamic societal processes in European states. No one precisely knows where they are going; even if the Convention shows a map clearly indicating the direction, there are no predefined or generally accepted answers to all the questions that might be raised in the context of human-rights protection. Controversial debates about interpreting the Convention, about redefining individual rights and freedoms *vis-à-vis* new challenges, about improving the mechanism of implementation of the Convention will re-emerge again and again. And, although Russia might be unique in size, history and culture, might be "tiptoeing on the edge of the European system", it is in the same boat as all the other European states.

This *Law in Eastern Europe* volume talks about progress, tensions, and perspectives. Progress is being made, yet tensions remain, and—according to the findings in this volume—future perspectives are not evident. The Russian bear might not be in an 'imaginary cage' as some have put it; but, for the time being, it might be reluctant to run.

Strasbourg,
January 2014

Russia and European Human-Rights Law: Progress, Tensions, and Perspectives

Introduction

Lauri Mälksoo

This volume of the series *Law in Eastern European* focuses on the general theme "*Russia and European Human-Rights Law: The Rise of the Civilizational Argument*".[1] As guest editor of this volume, I dare to argue that this is a very timely topic. On 7 October 2010, the First Section of the European Court of Human Rights (ECtHR) delivered its judgment in *Konstantin Markin v. Russia*.[2] In this case involving discrimination based on gender in social-security matters in the Russian Army, the ECtHR found that Russia had violated the European Convention on Human Rights. Moreover, the ECtHR dismissed an earlier interpretation of the Constitutional Court of the Russian Federation and suggested that the Russian government—in order to comply with the European Convention—would need to initiate a legislative amendment in the State *Duma*.

Upon the request of the Russian government, the *Markin* case was referred to the ECtHR's Grand Chamber. The Grand Chamber's judgment was rendered on 22 March 2012—soon after Russia's presidential elections.[3] However, even before the Grand Chamber judgment was handed down, the *Markin* case had become famous. Soon after the initial Markin judgment in 2010, the President of the Constitutional Court of the Russian Federation, Valerii Zor'kin, published an emotional article in the daily newspaper *Rossiiskaia gazeta*, entitled "The Limit of Giving In", in which he essentially suggested that the ECtHR had crossed the red line of Russia's sovereignty.[4] Moreover, Chief Justice Zor'kin warned that if Russia's "historical, cultural and social situation" were to be further ignored in the European system of human-rights protection, Russia might be forced, in the future, to bypass judgments of the ECtHR.[5]

The whole issue continued to be hotly contested during the months preceding the elections to State *Duma* in December 2011. In June and July 2011, the talk of the town among the political elite in Moscow was a legislative initiative by

1 Research for this volume was supported by grants from the European Research Council and the Estonian Science Foundation (Grant No.8087).

2 Case of *Konstantin Markin v. Russia* (7 October 2010) No.30078/06.

3 Case of *Konstantin Markin v. Russia* (22 March 2012) No.30078/06 (Grand Chamber).

4 "Predel ustupchivosti", *Rossiiskaia gazeta* (29 October 2010), available at <http://www.rg.ru/2010/10/29/zorkin.html>.

5 *Ibid.*

Lauri Mälksoo, ed.
Russia and European Human-Rights Law: The Rise of the Civilizational Argument 5-14

Aleksandr Torshin—the then-acting Chairman of the Federation Council—which suggested that the judgments of the ECtHR could only be implemented in Russia if first checked and approved by the Constitutional Court. Although the draft law was put on hold and Russia's media reported negative reactions (in particular among Russia's expert society but, also, among other parliamentarians[6]), Torshin's initiative was seen as a targeted provocation *vis-à-vis* the Strasbourg system.[7] When then-Prime Minister Putin—announcing that he would run again for the presidency in 2012—suggested in a newspaper article that a Eurasian union be created, Mr. Torshin immediately hooked up to the idea and suggested that Russia should also create a separate human-rights court for CIS countries.[8]

Of course, the Russian Federation is neither the first nor the only country that has developed a certain disliking of the ECtHR. In January 2012, British Prime Minister David Cameron, in Strasbourg, strongly criticized the ECtHR for its judgments in anti-terrorism cases involving Britain.[9] As far as Russia is concerned, it was only a matter of time before a case such as Markin came up. There have been a number of much more politically laden cases involving the Russian Federation: from Ilaşcu to Chechen cases, from Kononov to Yukos, not to mention cases involving Georgia that are still pending. Yet perhaps because the subject matter in Markin's case was relatively 'non-political' (at least, it did not involve major historical events such as World War II or the collapse of the USSR), the ECtHR chose a straightforward and head-on approach *vis-à-vis* the human-rights violations in question. It was a way to ask the government of Russia: what is your intent with the European consensus on human rights?

***

This is the context in which the present volume will be presented to the reader. However, the idea of this volume is older than the landmark case of *Markin v. Russia*. In order to lay out the writers' perspective, I would like to describe how this project came about.

6 Svetlana Sukhova, "V PASE protiv popravok Torshina", *Nezavisimaia gazeta* (24 June 2011), available at <http://www.ng.ru/world/2011-06-24/2_pase.html>.

7 See, *e.g.*, Ian Gordeev, "Rossiia prigrozila Evropeiskomu sudu", *Nezavisimaia gazeta* (11 July 2011), available at <http://www.ng.ru/politics/2011-07-11/3_sud.html>. See, further, Maksim Ivanov, Vladimir Solov'ev, Kristina Volobueva, "Aleksandr Torshin otlozhil Evrosud na osen'", *Kommersant* (18 July 2011), available at <http://www.kommersant.ru/doc/1681064>.

8 Nataliia Gorodetskaia, Anna Pushkarskaia, "Stat'ia prem'era nashla svoego chitatel'ia", *Kommersant* (6 October 2011), available at <http://www.kommersant.ru/doc/1788610>.

9 Nicholas Watt, "David Cameron Calls for Reform of European Court of Human Rights", *The Guardian* (25 January 2012), available at <http://www.guardian.co.uk/law/2012/jan/25/david-cameron-reform-european-court?INTCMP=SRCH>.

In November 2003, a fax from Venice arrived on my desk at the Faculty of Law at Tartu University in Estonia. The European Inter-University Centre, with its headquarters in the medieval monastery of San Nicoló on the Venice Lido, wanted to take into account the enlargement of the European Union to the East and invited the Tartu Law Faculty to represent Estonia in the European Master's Programme in Human Rights and Democratisation (<www.emahumanrights.org>). The invitation was gladly accepted, and the University of Tartu—along with a number of other universities from former socialist countries—joined the 'Venice programme'.

Currently, the European Master's Programme in Human Rights and Democratisation is a network of forty-one European universities. The programme, subsidized by the European Union, has fostered the emergence of a unique interdisciplinary collaboration among different European universities, departments and scholars.

One challenge that the Eastern European universities faced when joining the programme was that they were latecomers. They needed to reflect on what they could contribute to existing structures of teaching and research in the areas of human rights and democratization. Western European universities were better equipped in terms of material resources and had historically stronger traditions in research and teaching in the fields of human rights and democratization. It seemed that human rights and democratization were exactly what the Cold War had been about. Now since the West happened to win that ideological confrontation, there had to be losers as well. It was clear that, since 1989, the Eastern Europeans—having been subjects of Communist rule—had themselves been disciples, not teachers, of liberal ideology and values, including human rights and democracy. The whole Strasbourg system of human-rights protection needed to be understood, absorbed, and implemented. Again, this was a classic disciple's situation—not a teacher's situation.

Yet in terms of setting the research agenda, Eastern European scholars had another sort of legitimacy for talking about human rights: the experience of a different history and a different knowledge of their own region. Knowledge of the Russian language became an asset too. Many exciting and transitional developments in Europe were now taking place precisely in the East. The US Secretary of Defense in the George W. Bush administration, Donald Rumsfeld, provocatively captured this sentiment when he coined the terms 'old Europe' and 'new Europe'. Whether liberalism really marked 'the end of history' had come to be tested primarily in Eastern Europe. Things are now again starting to change with the financial crisis and the rise of anti-immigrant movements primarily affecting Western Europe and questioning liberal democracy as the 'end of history'.

If it ever made sense to speak about 'old' and 'new' Europe, the 'newest' Europe was the Russian Federation. Countries such as Estonia or Poland had been relatively successful converts to liberalism and 'European values', whereas Russia had proven to be a bigger challenge. The Russian Federation ratified the European Convention on Human Rights in 1998, but news about Russia's difficulties in the European Court of Human Rights and backlashes in implementing the Convention in Russia have become relatively frequent.

In any case, as historical Venice built its success on trade with the Orient,and the Portuguese, Spanish and the British still have unique links with, and expertise about, their former colonies, it was clear that the Baltic states—and, in the particular context of this initiative, Estonia—could serve as a bridge between Russia and Western Europe.[10] The history of Russia's laws had fascinated Tartu's (Dorpat's) legal scholars already in the early nineteenth century, after Tsar Alexander I had reopened the university in 1802.[11] Within the European Master's Programme, it was soon evident that the latecomer-universities from Eastern Europe did not simply need to follow their elder peers in what they were doing. In order to be competitive or even be taken seriously by their colleagues, they needed to offer a different perspective, to add some value. Thus, at Tartu we decided to focus our research on the human-rights situation in the former USSR, especially in the Russian Federation.

We would like to think that this approach proved fruitful—or at least interesting. The bulk of this volume consists of three master's theses written at the University of Tartu in the framework of the European Master's Programme. Dorothea Schönfeld and Petr Preclik defended their master's theses in 2008; Dara Hallinan in 2009. I had the honor to supervise all three theses.

One possible danger with studying human rights in Russia 'from the outside' is Orientalism. One may not fully understand 'the Other' and too easily fall into the trap of moral judgmentalism. The problem may be particularly relevant in the Baltic states which—perhaps more than any other member states in the European Union—may have historical scores to settle with the former imperial centre: Russia. Having oscillated from Russia's imperial control to the West's orbit, the Balts may have particular reasons to demonstrate and prove their faithfulness to Western values—whatever those are in a given historical period. They may also want to prove that Russia is 'bad', whereas they are 'better'. The British scholar

10 See, further, Lauri Mälksoo, "The Science of International Law and the Concept of Politics. The Arguments and Lives of the International Law Professors at the University of Dorpat/Iur'ev/Tartu 1855-1985", 76 *British Year Book of International Law* (2005), 383-502.

11 See, *e.g.*, Johann Philip Gustav Ewers, *Vom Ursprunge des russischen Staats: Ein Versuch, die Geschichte desselben aus den Quellen zu erforschen* (J.G. Hartmann's Buchhandlung, Riga, 1808); and *id.*, *Das älteste Recht der Russen in seiner geschichtlichen Entwickelung* (A. Sticinsky, Dorpat, 1826). Further, see, *e.g.*, Fedor Witte, *Ein Blick auf die geschichtliche Entwicklung des älteren russischen Erbrechts, bis zum Gesetzbuche des Zaren Alexei Michailowitch (1649)* (J.C. Schünmann's Wittwe, Dorpat, 1848).

(and then journalist) Anatol Lieven followed the 'Baltic revolution' on the spot in 1988-1991 and made the observation that—even though their own socio-economic and other crises may have been extremely difficult—Baltic leaders took particular comfort in affirming to themselves and their peoples that "at least we are better than Russia".[12] According to Lieven, this had almost become part of people's identity in the Baltic states. Maria Mälksoo demonstrated in her doctoral dissertation that the post-Communist Baltic states and Poland, on the one hand, and Russia, on the other hand, have struggled about the history of World War II for partly political reasons—to fight against their own liminality in Europe by singling out their neighbor as even less European and, thus, more liminal.[13]

It is up to the reader to decide whether we, the authors of these chapters, are (or have not been) similar to the man who has a hammer and, therefore, sees nails everywhere. As far as the danger of Orientalism goes, the only way to deal with it was to become aware of it. Human rights are a very normative field, of course, and one cannot and should not avoid taking firm positions, critical, if necessary. Yet, in writing these chapters and exercising the criticism that can be found here, we do not speak from a position of ultimate truths. We may have misunderstood certain matters, not known certain things, or simply failed to grasp all the complexity of the topic. These here are our views; there may be other, perhaps better reasoned or more justified ones. Yet the authors in this volume have explored the subject matter in good faith and share the belief that these issues must be discussed and talked about. An alternative that can sometimes be encountered, a polite and 'diplomatic' refusal to talk about these things frankly, was unattractive for us.

Nor do we imply that when Russia has the problems it has, everything is fine and rosy in our own home countries. Surely Estonia, Germany, the Czech Republic and Great Britain—among other EU member states—have their own problems in the field of human-rights protection.[14] These problems should not be downplayed, and serious scholarly research should be conducted on them.

Yet this particular volume is about the Russian Federation's attitude towards, implementation of, and dialogue with European human-rights law. Note that we have narrowed down the subject matter—referring consciously to the European regional understanding of human-rights law and the Strasbourg system of human-

12 Anatol Lieven, *The Baltic Revolution* (Yale University Press, New Haven, CT, 1994).

13 See Maria Mälksoo, *The Politics of Becoming European: A Study of Polish and Baltic Post-Cold War Security Imaginaries* (Routledge, London, 2010).

14 For example, Russian authors often have criticized citizenship legislation in Estonia and Latvia; namely, the fact that since 1991, it is based on the idea of state continuity with the pre-1940 republics and, consequently, no automatic citizenship was granted to the (Russian-speaking) Soviet era settlers. See, *e.g.*, Aslan Abashidze, Ekaterina Alisevich, Aleksandr Solntsev, *Regional'nye sistemy zashchity prav cheloveka* (Rossiiskii Universitet Druzhby Narodov, Moscow, 2012), 165-166.

rights protection. This volume is not about universal instruments such as the universal periodic review in the UN Human Rights Council; nor is it about Russian domestic protection of human rights such as the Russian ombudsman institution or the work of the RF Constitutional Court. Moreover, the general topic of Russia's interaction with European human-rights law is not entirely exhausted with sub-problems and issues as presented here. One could write chapters on other civic, political, social, economic, and cultural rights than those which are contained herein. Yet one ought to start somewhere, and this is our start. We believe that something historically significant happened in 1998 when the Russian Federation ratified the European Convention and became a member of the Strasbourg system. What exactly this significance would be is contested, and that contestation is what this volume is about.

One relative difficulty that we faced when preparing this study was that the object of the study has been—and inevitably remains—in constant flux. For example, the elections to the State *Duma* in December 2011 and mass protests regarding the alleged falsifications, that took place during the elections, created again a new situation, a new momentum. In Russia's case, the connection between the state of democracy and the state of human rights is particularly revealing. On 12 April 2011, the First Section of the ECtHR found that the liquidation of the Republican Party of Russia by the Russian government just before the 2003 State *Duma* elections violated the right to assembly of the party members.[15] Each new major judgment issued in Strasbourg will cause shifts in the discourse. Our volume has not been conceived to predict all important new developments; nor does it claim to tackle everything that has already been significant in the field. Rather, we have taken a few mental steps back and have made attempts to generalize about certain trends and perspectives. Of course, these chapters have been updated since the MA theses were defended in 2008 and 2009; yet, the main points that were made in theses back then remain the same.

***

After my own analysis of the human-rights concept of the Russian Orthodox Church and its Patriarch Kirill, the first chapter is by Petr Preclik, who takes an international-relations-theory perspective on the human-rights situation in Russia. Preclik makes the point that international-relations theory has not been too eager to include insights into human rights, considering it primarily the realm of lawyers. However, the opposite is true as well: the mainstream of human-rights scholarship often does not bother to go beyond the dichotomy of legal/illegal.

15 Case of the *Republican Party of Russia v. Russia* (12 April 2011) No.12976/07. See, further, Maria-Luiza Tirmaste, Ol'ga Pleshanova, Seda Egikian, Tamila Dzhodzhua (Geouga), "Evropeiskii sud vypolnil partiinoe sozdanie", *Kommersant* (13 April 2011), available at <http://www.kommersant.ru/doc/1620520>.

In contrast, Preclik's approach is general and even philosophical; he offers an interesting interpretation of why things are the way they are between Moscow and Strasbourg. His application of the theory of contestation is something that lawyers, in that form, are unable to offer. Preclik's approach is strongly influenced by the Constructivist theory of international relations. Preclik's work was reviewed by Viatcheslav Morozov, Professor of EU-Russia Studies at the University of Tartu and a well-known Constructivist scholar. Together with Petr Preclik, we would like to thank Professor Morozov for his important editorial input. An earlier version of Preclik's thesis was distinguished as one of the five best theses in 2008 in the European Master's Programme.

The second chapter is by Dorothea Schönfeld. She partly tackles the same themes as Preclik but has less patience with the Russian cultural-relativism argument. Schönfeld has taken a particular rights situation—the relative lack of media freedom in the Russian Federation—and studies its dynamic aspects, *i.e.*, how the situation has been dealt with by European human-rights institutions. The author interviewed Russian journalists and NGO representatives. The result is a passionate *Streitschrift* with the Russian government. Of course, the situation with the media is one area where changes are almost constant. Thus, commentators have pointed out that in terms of news consumption, the Internet is increasingly competing with public TV among Russia's urban middle class. In a number of cases, the blogosphere has played a pivotal role in 'breaking the news' when the state media has tried to present an idiosyncratic version of what happened. In December 2011, leading daily newspapers such as *Kommersant* reported on alleged election fraud and on the mass demonstrations that followed in a promisingly transparent and open way. The relative mildness of European responses to systematic violations of media freedom in Russia can be interpreted as the perennial primacy of economic and other pragmatic interests over concerns with the rights situation. Perhaps, too, a silent recognition exists in Old Europe that, indeed, Russia significantly differs from the rest of Europe so that the famous 'margin of appreciation' must be interpreted particularly liberally. The crucial question remains: should the main impulse for more media freedom come from inside or outside a country?

The third chapter in the volume, authored by Dara Hallinan, deals with religious freedom in the Russian Federation. Religion is a particularly sensitive area of life where one should be cautious with too easy a critique and moral 'interventionism'. Yet, at the same time, freedom of religion is one of the pillars of the Strasbourg system of human-rights protection. If one religion is prioritized over others, religious freedom is *ipso facto* endangered. This problem has particularly interesting aspects in Russia which, during the Communist period (1917-1991), was governed by a militantly atheist ideology. (As all diligent tourists learn in St. Petersburg, the Kazan' Cathedral in Leningrad/St. Petersburg was turned into a massive Museum of Atheism during the Communist era.) After the collapse of Communism, Orthodox Christianity returned to fill the ideological vacuum left by the demise of Marxism-Leninism. Whether other denominations of Christianity and other religions are—or can be—truly 'equal' to Orthodoxy has become a hotly contested issue in Russia. A report on the state of religious freedom in the Russian Federation—prepared by the Institute of Freedom of Conscience together with Moscow Helsinki group and published in February 2012—corroborates Hallinan's main findings: that the Russian government seems to have a systemic bias in favor of the Russian Orthodox Church.[16] What complicates the matter further is that the very notion of freedom of religion seems to be very much contested in Europe. For example, at the end of 2011, intense debates were carried out about whether the new Constitution in Hungary—among other contested aspects—would effectively restrict religious freedom in Hungary. Here is a field where post-Communist Russia may influence secular Europe even more than the Strasbourg system has influenced Russia. Conservative traditionalism stemming from Russia may yet balance some post-modern and ultra-progressive interpretations of rights in 'old Europe'. Was it not the dream of the nineteenth-century Slavophiles that Russia would 'save' Europe?

The fourth chapter is a shorter one. It is a reply by Vladislav Starzhenetskii, a scholar and practitioner in the field of human-rights law from Moscow. The idea of including a Russian scholar—among other reasons in order to diminish the dangers of one-sidedness or Orientalism—came from the *Review*'s general editor, Professor William B. Simons. By chance, I had just met Vladislav Starzhenetskii at an annual conference of the Russian Association of International Law in Moscow, already knew some of his work,[17] and was very impressed by his open-minded and well-informed presentation about the implementation of European human-rights law in Russia. Starzhenetskii kindly agreed to write a reply to Preclik, Schönfeld and Hallinan. As far as human rights in Russia are concerned, Starzhenetskii encourages one to see the glass as half-full rather than half-empty. He also points out that the authors represented in this volume have been mostly preoccupied with tensions in the relationship between Russia and Strasbourg and less with the progress that Russia has made over the last two decades.

Finally, in the fifth chapter, I offer the reader a conclusion to the present volume. In such a subjective and normatively charged field as human-rights law and policy, it cannot be the task of the editor to distill ultimate truths. The chapters included and arguments made in the volume speak for themselves. Instead of picking and highlighting certain particularly relevant aspects from

16 See Andrei Kozenko, Aleksandr Chernykh, Pavel Korobov, "Pravozashchitniki dolozhili na sovest'. Opublikovan doklad o svobode veroispovedeniia v RF", *Kommersant* (8 February 2012), available at <http://kommersant.ru/doc/1868115/print>.

17 See, *e.g.*, Vladislav Starzhenetskii, *Rossiia i Sovet Evropy: pravo sobstvennosti* (Gorodets, Moscow, 2004).

previous articles, I compare how contemporary Russian scholarly discourse on European human-rights law might enter into dialogue with or differ from, the 'view from the outside' as offered in this volume. The interesting thing is that leading Russian scholars themselves—for instance, Elena Lukasheva—have raised the civilizational aspect when explaining the deeper reasons for the situation with human rights in Russia.

When editing this volume, I finally decided not to compile a common bibliography. On the one hand, it did not seem to add much value for the reader for us to simply reproduce the references that are already contained in the chapters of each of the contributors. In any case, the footnotes of the chapters represent our collective bibliography. In particular, my own concluding chapter contains references to recent Russian scholarly treatises on international and European human-rights law. The biggest problem for the non-Russian student remains that such works are usually available only in the Russian Federation or, rather, in the best, specialized bookstores of major Russian cities. One reason why I decided not to venture further from the bibliography—already contained in the footnotes—is because I believe that such a bibliography on "Human-Rights Law and Russia" should aim at comprehensiveness. For example, the Chechen cases in the ECtHR have generated interesting scholarly commentary;[18] however, these aspects are covered only in passing in our volume. In this volume, we do discuss a number of ECtHR cases but do not claim that these are the only 'most important' ones. In other words, compiling a comprehensive bibliography on "Human-Rights Law and Russia" would constitute a major scholarly work in its own right; one that hopefully can be undertaken soon in the future. Even while finalizing the editing of this Volume, for example, a new study has been published containing an important comparative collection of how ex-Communist countries in Eastern and Central Europe have been faring in the Strasbourg system.[19]

As emphasized earlier, this volume is interdisciplinary, which had a significant impact on the methods chosen. Petr Preclik approaches the field of human rights from the disciplinary angle of international-relations theory, particularly its constructivist branch. This enables a more philosophical approach to the whole subject matter. (Some lawyers would argue that international-relations theory is nothing but good old political philosophy with a fancy new name; this, however, should not diminish its importance for the understanding of aspects that pure legal analysis is unable to enlighten.) Dorothea Schönfeld takes a more policy-oriented approach in that she takes Russia's non-compliance with law as

18 See, *e.g.*, William Abresch, "A Human Rights Law of Internal Armed Conflict: The European Court of Human Rights in Chechnya", 16 *European Journal of International Law* (2005), 741-767.

19 See Leonard Hammer and Frank Emmert (eds.), *The European Convention on Human Rights in Central and Eastern Europe* (Eleven International Publishing, The Hague, 2012). The chapter on Russia has been written by Dr. Anton Burkov.

an already relatively well-established starting point. She then explores the relative failure of Western policy to address Russia's non-compliance. Finally, the lawyer among the main authors, Dara Hallinan, proceeds from the classic positivist legal method. In his narrative, he establishes what the law is and looks critically at compliance with it. Vladislav Starzhenetskii, the author of a response to all three, also is a lawyer.

In this way, the chapters are quite different from one other; each of them reflects the personality and disciplinary focus of the respective author. Yet, the idea behind the whole volume project was to put these chapters together so that they would enter into dialogue and speak with each other. This would tear the individual chapters out from their isolation and create a larger forum of ideas where individual chapters, too, can be seen in a new dialogical light. However, the possibility remains that just as there may be a tension between Russian and non-Russian approaches to human-rights law, there may also be tensions between legal and non-legal approaches.

We would like to express our appreciation for the support of the institutions and funds that have facilitated the research and writing of this volume. The European Master's Programme in Human Rights and Democratisation with headquarters in Venice already has been mentioned. It is thanks to the *e.ma programme* that Dorothea Schönfeld, Petr Preclik and Dara Hallinan—three intellectually curious and open-minded MA students from Central and Western Europe—came to study in Tartu. Furthermore, the editing of this volume was supported, in part, by a grant from the European Research Council to study contemporary Russian understanding of international law and human rights and, also in part, by Grant No.8082 from the Estonian Science Foundation.

Finally, the general editor of the *Review*, and of the series in which this volume now appears, Professor William B. Simons, has been a wise, patient and generous source of help and encouragement who, among other things, has helped me to understand how much visible and hidden work is involved in running such an international journal and book series.

Tartu,
January 2014

The Human Rights Concept of the Russian Orthodox Church and its Patriarch Kirill I: A Critical Appraisal*

Lauri Mälksoo

Introduction

The debate on the universality of human rights recently has acquired an inner-European dimension. When previously, criticisms on the universalization of the European (Western) particularity were conducted mostly either in the name of the Asian values or from the perspective of third-world approaches to international law (TWAIL),[1] one of the most recent systemic criticisms comes from the heartland of Orthodox Eastern Europe, Russia.

On 6 April 2006, the Tenth World Russian People's Council adopted the "Orthodox Declaration of Human Rights. Declaration on Human Rights and Dignity".[2] Formally, the World Russian People's Council is an international non-governmental organization which has consultative status at the UN (ECOSOC). Patriarch Kirill I of Moscow explains that "the annual meetings bring together representatives of Russia's traditional religions, government and society but also representatives of the Russian diaspora from all over the world".[3] One might ask, however, what exactly the interest of representatives of Russia's other traditional religions—beyond Orthodox Christianity—would be to co-adopt the Orthodox Declaration of Human Rights? It seems that, substantively, the World Russian People's Council has been under the influence of the Russian Orthodox Church (ROC).

At the time of the adoption of the Orthodox Declaration in 2006, the World Russian People's Council was chaired by Patriarch Alexius II (1929-2008). Nevertheless, the current Patriarch Kirill I gave the programmatic speech "Human Rights and Moral Responsibility" there, and Kirill's own subsequent involvement with the Orthodox Declaration reveals that he has been the ideological

* Research for this chapter was supported by a grant of the ERC.

1 See, *e.g.*, Onuma Yasuaki, "In Quest of Intercivilizational Human Rights: Universal vs Relative. Human Rights Viewed from an Asian Perspective", 1(1) *Asia-Pacific Journal on Human Rights and the Law* (2000), 53-88; and Makau Mutua, *Human Rights: A Political and Cultural Critique* (University of Pennsylvania Press, Philadelphia, PA, 2002).

2 See the Bulgarian Orthodox Portal, "Orthodox Declaration of Human Rights. Declaration on Human Rights and Dignity" (2006), available at <http://www.pravoslavieto.com/docs/human_rights/ decla ration_ru_en.htm>.

3 *Moskva ja Kogu Venemaa Pühim Patriarh Kirill, Vabadus ja vastutus. Harmoonia otsinguil. Inimõigused ja isiksuse väärikus* (Tallinna Raamatutrükikoda, Tallinn, 2012), 104 (hereinafter referred to as "Kirill (2012)"). For the purposes of writing this chapter, I have used the Estonian version and translated the respective passages into English.

Lauri Mälksoo, ed.
Russia and European Human-Rights Law: The Rise of the Civilizational Argument 15-29

driving force leading to the Declaration's adoption.[4] Furthermore, in mid-2008, the ROC adopted its "Foundations on the Teaching on Dignity, Freedom and Human Rights" which elaborates, in further detail, ideas expressed in the 2006 Orthodox Declaration.[5]

More recently, the ROC published a collection of Patriarch Kirill's essays and speeches on human rights which reads like an extended commentary to the Orthodox Declaration of 2006. Patriarch Kirill's work has been translated in a number of languages, including English,[6] Japanese,[7] and Estonian.[8]

This chapter has a simple structure. In the following section, the 2006 Orthodox Declaration and Patriarch Kirill's views on human rights are introduced. Then, I will critically reflect on some of the points raised by the Orthodox Declaration and Patriarch Kirill I. Finally, I will offer the reader some conclusions.

Human Rights in the 2006 Orthodox Declaration and in Patriarch Kirill's Writings

The 2006 "Orthodox Declaration of Human Rights. Declaration on Human Rights and Dignity" starts with the statement that there exists a "unique Russian civilization" in the name of which the Declaration has been adopted.[9] It then turns to the concept of human dignity which it sees as foundational for human rights and makes the following claim:

> "It is by doing good [things] that the human being gains dignity. Thus we distinguish between human worth and dignity. Worth is given, while dignity is acquired."[10]

Human rights cannot be separated from morality; there cannot be such a thing as immoral dignity. The Declaration goes on to emphasize:

> "There are values no smaller than human rights. These are faith, morality, the sacred, motherland. Whenever these values come into conflict with the implementation of human rights, the task of the society, state and law is to bring both to harmony."

Moreover,

4 Kirill (2012), *op.cit.* note 3, 63-83, 86.

5 Moscow Patriarchate, "Osnovy ucheniia Russkoi Pravoslavnoi Tserkvi o dostoinstve, svobode i pravakh cheloveka" (26 June 2008), available at <http://www.patriarchia.ru/db/text/428616.html>.

6 Patriarch Kirill of Moscow, *Freedom and Responsibility. A Search for Harmony: Human Rights and Personal Dignity* (Darton, Longman and Todd, London, 2011).

7 Moscow Patriarchate, press release on the book presentation in Tokyo, available at <http://www.patria rchia.ru/db/text/2474890.html>.

8 *Op.cit.* note 3.

9 *Op.cit.* note 2.

10 *Ibid.*

> "It is unacceptable, in pursuit of human rights, to oppress faith and moral tradition, insult religious and national feelings, cause harm to revered holy objects and sites, jeopardize the motherland. Likewise we see as dangerous the 'invention' of such 'rights' as to legitimize a behavior condemned by both the traditional morality and historical religions."

The Declaration also makes an offer to the Russian state to cooperate:

> "We are willing to cooperate with the state and all benevolent forces in ensuring human rights."

These ideas now have been further elaborated in the collection of articles and speeches of Patriarch Kirill I of Moscow. This collection reveals how Kirill's thinking on human rights has evolved over more than a decade. Thus, in an article first published in 1999, Kirill already juxtaposed neo-liberal and traditional modes of thinking:

> "At the battleground of ideologies, a new confrontation is beginning to take shape, globalism and universalism against conservatism and rationalism."[11]

According to Kirill, the Enlightenment thinkers of the XVIII century—such as Holbach, Helvetius and Diderot, building on the Renaissance pagan rebirth—were responsible for the victory of the anthropocentric world-view in the West. The human being became the measurement of all things; however, this was not just human being as such but the fallen one, the one who was sinful. Liberalism rejected the notion of sinful and spoiled human nature. According to Kirill, an important role in the formation of liberal anthropocentric ideas also has been played by Judaist theology (Maimonides, Crescas, Ibn Ezra) and Jewish critical philosophers (Spinoza).[12] This liberal anthropocentric vision was first enshrined in the French Declaration of the Rights of Man and of the Citizen (1789) and finally in the Universal Declaration of Human Rights (1948).

At the time when the UDHR was elaborated in the UN, the USSR chose not to fully participate in the discourse of human rights and as a consequence, the Russian Orthodox spiritual and cultural tradition was not reflected in the works and in the negotiations leading to the adoption of the UDHR. As a consequence, asserts Kirill, contemporary universal standards on human rights by their nature are exclusively liberal Western standards.[13] In our time, particularly the Protestants—by starting to accept female priests and homosexual marriages—have succumbed to liberal standards with which Orthodox Christians will not be able to agree.[14] Theocentric spiritual tradition will not accept uncritically the views of the anthropocentric liberalism.[15]

11 Kirill (2012), *op.cit.* note 3.

12 *Ibid.*, 5.

13 *Ibid.*, 6.

14 *Ibid.*, 9.

15 *Ibid.*, 10.

The liberal concept wants to liberate the human being from everything that s/he might understand as the restriction of her/his will or rights. For Apostle Paul, however, freedom means something quite different; namely, freedom from sin and the force of the evil, from the instinct that burdens the human being. In liberalism, however, sin is actually permitted to the extent that it does not violate laws or restrict other individuals' freedom.[16] This extensive idea of freedom is in plain contradiction with Christianity, concludes Kirill.

Kirill then asks how traditionalist Christian countries should deal with such liberal ideas?[17] According to Kirill, two extreme options seem to be available for Russia: isolationism and closing off from the rest of the globalizing world on the one hand, and accepting the liberal premises mechanically and 'from above' on the other.[18] Kirill contends that it must be the role of the Orthodox theology to demonstrate that liberal ideas—while possibly acceptable in international relations—should not be imposed on inter-personal relations; in any case, not in Russia.[19] ROC should never accept the idea that religion is just a personal matter and that religious organizations are outside the political life. Kirill also reminds the reader that for centuries, the Orthodox tradition used to favor monarchy as the preferred system of state government. In that context, Kirill asks:

> "Perhaps in this ancient Orthodox political ideal there are some principles of how to relate to state power in terms of serving [...] that are topical also today?"[20]

In 2005, Kirill elaborated further on his views of human rights:

> "Ask contemporary European bureaucrats in Brussels or Strasbourg in what they see their task. They say: in the first place in the protection of human rights and freedoms because they think that all existing problems come from non-compliance with such rights in one country or another. I too am convinced of the need to protect human rights and freedoms. But I am also convinced that human beings are not born sinless. [...] Sometimes our opponents say: you, Orthodox people, simply have a hidden allergy towards the topic of rights and freedoms. No, it is not like this."[21]

In his speech "Human Rights and Moral Responsibility", delivered on 4 April 2006 at the Tenth World Russian People's Council, Kirill asserted that on the one hand, human rights were valuable and it was also because of human rights that religious communities in Eastern Europe could be liberated from the constraints of state atheism.[22] However:

16 *Ibid.*, 17.

17 *Ibid.*, 18.

18 *Ibid.*, 18.

19 *Ibid.*, 19-20.

20 *Ibid.*, 23.

21 *Ibid.*, 57.

22 *Ibid.*, 63.

> "On the other hand, we are witnessing how—with the concept of human rights—cover is provided to lying, and hurting religious and national feelings. Moreover, little by little ideas are integrated in the concept of human rights that are not acceptable not just for Christians but, generally, to the traditional moral understanding of the human being."[23]

The often-claimed universality of human rights must mean that these rights are really universal; but "are they?", asks Kirill. In reality, the concept of human rights was developed in the West.[24] The foundational concept for human rights in the West is human dignity. Kirill then gives his own meaning to the concept of human dignity; it means two things. On the one hand, dignity traditionally means what deserves respect and high status. On the other hand, it also means behaving according to one's status, to behave in a dignified way.[25] By being sinful, the humans lost their natural dignity; they can regain it only by doing good—should they choose to do evil, they will degrade their dignity.[26]

> "Nowadays, instead of seeing in the State the absolute like in the early modern era, the autonomy and rights of the individual beyond moral responsibility are taken as absolutes."[27]

Kirill then criticized the European Parliament's 2006 resolution on homophobia in Europe:[28]

> "In the end result, such propaganda will lead to temptation those who could have fought with this disease and created a healthy family."[29]

Another example referred to by Kirill was a 2005 resolution of the Parliamentary Assembly of the Council of Europe,[30] stating that freedom of religion was restricted by human rights. Kirill further warned:

> "If now such military activism of a secular humanist approach intervening in international law will not be tamed down, there will automatically be a conflict. Thank God, resolutions of the Council of Europe are not legally binding, but they shape opinions in society."[31]

Finally, Kirill asserted that:

23 *Ibid.*, 64.

24 *Ibid.*, 64.

25 *Ibid.*, 65.

26 *Ibid.*, 65.

27 *Ibid.*, 68.

28 European Parliament, Resolution on homophobia in Europe (18 January 2006), available at <http://www.europarl.europa.eu/sides/getDoc.do?pubRef=-//EP//TEXT+TA+P6-TA-2006-0018+0+DOC+XML+V0//EN>.

29 Kirill (2012), *op.cit.* note 3, 70.

30 Parliamentary Assembly of the Council of Europe, Resolution 1464 (2005) Women and Religion in Europe (4 October 2005), available at <http://assembly.coe.int/Main.asp?link=/Documents/ AdoptedText/ta05/ERES1464.htm>.

31 Kirill (2012), *op.cit.* note 3, 71.

> "Orthodox people are willing to accept human rights norms and to work towards their consolidation. But this they do only in the case when these norms help to perfect the human being, not when they justify his sinful condition."[32]

At the meeting of the European Council of Religious Leaders in Oslo in November 2002, Kirill repeated the idea that the Orthodox civilization differed in some crucial aspects from the Western tradition. Orthodox Christianity emphasizes not just the personal but, also, the societal life, family, collective, nation and state.[33] In our own time, when European integration no longer takes place only in the West but in the Orthodox East as well, liberal standards need to be supplemented by other cultural systems whereas such world-views must be recognized as equal.[34]

> "Otherwise, the new form of ideological imperialism will provoke even bigger clashes than are known from the history of the colonial era. [...] One needs to understand that Eastern lands of Europe do not want to blindly follow the rules that have once been worked out by someone without their participation and without taking into account their world-view. They do not want to follow such rules just because they are currently applied in the Western countries that are materially well off."[35]

A number of Kirill's post-2006 speeches abroad, including in the Council of Europe, have popularized further the Orthodox Declaration and have defended it from criticism that "Russians wanted to justify with it all their activities".[36]

In 2007, at a Dialogue of Civilizations seminar in Paris, Kirill maintained:

> "Unfortunately contemporary international law often develops towards imposing views of different minorities on the majority of the humankind. [...] In the private sphere, the freedom of moral choice must be as complete as possible. [...] However, in every state's public sphere, only such values should be spread and supported as are supported by the majority of the people."[37]

On 21 June 2011, Patriarch Kirill held a speech at the European Council of Religious Leaders which had gathered in Moscow.[38] In his speech, Patriarch Kirill criticized European countries for their predominantly secular concept of human rights and made a plea to modify it in the future.

In addition, one could also mention the recent publications of Igumen Phillip (Riabykh), the representative of the ROC in Strasbourg. Igumen Phillip has criticized the Western notion of the separation of the Church and the State and suggested that instead Russia should follow the concept of "symphony of

32 *Ibid.*, 73.

33 *Ibid.*, 74-75.

34 *Ibid.*, 77.

35 Kirill (2012), *op.cit.* note 3, 77-78.

36 *Ibid.*, 89.

37 *Ibid.*, 105.

38 Russian Orthodox Church, Vystuplenie Sviateishego Patriarkha Kirilla na zasedanii Evropeiskogo soveta religioznykh liderov "Prava cheloveka i traditsionnye tsennosti v Evrope" (21 June 2011), available at <http://www.patriarchia.ru/db/text/1546416.html>.

powers" developed in the VI century by the Byzantine Emperor Justinian I.[39] In other words, instead of emphasizing the clear separation of the state and religious authorities, their harmonious coexistence and inter-dependence should be emphasized. Moreover, as further background information one could add that some Orthodox legal scholars have begun suggesting that Russia should amend its Constitution of 1993, emphasize the special role of Orthodox Christianity for its identity, and even make reservations to that effect to international and European human rights instruments.[40]

Critical Discussion of the ROC's and Patriarch Kirill's Human-Rights Views

Carl Schmitt (1888-1985) once famously argued that all precise notions of modern constitutional-law scholarship were secularized notions of theology.[41] However, Schmitt did not specify whose theology. The 2006 Orthodox Declaration and Patriarch Kirill's writings make one wonder what the impact of different religious traditions on the post-World War II (and post-Cold war) European doctrine and practice of human rights has been. Reading Patriarch Kirill I, one may be reminded of historical dates like 1054 (the schism of the Roman Catholic and Eastern Orthodox churches) and 1439 (the date of the Council of Florence's decision to reunite both Christian churches which the Eastern Church ultimately rejected).

Perhaps the West has been too triumphalist, naïve and patronizing to think that the Communist ideology in Russia was something so idiosyncratic that when it suffered its defeat in 1991, Russia was simply and unproblematically predestined to rejoin the "common European house" and catch up on liberal European values. There has been much optimism about the narrative of universal progress and the idea that institutional arrangements, such as the Helsinki Final Act of 1975, were capable of fundamentally changing the human rights performance of countries.[42] Instead, culture and historically developed patterns may be much more resistant factors in the thinking on and implementation of human rights. We should at least be aware of the controversial thesis of the exiled Russian philosopher Nikolai Berdyaev (1874-1948), expressed in his book *The Origin of Russian Communism*

39 Igumen Phillip (Riabykh), "Grazhdanskaia simfoniia zvuchit po-novomu", *Nezavisimaia Gazeta* (5 December 2012), available at <http://religion.ng.ru/society/2012-12-05/5_symphony.html>. For his views in English translation, see <http://www.pravoslavie.ru/english/49391.htm>.

40 Aleksandr M. Ivanov, "Russkaia pravoslavnaia tserkov' v kontekste osnovnykh prav cheloveka i grazhdanina v sovremennoi Rossii", *Pravodevenie* (2008) No.4, 19-35, at 35.

41 Carl Schmitt, *Politische Theologie. Vier Kapitel zur Lehre von der Souveränität* (Duncker & Humblot, Berlin, 1934, 2nd. ed.), 49.

42 See Daniel Charles Thomas, *The Helsinki Effect: International Norms, Human Rights, and the Demise of Communism* (Princeton University Press, Princeton, NJ, 2001).

that certain historical roots of the Communist experiment in Russia may have lied in the Orthodox Messianism and collectivism[43]—a paradoxical possibility because the Bolsheviks were ferociously anti-Christian and anti-religious.

Another important influence preparing mentally the ground for today's views of the Russian Orthodox Church appears to be the thinking of Aleksandr Solzhenitsyn (1918-2008), the Russian writer and exiled dissident during the Communist period. In his Harvard address of 1978, Solzhenitsyn had argued that Russia constituted an autonomous world, apart from the West, and had criticized the liberal Western concept of human rights for its detachment from Christianity.[44] Solzhenitsyn's memoirs reveal a deep intellectual difference in thinking about human rights with another Soviet dissident, Andrei Sakharov (1921-1989). When Sakharov unequivocally supported the "ideology of human rights", Solzhenitsyn compared it—in the first and only place—with the metaphor of cancer.[45]

By the way, it is only partly true—contrary to what Patriarch Kirill I has argued—that the USSR played only a modest role in the elaboration of international human-rights law after World War II. The USSR abstained when the UDHR was adopted in the UN General Assembly 1948, but this does not necessarily reflect Soviet passivity. It rather accurately sums up the Soviet ambivalent attitude towards international human rights at that time and later. However, in 1966 when the two UN human rights covenants were adopted, the Soviet global influence was already crucial—in particular with respect to the recognition of social and economic rights as internationally protected human rights. The very adoption of two separate human rights covenants (instead of one) in 1966 reflected the Soviet disagreement with the Western emphasis on freedom rights. It seems thus a stretch to say that the USSR did not participate in the global human rights discourse during the Cold War.

Post-Soviet Russia adopted a democratic constitution in 1993 and ratified the European Convention of Human Rights in 1998. Yet since then, the political debates in the Parliamentary Assembly of the Council of Europe, the extensive Russian practice in the European Court of Human Rights and its political reception in Moscow have been far from easy.[46] Conservative forces in Russia apparently have concluded that because of the way in which the Council of Europe

43 Nicolas Berdyaev, *The Origin of Russian Communism* (University of Michigan Press, Ann Arbor, MI, 1960, first published in 1937), 158ff.

44 Aleksandr Solzhenitsyn, "A World Split Apart "(8 June 1978), address at Harvard Class Day Afternoon Exercises, available at <http://www.lib.ru/PROZA/SOLZHENICYN/s_world_engl.txt_with-big-pictures.html>.

45 Alexander Solschenizyn, *Meine amerikanischen Jahre* (Langen/Müller, Munich, 2007, transl. Andrea Wöhr and Fedor B. Poljakov), 77.

46 See, further, Lauri Mälksoo, "Russia and European Human-Rights Law. Margins of the Margin of Appreciation", *infra*, 217ff.

system for the protection of human rights functions—and prioritizes—its values, Russia is condemned to remain the disciple: being in the role of the one who needs 'to be civilized'. Ultimately, problems in the European Court of Human Rights always remain the tip of the iceberg—reflecting far larger practices and, ultimately, predominant thinking in state and society.

Seen in this light, the 2006 Orthodox Declaration and the views of Patriarch Kirill I symbolize increasing traditionalist resistance from Russia to the liberal notion of human rights. It is noteworthy that Kirill starts with the deconstruction of the foundational concept of human rights: that of human dignity. The UDHR recognizes in its preamble the "inherent" dignity of all human beings and emphasizes further in Article 1 that: "All human beings are born free and equal in dignity and rights." This is a quite different concept from Patriarch Kirill who emphasizes that human beings are born in sin, and that dignity is something that can be acquired and lost. If the person is not acting in a "good" way, she can lose her dignity, and—as can be logically inferred from Kirill's argument—the foundation of her human rights.

To highlight this dilemma in concrete terms, one contemporary example would be the human rights of terrorists. Although there is no clear-cut global detailed consensus on what terrorism means, there is a consensus that terrorism as such is evil. But do bad people, terrorists, by their acts lose all their human dignity and rights? One can think of the killing (and awkward burial) of Osama Bin Laden but, also, of the judgment of Russia's Constitutional Court of 28 June 2007, regarding the constitutionality of a stipulation in the 1996 RF Federal Act on Burials.[47] The Act foresees that burial sites of terrorists may not be revealed to their relatives, and the applicants lost their appeal in which they challenged the constitutionality of such a provision. Apparently, terrorists (or those suspected of terrorism) who have been killed do not have enough dignity so that their relatives could learn about where the state buried them.[48] Terrorist crimes are perhaps the most dramatic example, and at least common-law lawyers know by experience that hard cases make bad law. Nevertheless, one also can wonder whether—according to Kirill's understanding of human dignity—the members

47 RF Constitutional Court Judgment, "Po delu o proverke konstitutsionnosti stat'i 14.1 Federal'nogo Zakona 'O pogrebenii i pokhoronnom dele' i Polozheniia o pogrebenii lits, smert' kotorykh nastupila v rezul'tate presecheniia sovershennogo imi terroristicheskogo akta, v sviazi s zhaloboi grazhdan K.I. Gusieva i E.Kh. Karmovoi" (2007) No.8-P, *Vestnik Konstitutsionnogo Suda* (2007) No.4; and Federal'nyi Zakon "O pogrebenii i pokhoronnom dele" (1996) No.8-FZ (as amended), *Rossiiskaia Gazeta* (1996) No.12.

48 See Valerii D. Zor'kin, *Konstitutsiia i prava cheloveka v XXI veke". K 15-letiu Konstitutsii Rossiiskoi Federatsii i 60-letiiu Vseobshchei deklaratsii prav cheloveka* (Norma, Moscow, 2008), 91-98. See, also, Lauri Mälksoo, "Continuity and Change in the Russian Federation's Human Rights Policies in the Fight against Terror", in Michael Goodhart and Anja Mihr (eds.), *Human Rights in the 21st Century. Continuity and Change since 9/11* (Palgrave Macmillan, New York, NY, 2011), 86-104.

of the Pussy Riot punk band deserved their 2012 harsh criminal sentences because, by bringing their punk performance to Moscow's Orthodox Cathedral, they themselves had diminished their own human dignity? If so, then such a notion of human dignity might conveniently explain and justify some of the recent Russian cases and practices in the field of human rights which have been harshly criticized in the West.

The ultimate effect of such re-thinking of the notion of human dignity is evident: philosophical relativization of the validity of human rights. Instead of—at least fundamental—human rights being inalienable, they can in fact be taken away (or taken back) by state and society if the person herself is understood to have undermined her own human dignity. The crucial "liberal" question remains, though: who gets to decide about the nature of good and bad, and the question why and when dignity—or the main source for one's human rights—has been lost? For example, the Orthodox Declaration emphasizes that "fatherland"—or rather, what seems to be meant there, "love for fatherland" because "fatherland" as such cannot be a value—is no less important a value than are human rights. I, for one, sympathize with this view in principle but, nevertheless, the question remains: who gets to determine what suits the fatherland and what counts as patriotic? If the ruler does not (sufficiently) care about democratic legitimacy, is his self-serving interpretation of patriotism fully binding for all citizens?

Another significant trait in the Orthodox Declaration is the claim that Russia constitutes a unique civilization, *i.e.*, is *foundationally* different from (Western) Europe. Secular human-rights scholars in Russia such as Elena A. Lukasheva (from Moscow's Institute of State and Law) also have referred to a civilizational difference, partly in order to explain Russia's relatively poor performance in the Strasbourg human-rights protection system.[49] Yet Kirill's point seems to be that Russia should not be patronized by the West but, instead, that it has all the right to proudly remain normatively "on its own". One should add that the idea that Russia is a unique civilization—and, thus, existentially different from the rest of Europe—is a continuously contested question in modern Russian intellectual history. Yet, the perspective of Russia as a unique civilization is by far not representative of all Russian scholars and opinion leaders; a point made in the context of intense inner-Russian debates and struggles. From the point of view of Russian legal scholars who emphasize the priority of human rights, also in the Russian Constitution of 1993,[50] the argument of Russia's civilizational

49 See Elena A. Lukasheva, *Chelovek, pravo, tsivilizatsii: normativno-tsennostnoe izmerenie* (Norma, Moscow, 2009); and *id.*, (ed.), *Prava cheloveka i protsess globalizatsii sovremennogo mira* (Norma, Moscow, 2007).

50 See, *e.g.*, Sergei Alekseev, "K konstitutsii cheloveka. Rossiiskii Osnovnoi zakon: real'nost' i perspektivy", *Nezavisimaia Gazeta* (16 November 2012), available at <http://www.ng.ru/ideas/2012-11-16/5_konstitutsia.html>.

difference from the West must seem like a lousy excuse for the government's under-performance in the field of human rights.

It generally is worth highlighting that Patriarch Kirill's views are not just—or not even primarily—directed towards the world outside Russia; they are expressed in the framework of ideological contestations within Russia. The context of this may differ from Western contexts: for example, a leading Russian independent daily newspaper *Nezavisimaia Gazeta* each month measures Patriarch Kirill in the ranking of the country's leading politicians. In January 2013, for instance, he occupied place 13; in February 2013, place 10 in these rankings.[51]

A particularly sensitive part in the Orthodox Declaration and Kirill I's views are the rights of homosexual people which he sees suffering from a "disease".[52] Currently, there is no all-European normative consensus on the right of homosexuals to marry one other; the issue is debated and decided in each state individually and resolved, if at all, on the level of state's own constitutional (fundamental) rights. Therefore, it is an exaggeration to make the point that the European liberal concept of human rights is flawed because it automatically brings along, *e.g.*, the acceptance of the right of homosexuals to marry one another.

In countries where there is no broad support for fully equal rights to homosexual individuals or couples, the topic exposes a huge populist potential. A case at point can be seen in the rhetorical skirmishes exchanged within the framework of the *Markin v. Russia* case in which the Constitutional Court of Russia and the European Court of Human Rights clashed in their interpretation of whether gender equality in the army (or the lack of it) should constitute of margin-of-appreciation situation. When in 2010, the ECtHR's Chamber effectively overruled Russia's Constitutional Court's position and suggested that Russia should amend its respective laws,[53] the Constitutional Court's Chief Justice, Valerii Zor'kin, directed his frustration at the issue of the rights of homosexuals (which was not the actual controversy in *Markin*). Chief Justice Zor'kin published an emotional article in the fall of 2010 in *Rossiiskaia Gazeta*, entitled "The Margin of Giving In".[54] He criticized the ECtHR's reliance on its earlier decision in its 1999 *Smith and Grady v. United Kingdom* decision[55] which concerned the rights of homosexual men in the army, arguing that the preoccupation of contemporary European lawyers with homosexual rights was taking "grotesque forms" that sometimes turned into a "tragedy" (such as in Serbia where organizing a gay

51 Dmitry Orlov, "100 vedushikh politikov v fevrale 2013 goda", *Nezavisimaia Gazeta* (1 March 2013), available at< http://www.ng.ru/ideas/2013-03-01/5_top100.html>.

52 Kirill (2012), *op.cit.* note 3, 70.

53 *Markin v. Russia* (Chamber judgment 7 October 2010), Application No.30078/06.

54 Valerii Zor'kin, "Predel ustupchivosti", *Rossiiskaia Gazeta* (29 October 2010), available at <http://www.rg. ru/2010/10/29/zorkin.html>.

55 *Smith v. United Kingdom* (1999) Application Nos.33985/96, 33986/96, 1999-VI Eur. Ct. H.R. 45.

parade in a "traditionally Orthodox country" led to "mass riots").[56] While in the West it may have been tempting to condemn Serbian riots as ignorant, according to Chief Justice Zor'kin, they also could be a protest of the reasonably upset majority against a minority that "violates cultural, moral and religious code".[57]

In response to such judgments, Chief Justice Zor'kin argued that Russia had three alternatives. The first two were practically unwise: self-isolation, on the one hand, and servile subjugation of sovereignty to international institutions, on the other. (Compare this point with an earlier quotation from Patriarch Kirill I, about the alternatives which traditionalist countries currently have![58] It is a thinking that is reproduced almost verbatim.) The right way, in Chief Justice Zor'kin's view, would be to put delicate but firm domestic constitutional limits to judgments of the ECtHR concerning Russia.[59]

Thus, it can be argued that Kirill's traditionalist-religious interpretation of human rights has become quite influential, both within Russia and beyond. On 1 July 2013, an amendment to the 1996 Criminal Code of the Russian Federation entered into force which provides that "acts in public, demonstrating clear disrespect [*iavnoe neuvazhenie*] for society and committed with the intent to insult the religious feelings of believers" are punishable by fines of up to 300,000 rubles or by prison sentences of up to one year.[60] However, if such acts are committed "in a specially designated place of worship", then the maximum fine is 500,000 rubles (or three years in prison).[61] In principle, President Putin seems to hold the view that the feelings of the religious individuals must be protected by law and that a "vulgar, primitive" understanding of secularism must be abandoned.[62] However, Russian historians of religion have expressed their concern about the effects of the law,[63] and a 2013 editorial of *Nezavisimaia Gazeta* comes to concluding that the shift from a secular state to clerical state could not legitimately

56 Zor'kin (2008). *op.cit.* note 48.

57 *Ibid.*

58 Cf. *op.cit.* note 19.

59 See, further, Lauri Mälksoo, "Case Note on Markin v. Russia", 106 *American Journal of International Law* (2012), 836-842.

60 Federal'nyi zakon RF (29 June 2013) No.136-FZ, *Rossiiskaia gazeta* (2 July 2013) No.6117, amendment to Art.148(1), RF Criminal Code.

61 *Ibid.*, amendment to Art.148(2), RF Criminal Code.

62 Aleksandra Samarina, "Razmyvateli i ukrepiteli. Opponentov vlasti obviniaiut v beznravstvennosti i bezdukhovnosti", *Nezavisimaia Gazeta* (4 February 2013), available at <http://www.ng.ru/politics/2013-02-04/1_opponenty.html>.

63 Valerii Viatkin, "Nauka pechal'nogo obraza. Zakonoproekt o zashchite chuvstv veruiushikh mozhet udarit' po istorikam", *Nezavisimaia Gazeta* (6 March 2013), available at <http://www.ng.ru/ society/2013-03-06/6_science.html>.

take place without a referendum because Article 14 of the Russian Constitution is unambiguously clear about the secular nature of the Russian Federation.[64]

In Europe too, the clash of traditionalist and strictly secular notions of human rights has led to surprising results and turn-arounds, for example the famous 2011 *Lautsi v. Italy* case before the ECtHR[65] involving the use of crucifixes in Italian schools. In this case, the Russian Federation together with Armenia, Bulgaria, Cyprus, Greece, Lithuania and Malta (an alliance of some Orthodox and Catholic countries) submitted joint observations to the Grand Chamber. It must have been also thanks to the energy of these governments that the ECtHR entirely changed its mind: while the Chamber had been unanimously supporting the applicant against the Italian state, the Grand Chamber reversed the opinion.

Finally, there also has been a noteworthy initiative demonstrating new thinking in the UN Human Rights Council. On 24 March 2011, UN Human Rights Council passed a resolution[66] which welcomes the holding of a

> "workshop for an exchange of views on how a better understanding of traditional values of humankind underpinning international human rights norms and standards can contribute to the promotion and protection of human rights and fundamental freedoms".[67]

The resolution affirms that "dignity, freedom and responsibility are traditional values, shared by all humanity and embodied in universal rights instruments".[68] The resolution goes on to recognize that the better understanding and appreciation of these values contribute to promoting and protecting human rights and fundamental freedoms.[69]

However, the main thing that stood out in the 2011 resolution of the UN Human Rights Council was that just 24 countries in the Council were in favor of it, 14 countries voted against while 7 abstained. The Russian Federation—together with a number of non-Western countries—voted in favor whereas European countries—and the US—cast negative votes.[70] In his speech of 21 June 2011, Patriarch Kirill emphasized the active role of the ROC in bringing forward this resolution at the UN.[71] However, Patriarch Kirill also regretted that "a number

64 Editorial, "Est' vyshii sud – Konstitutsionnyi", *Nezavisimaia Gazeta* (14 March 2013), available at <http://www.ng.ru/editorial/2013-03-14/2_red.html>.

65 *Lautsi v. Italy* (18 March 2011) Application No.30814/06.

66 Human Rights Council, Resolution 16/3, "Promoting Human Rights and Fundamental Freedoms through a Better Understanding of Traditional Values of Humankind", UN Doc.A/HRC/RES/16/3 (24 March 2011).

67 *Ibid.*, 1.

68 *Ibid.*, 3.

69 *Ibid.*, 4.

70 See the voting record on Resolution 16/3 at <http://www.un.org/ga/search/view_doc.asp?symbol=%20A/HRC/RES/16/3>.

71 ROC, Patriarch's speech (21 June 2011), available at <http://www.patriarchia.ru/db/text/1546416.html>.

of European countries" continued on the path of the secular notion of human rights which appeared particularly erroneous at the backdrop of moral crisis in contemporary society.[72]

Conclusions

In 1984, the Soviet Georgian film director Tengiz Abuladze made a movie titled *Pokaianie* (Repentance) which was seen as bold allegory of Stalin's (and Beria's) dictatorial rule and crimes. The film initially was banned in the USSR and only publically shown in the final years of the *perestroika* period. The film ends with a famous scene in which an old woman asks for a way to the temple and, learning that the road does not lead to the temple, says: "What good is a road if it does not lead to the temple?"

Now, Patriarch Kirill I asks essentially the same question about the Council of Europe's human-rights protection system. It is well known that the most outstanding representatives of the Russian intellectual and literary tradition always have been fascinated by the "Big Questions" of human existence. In this context, it is a welcome phenomenon that the ROC and, in particular, Patriarch Kirill I have turned their attention to the concept of human rights: a concept that increasingly constitutes the language of international relations (a role that, in preceding centuries, was played by public international law). The European consensus on human rights can gain from a dialog among different partners with well-reasoned opinions. In this sense, the reception of liberal ideas in Russia is akin to a useful litmus test for West: if an idea encounters resistance in Russia, chances are good that the same idea also would be ideologically rejected in some other 'traditionalist' places outside the West. Western activists and scholars dreaming of a World Court of Human Rights, therefore, should take quite seriously such historic and cultural differences in the understanding of human rights.[73]

Patriarch Kirill's critical views on the Western culture of human rights also raise some uncomfortable and usually suppressed questions: for example, what, if any, is the interrelationship between the culture of human rights and the anthropocentric world-view on the one hand, and the negative demographic processes in the West and Russia on the other? While Patriarch Kirill makes an attempt to contrast the Orthodox world-view in Russia with liberalism in the West, both geographical-political spaces share a number of fundamental challenges—including the demographic decline. Nevertheless, Kirill's argumentation leads to a question that remains an important one and must be reflected more vigorously in the human-rights discourse: can (too much) freedom lead to self-destruction?

72 *Ibid.*

73 Philip Alston, "Against a World Court of Human Rights", 28(1) *Ethics and International Affairs* (2014), 197-212.

Yet while dialog on the nature and limits of human rights is good and needs in principle to be promoted, the outcome of such dialogs also matters hugely. For example, if Russia was admitted as member of the Council of Europe's human-rights protection system in 1998 under the—sometimes explicit, sometimes implicit—presumption that it must "get in line" with standards already worked out in liberal European countries, now Russia's political elites increasingly have concluded that European human rights-standards are based on questionable ideas and premises. Thus, Russia and other Council of Europe countries have a common problem which should not be ignored politically. Should Russia no longer want to transform itself in terms of approximation with Western Europe, the parting of ways in the Council of Europe should not be entirely ruled out as option. Should Russia indeed come to the conclusion that it wants to be (or remain) an independent "civilization" in its present historical formation, it would be free to do so, of course. In this sense, we live in an era of the right to (ideological) self-determination. However, unless the other European countries would agree to re-conceive the CoE system as a looser system of "inter-civilizational dialog", which is unlikely, Russia should then also simultaneously decide whether its new/old concept of the uniqueness of its own civilization and its impact on human rights is compatible with CoE premises. Moreover, the other European countries should not shy away from this question either.

However, the present chapter also points out that the ROC's and Patriarch Kirill's views on human rights reflect intense inner-Russian debates and struggles on the post-Soviet national idea and the future of the country. In the early 1990s, the rightness of the liberal discourse was decided from above; in the new millennium, we have witnessed a conservative traditionalist backlash to ideas imported "from abroad" and implemented "from above". The West should observe this evolving Russian debate with sincere and benevolent attention but remain resolute in its own underlying constitutional principles of which respect for human rights constitutes a core.

Culture Re-introduced: Contestation of Human Rights in Contemporary Russia*

Petr Preclik

Introduction

By the end of the twentieth century, Russia had signed most of the global UN treaties and European instruments for the protection of human rights, had become a member of the Council of Europe (CoE), and for the first time in its history had allowed an international court, that is, the European Court of Human Rights (ECtHR), to exercise its authority over internal Russian matters. One could have said that Russia had accepted the European notion of international law, including human-rights law. Indeed, the then president of the Russian Federation, Dmitrii Medvedev—in his inaugural speech—had pledged respect for human rights and freedoms as it was these "that determine[d] the sense and the substance of all state policy".[1] Similarly, then-President Vladimir Putin—while proclaiming in 2000 the infamous 'dictatorship of law'—had hoped to restore federal authority over Russia's regions but, rather, found himself, to his own displeasure, pressed to extend that phrase to meet the demands of Russia's membership in the Council of Europe.[2]

However, Russia is still often perceived as an impediment to the overall development of the Council of Europe, an autocracy, and ultimately a human-rights violator. On the other hand, Russia, finding itself too often on the defensive, shields itself by referring to alleged Western Russophobia, double standards, and a mentor style of communication.[3]

* Parts of the present contribution were revised for the author's 2009 Master Thesis at Masaryk University (Brno) Faculty of Social Science (Department of International Relations and European Studies International Relations), entitled "Assessing the Impact of the European Court of Human Rights on Russia's Conduct in Chechnya in the Context of the Judicialization of World Politics", available at <http://is.muni.cz/th/102905/fss_m/Preclik_thesis_final_clean.txt>.

1 Dmitrii Medvedev, Speech at Inauguration Ceremony as President of Russia (7 May 2008), available at <http://www.kremlin.ru/eng/speeches/2008/05/07/1521_type82912type127286_200295.shtml>.

2 J.D. Kahn, "Russia's 'Dictatorship of Law' and the European Court of Human Rights", 29(1) *Review of Central and East European Law* (2004), 1-14, at 2.

3 A good example is the 2008 Russian commentary on the US Department of State Report on Human Rights. See Russian Ministry of Foreign Affairs, "Kommentarii Departamenta informatsii i pechati MID Rossii v sviazi s dokladom Gosudarstvennogo departamenta SShA o polozhenii s pravami cheloveka v mire" (12 March 2008), available at <http://www.mid.ru/brp_4.nsf/0/57887EDFED23AB5EC325740A0061164B>.

Lauri Mälksoo, ed.
Russia and European Human-Rights Law: The Rise of the Civilizational Argument 31-89

How should we understand these obvious paradoxes? In the words of Jeffrey Kahn, written already a decade ago:

> "Russia is trapped: unwilling to quit one of the only European organizations willing to accept it as an equal member, the Russian government finds itself increasingly called to meet the requirements of membership."[4]

To put it differently, Russia—despite its tendencies towards autocracy—had to sign up to the international human-rights regime, as it lives in a predominantly liberal area and, thus, had to maintain the 'trappings of democracy'[5] in order to legitimize itself. Losing the recognition and the self-image of its European political identity would be disastrous.

The problem lies in reducing politics into a mere dichotomy: either adhering to or violating the rules of a human-rights regime. Any plausible analysis should focus on the process through which human rights are contested and possibly translated into the foreign policy of the individual state. Despite the frequency with which scholars talk about human-rights culture, they hardly ever explore human rights on that level. If they occasionally do so, rights are then usually criticized as hostile to local cultures and blamed for reducing the world's entropy;[6] or *vice versa*, culture is perceived as a shield that dictators around the world use to repulse the introduction of human rights into their societies.[7]

I argue that the often omitted or discarded cultural level of human rights should be re-introduced into rights scholarship and that attention should be turned to the dynamics of interaction between universal human rights and particular local culture systems. However, discussing differing notions of human rights and their cultural embeddedness became almost heretical after the UN World Conference in 1993 in Vienna and has been constantly discredited ever since. The conclusion at that time was clear-cut: All human rights are universal, indivisible, interdependent, interrelated, and despite "the significance of national and regional particularities and various historical, cultural and religious backgrounds, it is the duty of States, [...] to promote and protect all human rights and fundamental freedoms".[8]

What strikes me is the reluctance of human-rights discourse to acknowledge the role of various ideas and notions behind its concepts. Human rights are

4 Kahn, *op.cit.* note 2, 6.

5 Robert Kagan, "End of Dreams, Return of History", *Policy Review* (2007) No.144.

6 For examples see, *inter alia*, Viatcheslav Morozov, "Resisting Entropy, Discarding Human Rights: Romantic Realism and Securitization of Identity in Russia", 37 *Cooperation and Conflict* (2002), 409-429.

7 See, *inter alia*, Jerome J. Shestack, "The Philosophic Foundations of Human Rights", 20 *Human Rights Quarterly* (1998), 201-234.

8 United Nations General Assembly, Vienna Declaration and Programme of Action, application A/CONF.157/23 (judgment of 12 July 1993), Art.5; emphasis added by the author.

presented as "divorced from base materialism, self-interest, and ideology",[9] disregarding their ideational roots in Western European thinking[10] and their temporal roots in specific post World War II settings.[11] Human rights—having become the dominant global legitimizing vocabulary—tend to dismiss different concepts of universal human good, however deeply these are embedded in historical practices of individual cultures, and create a monopoly on the conceptualization of that good.

Despite my skepticism about the universal nature of human rights, this chapter does not support boundless cultural relativism. I argue (together with others) that there is a constitutive paradox of both international law and the human-rights movement, *i.e.*, neither international law nor human rights can ever be really universal; however, any concession from the universality claim would be mortal to the concepts as such.[12] In other words, I do believe in the universalism of human rights; however, I also believe that universality is discursive and constructed and cannot be considered epistemologically absolute. Human rights function as a modern conceptualization of human good and peaceful well-being, however imperfect and time-bound. Human rights serve as a Popperian approximation to universal truth—coming ever closer, but never reaching it.

Thus, there is a need for research that goes beyond that perspective. The purely legal perception of human rights fails to explain various attitudes that different cultures hold towards human rights. Human rights more and more noticeably possess a creational power to establish or influence the identity of actors across the globe. Identity is a cultural phenomenon and, thus, only an analysis starting from the cultural level can uncover the inner dynamics with which human rights influence the self-perception of states and societies. I argue that human rights enter national discursive space as new meanings and have to be contested within that space; that is to say, despite their universal drive, rights have to be contested locally.

Having balanced itself between the West and the non-West, Russia serves as a good case study to confirm the general idea that human rights need to be studied as discursive practices, as local answers to locally perceived threats and

9 Makau Wa Mutua, "Politics and Human Rights: An Essential Symbiosis", in Michael Byers (ed.), *The Role of Law in International Politics* (Oxford University Press, New York, NY, 2000), 149-176, at 149.

10 Martti Koskenniemi, *From Apology to Utopia: The Structure of International Legal Argument* (Cambridge University Press, Cambridge, 2005), chapter 2.

11 Kathryn Sikkink, "The Power of Principled Ideas: Human Rights Policies in the United States and Western Europe", in Robert O. Keohane and Goldstein, Judith (eds.), *Ideas & Foreign Policy: Beliefs, Institutions and Political Change* (Cornell University Press, Ithaca, NY, London, 1993), 139-170.

12 Emmanuelle Jouannet, "Universalism and Imperialism: The True-False Paradox of International Law?", 18 *European Journal of International Law* (2007), 379-407, at 380.

as values contested within regional semantic spaces. While sharing borders with one of the strongest world identities—Europe—Russia walks a tightrope while searching for a balance between being European and unique, open or isolated, opposing or supporting European attitudes. It is exactly this tiptoeing on the edge of the European system that makes Russia, in my view, the best example to study the dynamics of human-rights contestation within national space.

Taking Russia as a case study would, *first*, help to deconstruct the often-employed Russian claim that it possesses a unique notion of human rights and, *second*, would help to understand the inner processes within the Russian Federation that shape that claim. However, the notion applied of 'us' as opposed to 'them' should not be hoisted to the level of the uniqueness of one or even of all. This is a study of identity re-creation and processes within that re-creation, not a defense of one's uniqueness.

While discussing the cultural contestation of human-rights notions in Russia, I argue that the current state of Russian discourse is one of securitization. This securitization stems from the large number of high-profile cases that Russia has lost at the ECtHR in Strasbourg, each of which undermines the key claim by Vladimir Putin that his regime "brought law, order, and prosperity to Russia".[13] Moscow, on the one hand, recognizes its commitment to the European regime of human-rights protection, including the authority of the ECtHR, yet blames the Council for bending the original meaning of rights, for an unlimited broadening of the understanding of the ECtHR, or for undisguised use of double standards in assessing the situation in different CoE member states. In other words, Russia perceives itself as being outside the dominant world order and in need of self-protection from being absorbed into, and transformed within, that world order beyond its control.

Structure of the Study

Having introduced my main assumptions and in order to argue for the above-developed hypothesis, this chapter develops as follows:

Part 2 proposes that human rights need to be read on the cultural level and describes the main features of this level. I argue that human rights have creational power to influence national identity and the process of its creation. National identity, in my view, represents a localized subsystem of a culture, whereas human rights operate as semantic variables entering that subsystem.

Having discussed the need to re-introduce cultural level into human-rights scholarship, part 3 develops a theoretical model of national identity as a cultural subsystem within which human rights are contested against other legitimizing projects. The question to examine is how to include culture in foreign-policy research. What role does national identity (and human rights contested within)

13 Alexei Trochev, "All Appeals Lead to Strasbourg?", 17 *Demokratizatsiya* (2009), 145-178, at 146.

play in foreign-policy considerations? Is there a role at all? To answer these questions, the chapter analyzes the applicable scope of international-relations theories.

Part 4 analyzes Russian human-rights discourse as applied in the context of the Council of Europe. The task is to illustrate how Russia engages itself in advocating its own specific notion of human rights, which differs from mainstream Western discourse. I will demonstrate how "the concept is treated within the dominant foreign policy discourse; how it interacts with other fundamental concepts, and how new meanings and structures are produced in this process".[14] The aim of this part is to describe the oratorical stalemate that impedes, or even blocks, further cooperation between Russia and other CoE members in the field of human rights. Part 4 then examines the formation of national identity within the Russian context and its interactions with human-rights discourse. *First*, on the side of international influences, I discuss the constitutive nature of the thousand-year-long balancing of Russia between East and West and its impact on the Russian understanding of human rights. *Second*, on the level of domestic determinants, I try to illustrate the most significant domestic inputs into the process of national-identity creation. *Third*, I conclude this part by examining the state of securitization of domestic discourse.

Part 5 then summarizes the findings and draws implications for the CoE and other human-rights organizations on how to understand and read the human-rights record of Russia while including the cultural level in the research.

Methodology

As already mentioned, the main scope of my analysis is the discipline of international relations. Other disciplines discussed or involved in my research, namely those of international law and cultural studies, are used only to the extent applicable within international-relations research. International law from the perspective of international relations is only one of the factors determining a state's behavior and as such can be outweighed by other considerations; it can be breached or complied with according to a state's preferences, and it can be analyzed as a political concept.

In order to proceed with the above-outlined structure of my argument, I follow the idea that "[t]hings do not mean (the material world does not convey meaning); rather, people construct the meaning of things, using the sign system (predominantly, but not exclusively linguistic)".[15] In this sense, I believe that the foreign policy of any state needs to be studied as "an instrument for the realization

14 Morozov, *op.cit.* note 6, 410.

15 Jennifer Milliken, "The Study of Discourse in International Relations: A Critique of Research and Methods", 5 *European Journal of International Relations* (1999), 225-254, at 229.

of the self-image [and] may be studied as an identity producing practice".[16] In other words, foreign policy is largely conducted as a discursive practice and needs to be studied as such. A discourse, in this sense, works as "a shared set of concepts, categories, and ideas that provides its adherents with a framework for making sense of situations, and which embodies judgements, assumptions, capabilities, dispositions, and intentions".[17] Discourses are productive, as they "operationalize a particular regime of truth, while excluding other possible modes of identity and action".[18] The fact of discourse productivity engenders the need to study hegemonic or dominant discourses and the way they are structured. In other words, I analyze an 'elites' regime of truth that enables certain courses of action by a state, while excluding other policies as 'unintelligible or unworkable'.[19] More precisely, I examine the strategies that Russia applies toward the dominant discourse of human rights in recent years.

I borrow the explanation of the method from Commuri:

> "I address this question by juxtaposing discourses (expressions of national identity) and events (observable aspects of action). The rationale of combining discourse and events analysis is that while discourse analysis allows us to understand the narratives of self/other, event analysis (historical) allows us to examine actions and correlate the two."[20]

In analyzing discourse, I examine the position of authorized speakers[21] and "those possessing the social power to define the foreign policy agenda".[22] For the purpose of this chapter, I chose to focus on state practices in creating discourse.[23] I turn attention, *first*, to verbatim records from the sittings of the Parliamentary Assembly of the Council of Europe (PACE), as they show the primary Russian reaction to, and interaction with, the human-rights discourse stemming from the CoE.

16 Alla Kassianova, "Russia: Still Open to the West? Evolution of the State Identity in the Foreign Policy and Security Discourse", 53 *Europe-Asia Studies* (2001), 821-839, at 822; emphasis added by the author.

17 John S. Dryzek, "Transnational Democracy in an Insecure World", 27 *International Political Science Review* (2006), 101-119, at 104.

18 *Ibid.*

19 Milliken, *op.cit.* note 15, 236.

20 Gitika Commuri, "The Relevance of National Identity Narratives in Shaping Foreign Policy: The Case of India-Pakistan Relations", 4 *Journal of South Asian Development* (2009), 161-202, at 163.

21 *Ibid*, 233.

22 Morozov, *op.cit.* note 6, 411.

23 In the language of Kassianova, there is a tendency to "separate the state (or government) from the company of the identity-producing actors, assigning it the role of intervening, authorising *mediator* privileging some narratives over others, prone to be captured by a particular identity narrative, and possessing instruments strengthening or mitigating the competing discourses". She concludes, however, that a state should also be considered as the *producer* rather than as mediator or arbiter of the identity discourse. See Kassianova, *op.cit.* note 16, 825.

Second, I turn to domestic authorized speakers who further shape interactions between international human-rights discourse and domestic discursive answers.

The necessary external framework for this analysis is then provided by the theory of transnational discursive democracy, whose model rests "on the notion that discourses and their interactions are consequential in producing international outcomes through their influence upon and constitution of actors".[24] In this sense, as soon as one accepts the constraining and enabling power of external dominant discourses such as liberal economy, human rights, or sustainable development, one has to ask how these discourses actually influence domestic discursive spaces. How can one operationalize the alleged power of these dominant discourses while entering national space? How can one describe the functioning or resistance of alternative discourses?

To answer these questions, I argue that the discipline of international relations should analyze the notion of human rights as culturally bound discursive variables that enter the national space of the state and interact with domestic discourses. To operationalize such an interaction, I propose a model based on the contestation thesis, *i.e.*, human rights need to be contested against the already-proven dominant practices of the individual state and through such contestation become embedded in the national self-image and institutions.

Culture Re-Introduced

Human rights, surprisingly, are often omitted from the discipline of international relations as being purely of a legal nature (and thus a focus of a different discipline), mere soft-power instruments of negligible importance (realism), or instrumental tools used to achieve and to ease inter-state cooperation (neoliberalism). Within the human-rights literature,[25] the topic of translating human-rights commitments into foreign-policy actions is usually omitted. The role of human-rights proponents is given almost solely to civil society or international organizations and the state is reduced to a black box; the role of which is to protect, respect and promote human rights without contesting them.

Only at the end of the twentieth century, the "enormous expansion in the range of issues and problems that are subject to regulation and institutionalization"[26] rendered it impossible for international-relations scholars to ignore the role that international law plays in international politics and forced an increasing interest

24 Dryzek, *op.cit.* note 17, 102.

25 For an introductory discussion, see, *inter alia*, Philip Alston, Ryan Goodman, Henry J. Steiner, *International Human Rights in Context: Law, Politics, Morals* (Oxford University Press, New York, NY, 2000); Jack Donnelly, *Universal Human Rights in Theory and Practice* (Cornell University Press, New York, NY, 2003); or Manfred Nowak, *Introduction to the International Human Rights Regime* (Martinus Nijhoff Publishers, Leiden, 2003).

26 Andrew Hurrell, *On Global Order* (Oxford University Press, Oxford, 2007), 6.

in examining the overlap between the two disciplines. International-relations scholarship has only slowly come to appreciate an observation made much earlier by Max Weber that there is a "generally observable need of any power [...] to justify itself".[27] In other words, "power is not self-justifying; it must be justified by reference to some source outside or beyond itself".[28]

But where should one look for external justification of power? The re-discovered question of the role which normativity plays in international conduct has resulted in rich scholarly discussion, with questions of commitment, compliance and legitimacy regaining their status.[29] At the same time, no one can deny that the simple need to legitimize one's actions within international law together with a wish to maintain one's status does not prevent states from committing unlawful acts and the simple realist argument that 'where there is no power, there can be no law' maintains some of its original appeal. As Andrew Hurrell argues, we are "not dealing with a vanished or vanishing Westphalian world [...] but rather with a world in which solidarist and cosmopolitan conceptions of governance coexist, often rather unhappily, with many aspects of the old pluralist order".[30]

We have to realize that there have been significant changes in the international system that force us to reconsider the role of ideas, culture, and normativity in our understanding of world politics and the functioning of the state.

First, changes in the role and understanding of the state are no longer deniable. Despite the fact that states remain the main actors in the international system, they are also currently undergoing "part transnationalization, part de-nationalization, and part privatization", *i.e.*, processes that are all accompanied by, on the one hand, decentralization and devolution of powers to the local level, and transnationalization of law and policy, on the other.[31] To put it differently, as the state disaggregates:

27 Max Weber, *Economy and Society: An Outline of Interpretative Sociology* (University of California Press, Berkeley, CA, 1978), 953.

28 Hurrell, *op.cit.* note 26, 39.

29 See, *inter alia*, Kenneth W. Abbott, Robert O. Keohane, Andrew Moravcsik, Anne-Marie Slaughter, Duncan Snidal, "The Concept of Legalization", 54 *International Organization* (2000), 401-419; Andrew Moravcsik, "The Origins of Human Rights Regimes: Democratic Delegation in Postwar Europe", 54 *International Organization* (2000), 217-252, Christian Reus-Smit, "Politics and International Legal Obligation", 9 *European Journal of International Relations* (2003), 591-625; Oona A. Hathaway, "Why Do Countries Commit to Human Rights Treaties?", 51 *Journal of Conflict Resolution* (2007), 588-621; or Emilie M. Hafner-Burton *et al.*, "International Human Rights Law and the Politics of Legitimation: Repressive States and Human Rights Treaties", 23 *International Sociology* (2008), 115-141.

30 Hurrell, *op.cit.* note 26, 9.

31 See Shalini Randeira, "De-politization of Democracy and Judicialization of Politics", 24 *Theory, Culture & Society* (2007), 38-44, at 40.

> "The traditional maps of domestic checks and balances are also redrawn in the never-ending struggle to govern and to review government. In an era of inter-dependency, [...] the national government [...] must forge coalitions across national boundaries to remain effective domestically."[32]

Second, the international system is undergoing a normative change. As some scholars have declared, there is a tendency towards a global normative synthesis that would bring about the creation of a global community of communities. To put it bluntly, having dissimilated for millennia, "humankind is slowly and often reluctantly assimilating [again]".[33] George Ulrich, in this sense, sees human rights as increasingly working as a global ethical commitment and serving as a normative guide for the emerging global community, as unified answers to global threats, and as a threshold for newcomers to pass.[34]

In other words, within the scope of international relations, "the past two decades have seen increasing interest in extending democracy into an international system long inhospitable to democratic projects beyond the level of the nation-state".[35] Andrew Hurrell goes even further when he concludes that a "new *raison de système* [was] developing that [would] alter and ultimately displace the old-fashioned notion of *raison d'état*".[36]

Third, along with the evolution of the normative cascade within the international system came its enmeshment with international institutions. Never before was the range of institutions so broad, exponentially increasing in numbers, scope, and agendas. The network of institutions—of which almost any state in the system is a member and subject—is almost impenetrable. While discussing this institutional entanglement, "it is not difficult to highlight the weakness of particular institutions, it is harder to deny the cumulative impact of institutional enmeshment across an ever-increasing range of subjects and sectors".[37]

Lastly, the question of when and why states follow international law became even more complicated once scholars began to consider non-state actors and,

32 Eyal Benvenisti, "Reclaiming Democracy: The Strategic Uses of Foreign and International Law by National Courts", *Tel Aviv University Law Faculty Papers* (2008) No.59, 44.

33 Rein Müllerson, "Being Tough on Terrorism or Respecting Human Rights: A False Dilemma of Authoritarian and Liberal Responses", 48(12) *American Behavioral Scientist* (2005), 1626-1656, at 1626.

34 See George Ulrich, "Towards a Theory of Global Ethics in Support of Human Rights", in Wolfgang Benedek, Koen De Feyter, and Fabrizio Marrella (eds.), *Economic Globalisation and Human Rights* (Cambridge University Press, Cambridge, 2007), 39-66.

35 Dryzek, *op.cit.* note 17, 101.

36 Andrew Hurrell, "Hegemony, Liberalism and Global Order: What Space for Would-be Great Powers?", 82 *International Affairs* (2006), 1-19, at 7. The ECtHR has been very outspoken on this issue, proclaiming that democracy appeared to be the sole political model contemplated by the Convention and, consequently, the only one compatible with it. See case of the *United Communist Party of Turkey and others v. Turkey* (30 January 1998) No.19392/92, para. 45.

37 Hurrell, *op.cit.* note 26, 66.

more recently, also international citizenry as relevant for analysis. Together with the development of binding international human-rights norms, omitting states' citizens outside the decision-making and legitimacy-making process seems "entirely ruled out from the realm of possibilities",[38] which in turn makes modern democracies extremely wary of keeping their legitimacy *vis-à-vis* such third-party actors. As Karl Josef Partsch notes, "transformation of the position of the individual is one of the most remarkable developments in contemporary international law".[39]

One has to further abandon the artificial divide between international law (including human-rights law) and international politics. What I argue, alongside many others,[40] is that the artificial division of international law and international-relations theory in Morgenthau's way is obsolete and of little value to current research. No longer can political scientists think only in terms of interest defined as power, nor can lawyers think only in terms of conformity of action with legal rules.[41] No longer is it plausible or feasible for any political theory to strictly distinguish between the political, economic or legal—as Morgenthau had asserted in his theoretical design.

"Law, like politics, is a meeting place for ethics and power", exclaimed Edward H. Carr in 1946, while referring to the inherent link between the two fields.[42] However, as soon as Morgenthau divorced law from politics and Kenneth Waltz denied international law the status of a systemic force, it seemed that the law chose to accept ethics while refusing to have anything in common with notions of power, while politics did the exact opposite. Crude power was the only driving force; ethics had no place in state conduct. Consequently, the

38 Aristide R. Zolberg, "Immigration and Multiculturalism in the Industrial Democracies", in Rainer Bauböck, Agnes Heller and Aristide R. Zolberg (eds.), *The Challenge of Diversity: Integration and Pluralism in Societies of Immigration* (Avebury, Aldershot, UK, 1996), 57.

39 Karl Josef Partsch, "Individuals in International Law", in Rudolf Bernhardt (ed.), *Encyclopedia of Public International Law* (Max Planck Institute for Comparative Public Law and International Law, Heidelberg, 1995), 957-958, at 957.

40 For ongoing discussion on the relationship between law and politics, see Kenneth W. Abbott, "Modern International Relations Theory: A Prospectus for Lawyers", 14 *Yale Journal of International Law* (1989), 335-411; Anne-Marie Slaughter, "International Law and International Relations Theory: A Dual Agenda", 87 *American Journal of International Law* (1993), 205-239; Robert O. Keohane, "International Relations and International Law: Two Optics", 38 *Harvard International Law Journal* (1997), 487-502; Anthony Clark Arend, "Do Legal Norms Matter in International Law and International Politics", 38(2) *Virginia Journal of International Law* (1998), 107-154; Martha Finnemore and Stephen J. Toope, "Alternatives to Legalization: Richer Views on Law and Politics", 55 *International Organization* (2001), 743-758; Christian Reus-Smit (ed.), *The Politics of International Law* (Cambridge University Press, Cambridge, 2004); or Koskenniemi, *op.cit.* note 10.

41 See Hans Morgenthau, *Politics among Nations* (McGraw Hill, New York, NY, 1985), 13.

42 Quoted in Miles Kahler, "Conclusion: The Causes and Consequences of Legalization", 54 *International Organization* (2000), 661-683, at 661.

discipline of international relations excluded law from its analysis—despite calls from several prominent legal scholars for a mutual dialogue.[43]

Only at the end of the last century did the "enormous expansion in the range of issues and problems that are subject to regulation and institutionalization"[44] render it impossible for internationa-relations scholars to ignore the role that international law plays in international politics and forced increasing interest in examining the overlap between the two disciplines.

Similarly, human-rights activists and scholars only blind themselves if they perceive human rights as apolitical, as a trump answer to political bickering and fault play.

In sum, there is an intrinsic entanglement between law and politics that needs to be addressed by both international law and international relations; it is not possible to isolate one from the other. That is not only to embrace the realist point of view that "where there is neither community of interest, nor balance of power, there is no international law";[45] in other words, that international law is "mired in, and lacking force without politics".[46] Not only do politics influence the law, but the causal arrow goes both ways. As Christian Reus-Smit bluntly observes, "the discourse of politics is now replete with the language of law and legitimacy".[47] International law constrains political choices even in the hardest security issues, forcing states to legitimize their action within its vocabulary and to consider the political costs of a breach of the law.[48]

In recent decades, the international system has undergone several changes that challenge the initial assumptions of international-relations scholars. Disaggregation of the state, the normative cascade within global discourses, institutional enmeshment, and changes to the position of individuals within the system—all these changes force scholars to reconsider the ways in which the state works within the international community, accepts its rules and norms, and creates its foreign policy.

43 The almost legendary contribution and factual initiator of the discussion was Slaughter, *op.cit.* note 40.

44 Hurrell, *op.cit.* note 26, 6.

45 Morgenthau, *op.cit.* note 41, 296.

46 Reus-Smit, *op.cit.* note 40, 16.

47 *Ibid.*, 2.

48 Even the only remaining military superpower, the US, considers the costs of breaching international law, tries to legitimize its actions by using its vocabulary—consider US lawyers trying their best to read the anticipatory self-defense concept into the UN Charter—and has to consider which weapons to use and what targets to bomb in its war scenarios. See, respectively, Joseph S. Nye, *Soft Power: The Means to Success in World Politics* (Public Affairs, New York, NY, 2004); and Noam Chomsky, *Failed States* (Penguin Books, London, 2006).

However, despite the progress of cultural research in the last twenty years,[49] speaking about culture and history within international-relations research remains somewhat problematic. As Chabal and Daloz note, Western comparative politics is "singularly ill-equipped"[50] to integrate cultural variables into its research designs. Culture always remains a residual culture: it has to be taken into account but it never oversteps the threshold of being a mere spice or color to the objective political process and merely helps to "fine tune or refine an interpretation of politics in a specific setting, [but never amounts to] a primary or a causal factor of the changes that [took] place".[51]

My aim is to reinstate history and culture as constitutive and fundamental parts of analysis and, therefore, oppose the behavioral idea of ahistorical science. Through the behavioralist lens, history and culture have become unnecessary and non-scientific, serving only to search for evidence that the nature of the international system is *de facto* eternal and unchanging. To the contrary, I believe that one needs to focus on functional changes in international systems, notions of the state and sovereignty and discuss how these have changed over time. As one prominent scholar notes, "only a study of the conditions of international life at a particular time, and of its historical development, can elucidate the true international legal consciousness".[52]

Hitherto, embracing culture within social-science research, including human rights, has usually taken the form of one of two extremes. In the first extreme, cultural differences are considered superficial, merely masking similarities between all human beings. Conveyed into human-rights discourse, culture is dismissed as being in the service of human-rights violators as an excuse for not obeying their rights commitments,[53] or simply as irrelevant in the face of the universal nature of rights. The second extreme considers culture cleavages to be so deep that they call into question the very existence of a shared human nature. This approach is shared by many anthropologists who oppose any universal claim as imperialist and ill-fated.

49 Lane and Ersson emphasize namely multiculturalism, postmaterialism, postmodern nationalism, the politics of recognition, the trust society, or the clash of civilizations. See Jan-Erik Lane and Svante Ersson, *Culture and Politics: A Comparative Approach* (Ashgate, Aldershot, UK, 2005), 1.

50 Patrick Chabal and Jean-Pascal Daloz, *Culture Troubles: Politics and the Interpretation of Meaning* (Hurst & Company, London, 2006), 5.

51 *Ibid.,* 11. For a contradictory opinion, see Lane and Ersson, *op.cit.* note 49.

52 Vladimir E. Grabar, *The History of International Law in Russia 1647-1917: A Bio-Bibliographical Study* (Oxford University Press, New York, NY, W.E. Butler ed. & transl., 1990, translated from: V.E. Grabar', *Materialy k istorii literatury mezhdunarodnogo prava v Rossii (1647-1917)* (Izdatel'stvo akademii nauk SSSR, Moscow 1958), 385.

53 Shestack, *op.cit.* note 7.

How can we find a moderate, middle way? Are there indeed some notions, ideas, or vague concepts that are common to all human beings and that create a shared human nature? As Chabal and Daloz argue, every culture on Earth may contain an 'unconscious universal'[54] that can be embedded in religion, political ideology, ethics, or philosophy. Such an unconscious universal represents the conceptualization of the laws of the ontological objective world. However, as epistemological cognition depends on actors, so does the conceptualization of a universal. These concepts then act as an organized and closed archive of historical memory of the respective societies, and they are dominant and power-controlled in relation to a certain period.[55]

Why should human rights, the most recent claimant of universal good, concern itself with such an ever changing, unstable and evanescent phenomenon as culture? The aim of rights is to emancipate individuals from state power, to protect them against perceived threats, and allow them undisturbed development. Unfortunately, this approach too often falls into the trap of endless universalism as it supposes that people around the globe demand the same rights and that only stubborn governments are depriving them of these, so that cultural differences are disregarded.

I argue against the assumed naturalness of human rights—rights claim to be not only pre-institutional (they belong to people solely for their humanity) but, also, pre-cultural. For Fran Markowitz:

> "These symbolic attempts to supersede artificially created boundaries [that is, states and nations] by offering a more mobile, hybridized and authentic world of inherent fairness and dignity have done very little to forge an apparatus for dismantling the very real conditions of economic inequality and physical want."[56]

But how can we operationalize culture? Chabal and Daloz propose that culture should be studied as a system of meanings, not as a system of values. Values and their explanations are, in their view, ethnocentric and, moreover, cannot explain cultural differences within a single society. "To look at culture in terms of meanings [...] is to attempt to reveal the language in which people, who may disagree about values, or political ends, can do so within a shared perspective."[57] Culture can then be operationalized as a system of inherited conceptions expressed in symbolic forms; this system is essentially a semiotic one and helps to structure the meanings through which people give shape to their experience.[58]

54 Chabal and Daloz, *op.cit.* note 50, 58.

55 Peter L. Berger and Thomas Luckmann, *The Social Construction of Reality: A Treatise in the Sociology of Knowledge* (Penguin Books, London, 1966), 53.

56 *Ibid.*, 334.

57 Chabal and Daloz, *op.cit.* note 50, 21-22.

58 *Ibid.*, 23.

Even as one accepts the semantic nature of culture and the need to study it as a system of meanings, not of values, the question remains of how to include it in any possible international-relations research design. I argue that the focal point between culture and the foreign policy of any state is the concept of national identity. National identity, in this sense, is the ever-continuing cycle of the 're-recreation' of a system of shared meanings and redistribution of significance within that system. New meanings are contested against historically proven ones.

In such a design, human rights cannot escape interaction with, and inclusion in, the process of national-identity formation. National identity is a construction, "an elaborate palimpsest of stories, images, resonances, collective memories, invented and carefully nurtured by traditions".[59] It is a cultural norm that is "conceived not as a coherent structure but as a multiplicity of discourses, which emerges in relations with multiple others".[60] National identity unites the nation around a system of shared meanings and notions and divides one nation from another by nurturing ideas of distinctiveness, uniqueness, specialness or mere divergence. It helps to interpret the reality of state and society's everyday life, it determines the scale on which states perform rational cost/benefit calculations, and influences the perception of threats menacing the nation. However, the role of culture and national identity in foreign policy should not be taken as given, but as a part of a process that is often selective and often material.[61]

Human rights enter the semantic space of society and challenge the historically contested system of values and meanings within it and challenge power structures that are not in compliance with the emerging 'global ethical commitment' of rights.[62]

However, none of the above criticism aims to support and follow the cultural-relativism approach. François Jullien rightly wrote that:

> "Most often we waver between a naïve universalism (as if the concept of law had always existed everywhere) and a lazy relativism (as though human rights were not valid for Chinese, whereas experience shows us that since they discovered that concept, they have found it harder and harder to do without it)."[63]

But how should one overcome the gap between lazy relativism and naïve universalism? How should we distinguish the universal from the culturally bound? Which

59 Anthony Pagden (ed.), *The Idea of Europe: From Antiquity to the European Union* (Cambridge University Press, Cambridge, 2002), 33.

60 Alexander Bukh, "Identity, Foreign Policy and the 'Other': Japan's 'Russia'", 15 *European Journal of International Relations* (2009), 320-345, at 320.

61 Brenda Shaffer (ed.), *The Limits of Culture: Islam and Foreign Policy* (MIT Press, Cambridge, MA, 2006), 73.

62 Ulrich, *op.cit.* note 34, 39.

63 Francois Jullien, quoted in Charles Leben, "Is There a European Approach to Human Rights?", in Philip Alston (ed.), *The EU and Human Rights* (Oxford University Press, New York, NY, 1999), 69-98, at 79.

moral principles are to be followed globally? Jack Donnelly argued that human rights are, in fact, "only loosely [based] on abstract philosophical reasoning and *a priori* moral principles".[64] To the contrary, Donnelly argues that human rights emerge from concrete experience, suffering and political struggle to defend or realize the human dignity of real human beings. Human rights reflect a "politically driven process of social learning".[65] As a conclusion, there is no authority that can claim universality of any of the rights since all rights, respect for human life included, change their nature and content over time and space. We seek a general good, and we learn which concept can better approximate this aim. Human rights are one of the conceptualizations of the ways to achieve the general good.

In this part of my chapter, I have tried to demonstrate that both law and politics are forms of social activity and as such they are socially constructed; neither can be separated from values and normative views. This view is widely accepted for politics. However, it is rarely considered in the realm of law, which tries to be "quarantine[d] from politics in order to protect its assumed impartial character".[66] The point (in accord with normative theory of social sciences) is that no social concept can be neutral, apolitical and free of any ideology. As soon as one accepts that "all theories reflect values, the only question being whether or not the values are hidden",[67] one must ask about the origins and legitimacy of existing social and political institutions, human rights included. The domestic discursive contest of human rights is inevitable. Russian efforts to claim a specific—sometimes even unique—notion of human rights cannot be discarded so easily. The underlying argument of this chapter is, thus, that failure to create agreement on the exact scope and content of human rights with discussion raging over "cultural relevance, ideological and political orientation, and thematic incompleteness"[68] exists due to the reluctance of the human-rights movement to acknowledge its particular social and political background.

Paradoxically, only by accepting ties to certain non-neutral assumptions—to a certain period and world vision—can human-rights activists continue their quest for universal acceptance. I argue that human-rights scholarship should abandon the false perception that human rights can work outside the realm of politics (rights are not pre-institutional) and culture (rights are not pre-cultural). International human-rights law has to recognize inputs from both politics and culture in order not to fall into the trap of becoming technical or doctrinal.

64 Donnelly, *op.cit.* note 25, 58.

65 *Ibid.*

66 Reus-Smit, *op.cit.* note 40, 1.

67 John Baylis and Steve Smith, *The Globalization of World Politics* (Oxford University Press, Oxford, 1999), 172.

68 Mutua, *op.cit.* note 9, 149.

National Identity and Human Rights

In the previous part of this chapter, I presented an argument about the insufficiency of a purely legal reading of human rights within the discipline of international relations and proposed a cultural level that should be (re)introduced in analysis of the role that human rights play in foreign-policy considerations. The question remains: how should the cultural level be operationalized? Since the dominant role of the state within the international system remains generally accepted, and since the main goal of my research is to analyze the role of human rights within foreign-policy considerations, I propose that the national identity of any state can serve as a focal point or, rather, as a link between culture and the creation of foreign policy. I believe that national identity operates on the general level of culture, while it allows for the limitation of the broad term 'culture' into an operational concept that has clear temporal and spatial borders at the same time. Compressing culture into the concept of national identity allows me to connect the process of human-rights contestation with the process of foreign-policy creation. In that sense, I will be able to illustrate that the extent of human-rights' embeddedness in foreign policy relies significantly on the previous successful contestation of rights in the process of creating national identity.

In order to argue my point, the chapter will be developed as follows. *First*, I address the role that different international-relations approaches attribute to the concepts of culture, national identity, and various ideas in general. *Second*, I explore the possibilities of operationalizing the concept of national identity within my research and, *third*, I analyze how national identity is connected with concrete foreign policy; in other words, how a general and vague national identity influences the concrete foreign policy of the state.

National Identity and International-Relations Theory

This section analyzes the role that different approaches attribute to the place of the concepts of culture, national identity and generally to ideational variables. My aim is to put the cultural concept of national identity into the bigger picture of international-relations theory and to discuss its theoretical position within the discipline. I have consciously omitted the micro-theories of decision-making that, in my view, focus too much on specificity and the uniqueness of every case and, thus, reduce the possibilities of generalizing the role of ideas within the international system.[69]

In evaluating the capability of different theoretical approaches to incorporate the role of culture and different ideas, I use the description of politics as given by Christian Reus-Smit as a starting point. He describes four "cognitive reference

69 For discussion of these models, see, *inter alia*, Nicole J. Jackson, *Russian Foreign Policy and the CIS* (Routledge, London, 2003), 16-21.

points that frame political deliberation",[70] each bearing a different set of questions. Politics is then an interstitial of these four points. *First*, he recognizes the idiographic reference point that supervenes the other three points. Here, one asks who one is, how one defines and perceives oneself. *Second*, Reus-Smit names the purposive reference point with the main question being "what do I want?" In other words, one needs to define one's interests. However, without knowing who one is, the definition of what one wants is impossible. The same goes for the *third*, ethical point. Here the question is: How should one act? What is moral or at least acceptable behavior? The *fourth* and the final point is the instrumental point. Here one asks two sets of questions, the strategic-instrumental (How does one get what one wants?) and the resource-instrumental (What does one need to get what one wants?). As Reus-Smit argues, none of the latter sets of questions can be solved without answering the very first one; that is, the one of self-imagination and self-perception.

However, both realist and liberal approaches omit the idiographic point, as it focuses too much on the purposive and instrumental levels. The ethical level is negligible in such an analysis as a state can breach international norms—including international law and human-rights standards—any time it wishes to do so. The idiographic level is not approached at all, as states are seen as unitary, rational actors. Even in the view of neoliberal institutionalists, norms and shared identity matter only up to a point to ease co-operational and collaborational issues among states. Consequently, cooperation serves to ease the constraints put on states by the nature of the international system; that is, through anarchy and the unequal distribution of resources. Therefore, the main underlying factor for neoliberals is—in agreement with neorealism—the distribution of power and resources.[71] The international system is then shaped as a market where states want to maintain their position and take advantage of possible windows of opportunity.

Within such a paradigm, human rights create an unnecessary and unbinding constraint that can be disregarded any time the state decides to do so. As Nicole J. Jackson observes, the problem is that by dismissing other important variables "any argument can be constructed to prove that any action is intended to enhance or preserve the power of the state".[72] Some scholars go as far as to proclaim the concept of national interest to be "oversimplified and wrong-headedly dogmatic [as] it can be used to mean whatever the user wishes".[73] The concept of national interest then seems empty, as both liberal and realist approaches ignore the

70 Reus-Smit, *op.cit.* note 40, 25.

71 See Robert O. Keohane, *International Institutions and State Power* (Westview Press, Boulder, CO, San Francisco, CA, London, 1989).

72 Jackson, *op.cit.* note 69, 13.

73 Jutta Weldes, "Constructing National Interests", 2 *European Journal of International Relations* (1996), 275-318, at 275.

process through which it is shaped. Other factors such as ideology, the nature of government, and political culture can be used to specify the national interest, but never to contradict it or outweigh it in analysis.[74]

The arbitrariness of this approach to the concept of national interest has become obvious in the discussion about Russia. Throughout the 1990s, Russian policy-makers seemed to share the idea that national interests are not to be 'defined' but they needed to be 'found' as they exist somewhere outside the political contest.[75] Although national interests were believed to lie somewhere almost in the realm of natural law, fundamentally different orientations of Russian foreign policy were contested in domestic politics. Myriads of studies tried to categorize and generalize these orientations, usually breaking them down into three broad categories: Westernizers (liberal democrats, social democrats), Statists, and Civilizationists (communists, Eurasianists).[76] The unchallenged Westernism of Gorbachev and early Kozyrev, El'tsin's Minister of Foreign Affairs; the more cautious balancing of Primakov, El'tsin's second Minister of Foreign Affairs; and the pro-Western pragmatism of President Vladimir Putin all claimed to reveal and defend the 'genuine' national interest of Russia, yet these notions clearly contradict one another. Indeed, they are sometimes hostile to each other. Within the given context, the outcome can be described as the "agony of the Russian question";[77] that is, which European values should be endorsed in Russia, how quickly, and to what extent?

As Alla Kassianova has noted:

> "The problem of national identity was established as a centerpiece of Russian political and intellectual life and [it] continues to be evoked both as a routine observation and, more importantly, as a principal element of academic and political analysis."[78]

In that sense, the "oscillation between violent advance towards the West and no less violent reaction against the West"[79] seems to have evaded being grasped by realist and liberal writers. The idiographic question that had hitherto been avoided by many appeared to gain momentum together with the argument that there is a social structure to international politics where ideas and collective meanings

74 Andrei P. Tsygankov, *Russia's Foreign Policy: Change and Continuity in National Identity* (Rowman & Littlefield Publishers, Oxford, 2006), 9.

75 Christer Pursiainen, *Russian Foreign Policy and International Relations Theory* (Ashgate, Aldershot, UK, 2000), 59.

76 For an overview of the respective groups see, *inter alia*, Iver B. Neumann, *Russia and the Idea of Europe: A Study in Identity and International Relations* (Routledge, London, 1996), 159; Kassianova, *op.cit.* note 16, 825; Jackson, *op.cit.* note 69, 33 and 36; or Tsygankov, *op.cit.* note 74, 61.

77 Sebastian Kaempf, "Russia: A Part of the West or Apart from the West?", 24 *International Relations* (2010), 313-341, at 318.

78 Kassianova, *op.cit.* note 16, 830.

79 Kaempf, *op.cit.* note 77, 314.

play a pivotal role[80] and that the "the building blocks of international reality are ideational as well as material".[81] The categories of nation and national interest are, thus, not given but are "open to various meanings and interpretations" and "shaped by locally meaningful ideological debates".[82]

Scholars focused on international state practices, socially constructed national interests, collectively shared memories and narratives[83] and looked at "those historical and social processes through which the rules and norms that shape the present behavior of an actor in the international system are constituted".[84] Research focused on the dynamics of mutually enforcing and threatening identities, the mixture of defining oneselves and others, on the socialization of various norms in various local contexts.

Foreign policy, in such a view, then "functions as an instrument for the realization of the self-image through objectives determined by interests [and] may be studied as identity producing practice".[85] In other words, without analyzing the creation of the self-image of a state, one cannot successfully analyze its objectives and interests. Policy, first and foremost, serves as "a representational practice that secures and reproduces the identity".[86]

However, scholars quickly reached the problem that norms and identities matter only at certain times, whereas they are overlooked in other cases. Constructivists usually answer with attention either to the creative agents and the persuasive strategies they deploy[87] or to the gradual process of the socialization of states to the norms in question.[88] In the footsteps of Wendt, many constructivists focused solely on the interplay between different international Selves and Others, whereas they omitted the "locally meaningful ideological debates" as mentioned by the Tsygankovs.

80 See Ronald Jepperson, Alexander Wendt, and Peter Katzenstein, "Norms, Identity, and Culture in National Security", in Peter Katzenstein (ed.), *The Culture of National Security* (Columbia University Press, New York, NY, 1996), 33-75.

81 John Gerard Ruggie, "What Makes the World Hang Together? Neo-utilitarianism and the Social Constructivist Challenge", 52 *International Organization* (1998), 855-885, at 879.

82 Tsygankov, *op.cit.* note 74, 15.

83 See Alexander Wendt, *Social Theory of International Politics* (Cambridge, Cambridge University Press, 1999).

84 Pursiainen, *op.cit.* note 75, 158.

85 Kassianova, *op.cit.* note 16, 822.

86 Bukh, *op.cit.* note 60, 320.

87 See, *inter alia*, Martha Finnemore and Kathryn Sikkink, "Norms and International Relations Theory", 52 *International Organization* (1998), 887-917; or Jeffrey Checkel, "Norms, Institutions, and National Identity in Contemporary Europe", 43 *International Studies Quarterly* (1999), 83-114.

88 For examples, see, *inter alia*, Richard Price and Nina Tannewald, *Norms and Deterrence: The Nuclear and Chemical Weapons Taboos* (Columbia University Press, New York, NY, 1996).

Following a similar thread, Mark Laffey and Jutta Weldes proposed in their article to understand ideas as symbolic technologies. This would allow them to treat ideas as social, rather than individual, phenomena, as constitutional practices rather than causal variables, and as involved in the production of interests rather than detached from them.[89] According to Laffey and Weldes:

> "Symbolic technologies are, most simply, intersubjective systems of representations and representation-producing practices. [They are] symbolic machineries, that have developed in specific spatio-temporal and cultural circumstances and that make possible the articulation and circulation of more or less coherent sets of meanings about a particular subject matter."[90]

In this sense, symbolic technologies enable certain kinds of actions, as "they are 'mechanisms' by which meaning is produced";[91] however, they constrain other actions, as some meanings clearly preclude certain other meanings. In other words, while certain meanings become dominant and, thus, enable certain kinds of actions, they simultaneously preclude certain other actions.

I believe that national identity works exactly as such symbolic machinery, creating more or less coherent sets of meanings, within both domestic and international spaces. The operationalization of that machinery will be the content of the next chapter.

Operationalization of National Identity

To operationalize identity for the purposes of research design is a Sisyphean task. In my view, national identity has to be conceptualized as a semantic entity, a system of shared meanings and myths that helps its members to assign significance and sense to the surrounding reality. Its formation is, therefore, "a process of obtaining significance, or signification, through which newly emerged and highly contested meanings evolve into meanings that are little contested and institutionalized".[92]

To describe the process of identity creation better, I use the model proposed by Andrei P. Tsygankov (see Figure 1).[93]

89 Mark Laffey and Jutta Weldes, "Beyond Belief: Ideas and Symbolic Technologies in the Study of International Relations", 3 *European Journal of International Relations* (1997), 193-237, at 195.

90 *Ibid*, 209.

91 *Ibid*, 210.

92 Andrei P. Tsygankov, *Pathways after Empire: National Identity and Foreign Economic Policy in the Post-Soviet World* (Rowman & Littlefield, Lanham, UK, 2001), 17.

93 *Ibid.*

Figure 1: Tsygankov's model of national-identity creation

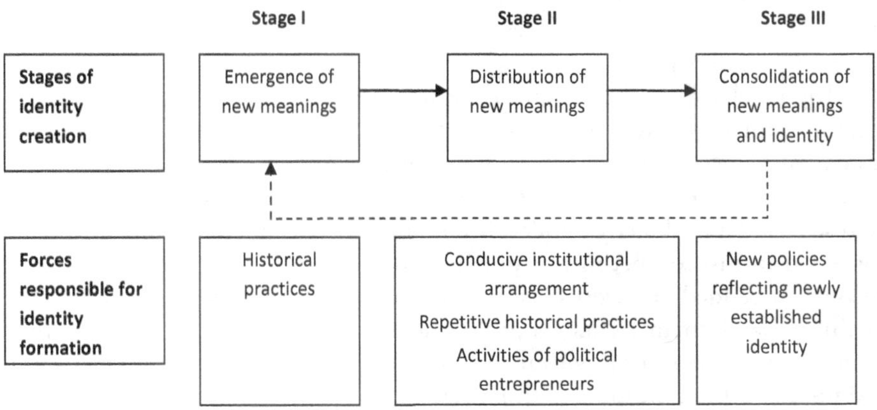

Tsygankov explains his model:

> "At stage I, as a result of historical practices, new meanings emerge in a society allowing room for new interpretations of its past and present. Here the newly emerged meanings/ interpretations are highly contested and marginal in their influence due to overwhelming power of hegemonic discourse. At stage II, however, the newly emerged meanings receive a chance to increase their influence. Due to conducive institutional arrangements, repetitive historical practices, and activities of political entrepreneurs, the new meanings get spread in a society thereby increasingly obtaining hegemonic status. Finally, at stage III, identity formation reaches the point when the new meanings are sufficiently consolidated and get exploited, both socially and politically, for the purpose of their further consolidation. In the meantime, history does not stop—new meanings emerge challenging the old identity's content and boundaries and encouraging change."[94]

The most important part of Tsygankov's model is the contestation thesis. When new ideas enter the process of national-identity formation, they are highly contested, challenged and questioned. Only as they acquire some support—be it political or societal, and consolidate their position within the cycle of the constant re-creation of shared meanings—do they become embedded in the societal order and its institutions and thus are challenged less (or hardly at all).

The problem with human rights is that they aim to emancipate individuals from authoritative state power and to disregard symbolic groupings such as nations. However, I believe that human rights not only regulate relations between the state and its citizens and individuals within its power,[95] but that rights are

94 *Ibid.*; emphasis added by the author.

95 In this sense, the concept of collective rights is still highly disputed and common mainly to the African system of human-rights protection and a few UN General Assembly resolutions but generally disregarded within the European system. Similarly, the question of the responsibility of private actors, that is, of transnational companies and NGOs among others, is still too heated to draw an unambiguous conclusion. Therefore, I continue to perceive human rights as determining relations between the state and individuals within its power.

intrinsically embedded in the societal order as well. In other words, human rights represent more than mere emancipatory vocabulary for marginalized groups and individuals; they work as a legitimizing project for whole societies and the power structures within.

Rights challenge the system of meanings and significance within society, *i.e.*, rights force their way of attributing significance to the historically contested system of values. I argue that human rights cannot escape the contestation cycle. In other words, human rights are not somewhere 'out there' waiting to be discovered and directly applied from 'point zero'. Human rights have to be contested against competing legitimizing projects and through contestation they become embedded in society's institutions and bound with the national identity. In this sense, human rights cannot be detached from national identity; they cannot resist contestation within the constantly repeating cycle of establishing and re-establishing meaning within society.

Once the tension between old and newly created meanings increases, the state reaches the point of identity crisis. That is what happened to the Soviet Union between 1985 and 1991, when the inability of its elite to resolve the crisis led to the dissolution of the whole bloc of states, the USSR included. The newly created Russian Federation then inherited the crisis. Today, according to some, the crisis is luckily over, and a new Russia has emerged on the scene and "for the first time in Russian history, national interest is not linked to sheer power and territorial control, but rather to domestic reform, prosperity and efficiency of governance".[96] For others, Russia is still being tossed between various extremes and ideas in its search of a new identity.[97] Russia, in that sense, is in the process of an incremental change of its identity.[98] The tension between newly created meanings (democracy, liberal market, human rights, or the rule of law) and old practices has resulted in a continuing identity crisis.

96 Sergei Medvedev, *Rethinking the National Interest: Putin's Turn in Russian Foreign Policy* (The George C. Marshall European Center for Security Studies, Garmisch-Partenkirchen, 2004), xiii.

97 As Dmitri V. Trenin has repeatedly argued in his latest articles; see, *inter alia*, Trenin, *Reading Russia Right* (Carnegie Endowment for International Peace, Washington, DC, 2005); *id.*, "Russia Leaves the West", 85(4) *Foreign Affairs* (2006), 87-96, available at <http://www.carnegieendowment.org/publications/index.cfm?fa=view&id=18467&prog=zru>; or *id.*, *Getting Russia Right* (Carnegie Endowment for International Peace, Washington, DC, 2007).

98 Tsygankov distinguishes two ways: incremental and revolutionary. Incremental change comes as a result of a country's adaptation to various domestic and international pressures. In contrast, revolutionary change comes as a result of societal revolution, war or other disaster of huge impact that destroys everything while imposing a new order at the same time. See Tsygankov, *op.cit.* note 92, 18.

National Identity in Foreign-Policy Considerations

This section examines the question of why one should consider national identity as constitutive of foreign policy. In order to describe these processes, I use one more model proposed by Andrei Tsygankov (see Figure 2).[99]

Figure 2: Tsygankov's model of foreign-policy creation

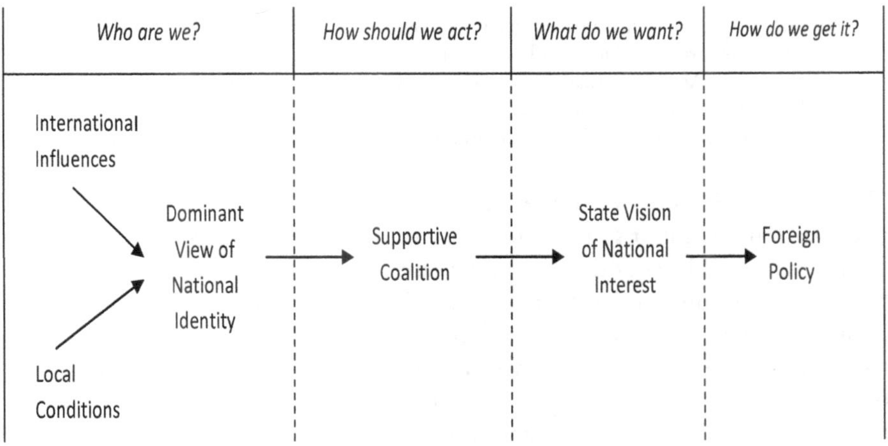

The connection between the previously mentioned definition of politics set forth by Christian Reus-Smit and Tsygankov's model is surprising. Tsygankov makes the concept of national identity as basis of his model. According to him, first, a dominant view of national identity is created combining both international and local influences so that Reus-Smit's idiographic question is answered. Then, a supportive coalition is drawn around the previously created dominant view of national identity. During this stage, the coalition is gathered (and divided) by the question of how one should act once one knows who one is; that is, the supportive coalition is rallied around the ethical reflective point. Once the supportive coalition is strong enough, the state embraces it and bases its understanding of national interest on the outcomes of previous stages. In that sense, both purposive (what do we want?) and instrumental (how do we get it?) sets of questions are answered. Once all these stages have been fulfilled, foreign policy is created. Only a foreign policy that has gone through all of these stages can claim legitimacy and stability, avoiding a defensive, unstable and reactionary character. Similarly, only human rights which have been contested at the beginning of this process may become embedded stably and fully into the foreign policy of the respective state.

99 Tsygankov, *op.cit.* note 74, 17.

The question remains as to how one should understand the process by which a state embraces the dominant view of national identity around which the strongest coalition is rallied. In this sense, one has to stop perceiving states as a unitary and rational black box whose international behavior is independent of domestic conditions. As Robert D. Putnam describes it, domestic and foreign policies are intrinsically intertwined, that is, which he famously calls Janus-headed. For Putnam, interstate relations should be seen as a bargaining on a two-level game board:

> "At the national level, domestic groups pursue their interests by pressuring government to adopt favourable policies, and politicians seek power by constructing coalitions among those groups. At the international level, national governments seek to maximise their own ability to satisfy domestic pressures, while minimising the adverse consequences of foreign developments. Neither of the two games can be ignored by central decision makers, so long as their countries remain interdependent, yet sovereign."[100]

The problem with such a complex game is that moves which may be rational for one board may seem unsuitable for the second one. Thus, moves convenient for the international level of the game may be discarded simply for their unwanted backfire on the domestic level. Therefore, political decision makers try to reconcile domestic demands and international imperatives simultaneously. Basically, Putnam's key concept is that of win-set; that is, "the set of all possible international bargaining outcomes that might win majority backing on the home front of a given player".[101] In this sense, a state searches for and tests possible win-sets that can bring about the strongest support. For Putnam, the larger the size of the win-set at the domestic level, the more likely is international agreement. The size of the win-set then depends on three factors: domestic preferences and coalitions, domestic institutions, and negotiator's strategies at the international level.[102]

Consider the precipitate decision by El'tsin and his suite to integrate Russia into Western structures. Not only was this done in the complete absence of the dominant view of the national identity, but, moreover, there was no strong supportive coalition to uphold the decision so that the ensuing shock that the Russian economy experienced severely damaged Westernizing projects. Similarly, at the time of the attempted putsch in 1991, the former Soviet elites lost the support of the grouping that had previously supported them: namely, the main part of the army and the general public. In both of these cases, the political leaders lost their games due to underestimating domestic preferences, the uncertain status of various domestic institutions, and unsuccessful strategies

100 Robert D. Putnam, "Diplomacy and Domestic Politics: The Logic of Two-Level Games", 42 *International Organization* (1988), 427-460, at 434.

101 Mette Skak, "The Logic of Foreign and Security Policy and Continuity in National Identity", in Jakob Hedenskog, Christer Pursiainen, Ingmar Oldberg, Bertil Nygren and Vilhelm Konnander (eds.), *Russia as a Great Power* (Routledge, New York, NY, 2005), 81-106, at 86.

102 Putnam, *op.cit.* note 100, 442.

at the international level, which never brought the support that both Gorbachev and El'tsin anticipated.

Talking about human rights, decision makers seem to have to fight domestic preferences yet may rely on domestic institutions, as the Constitution directly recognizes human rights and international treaties as applicable on Russian territory. Possible win-sets springing from such a setting are further discussed in the next section of this chapter.

To close this part, the question of how human rights can be included in this model should be addressed. Human rights work as an explanatory vocabulary on the level of principled ideas and, as such, come into the picture at the very beginning when they are contested within local semantic space or brought in by international influences. Including human-rights ideas as variables already at this level, they can shape the outcome of the "who are we?" question as put forward by Christian Reus-Smit. Moving to the next stage, human rights become a contested part of the dominant view of the national identity around which supportive coalitions are gathered. Support for, ignorance, or even conscious breaches of, human-rights commitments can be seen as parts of Putnam's search for a win-set to create a dominant view of state interests.

As I will show in the next part, the situation in contemporary Russia led to the creation of two conflicting win-sets, the illiberal centralized one for the domestic-level game (and, thus, hostile to broad human-rights inclusion and recognition) and, on the other hand, the liberal pro-Western one in the realm of foreign policy that favors the Western view of the fundamental position of human rights, including acceptance of ECtHR jurisdiction over Russian matters.[103]

However, a remark must be made at this point. To no extent do I claim that contestation of human rights continues solely in Russia or solely outside the EU or the West in general. This process is inherent to all cultures and identities, and I do not claim that the EU, OSCE or any European state—on its own—possesses a true understanding of human rights. As has already been stated, Russia serves only as an example to illustrate the process that takes place to some extent in every ideational space in the world.

Contestation of Human Rights in Russia

As already indicated in the introduction to this chapter, Russia to some extent has come to feel trapped in the CoE system. The situation might have been different at the beginning of the 1990s. El'tsin's government applied to the Council in 1992 during its 'honeymoon with the West' period when it contemplated joining not only the CoE but, also, NATO and potentially even the European Community. In the end, the Council of Europe was—despite several unfavorable

103 See Skak, *op.cit.* note 101.

voices—the only organization willing to accept Russia among its ranks and the Russian Federation acceded to the Council on 28 February 1996.

With admission, Russia committed itself to ratifying the European Convention on Human Rights and its Protocols and to accepting the jurisdiction of the European Court of Human Rights, which both formally happened on 5 May 1998. Thanks to the CoE regime, Russia has *de facto* (although not *de jure*) abolished the death penalty as a direct result of signing Protocol No.6,[104] and a growing body of European human-rights case law has become part of Russia's legislative framework.

Simultaneously, Russia pledged to pursue a series of law reforms in accordance with the recommendations made by PACE; most notably, to adopt a new criminal code and code of criminal procedure, a new civil code, a new law on the administration of its penal system, new legislation governing the functioning of the prosecutor's office and the office of the commissioner for human rights, and new legislation protecting national minorities, freedom of assembly, and freedom of religion. The Russian government also accepted commitments regarding its policy in Chechnia. In this sense, Russia's membership in the Council of Europe represents its deepest and most visible commitment to the European system of human-rights protection.

Things are far from being ideal, however, as one encounters numerous paradoxes. On the one hand, Russia has made 'giant strides'[105] in the direction of full implementation of rule of law, multi-party democracy, and protection of individual human rights. On the other hand, during the same period, two Chechen wars broke out.[106] In addition, cases from Russia currently make up a quarter of pending allocated cases—more than any other member state[107]—and relations between Russia and the Council have progressively deteriorated. The situation of a battleground between PACE and Russia led Bill Bowring to go

104 Since the Protocol has not been ratified, only a moratorium has been placed on execution of the death penalty, but effective and permanent legal abolition of the penalty never took place.

105 Bill Bowring, "Russia and Human Rights: Incompatible Opposites?", 1 *Göttingen Journal of International Law* (2009), 257-278, at 258.

106 The First Chechen War is dated between 1994 and 1996; the second conflict has dragged on with several breaks continuously from 1999. Human-rights organizations estimate the number of killed or missing civilians at up to 50,000 for the first Chechen war and up to 25,000 for the second and its aftermath. According to official figures, around 10,000 servicemen were killed in both wars, but experts and human-rights campaigners say the toll is much higher. See AlertNet, "Two Wars Fought since 1994" (28 July 2009), available at <http://www.alertnet.org/db/crisisprofiles/RU_WAR.htm?v=in_detail>.

107 Jennifer W. Reiss, "Protocol No.14 ECHR and Russian Nonratification: The Current State of Affairs", 22 *Harvard Human Rights Journal* (2009), 293-317, at 307.

as far as to ask whether there was, in fact, "a legal culture [in Russia] which [is] simply anathema to human rights".[108]

For the last fifteen years, the most egregious reminder of Russia's problematic human-rights record has been the Chechen conflict. Despite the fact that the number of applications to the Court originating from Chechnia is "miniscule compared to the overall number of applications from Russia",[109] these involve the gravest examples of human-rights violations, including summary executions, arbitrary killings, enforced disappearances, torture, abuse, undetermined and undocumented detentions, and wanton destruction of property, while no effective remedy or possibility of investigation exist.

As the report by PACE notes, the armed conflict has not gone away, with paramilitary groups set up by illegal combatants becoming increasingly organized, coordinated, widespread and technically well-equipped. This seems to be a major blow for the Russian government, especially in light of the alleviation of the special anti-terrorist rules which had applied throughout the Chechen Republic up to 16 April 2009. The federal army units deployed in the region were to be withdrawn and the task of combating terrorism was to be definitively handed over to local security forces run by the Chechen Minister of the Interior and certain battalions of Federal Russian interior troops.[110]

Despite the heartening statement by the Russian government, the situation continued to deteriorate as, during the summer of 2009 alone, 142 members of the security forces were killed, almost 300 injured, and the conflict threatened to spread to neighboring republics, namely Kabardino-Balkaria and North Ossetia-Alania.[111] The activity and the boldness of the terrorists mounted with a suicide-bomb attack on two subway stations in Moscow and on several trains and police stations in Dagestan in March 2010 and the terrorist attack at Moscow's Domodedovo airport on 24 January 2011—as a few notable examples of increasing and reappearing tension.

Most ECtHR judgments on Chechnia have undermined the key claim made by Vladimir Putin that his regime "brought law, order, and prosperity to Russia".[112]

108 Bowring, *op.cit.* note 105, 260.

109 Of more than 46,000 applications received by the ECtHR from Russia since 1998, only about 400 have originated from Chechnia. The majority of cases concern complaints about the excessive length of judicial proceedings and non-implementation of domestic judicial decisions. See Ole Solvang, "Chechnya and the European Court of Human Rights: The Merits of Strategic Litigation", 19 *Security and Human Rights* (2008), 208-219, at 211.

110 CLAHR, "Situation in the North Caucasus Region: Security and Human Rights" (29 September 2009), available at <http://www.londonmet.ac.uk/londonmet/fms/MRSite/Research/HRSJ/EHRAC/PACE%20report%20Sit%20in%20N%20Caucasus%20security%20and%20HR%2029_9_09.pdf>, para. 14.

111 *Ibid.*, paras. 3 and 4.

112 Trochev, *op.cit.* note 13, 146.

President Medvedev took the threat to the perception of his government's ability to guarantee order seriously when he told delegates of the All-Russian Congress of Judges that he was ready to consider "transformations" in the judicial system to make it "so effective that it would minimize complaints to the international courts".[113] In this statement, one can read the nature of the relationship between the Court and Russia: The latter will comply with the former's rulings as long as non-compliance damages the government's ability to foster supportive coalitions at both the domestic and international levels. In other words, the strength of the Court is in its ability to influence the reputation, reliability, and legitimacy of the government *vis-à-vis* both its domestic constituency and opposition groups and its international partners.

Having conveyed a theoretical analysis of the concept of culture, condensed into the notion of national identity, let me now turn to the practical application of the above-presented models. This part examines the current state of national-identity creation in Russia and its interaction with the notion of human rights.

I will *first* briefly describe the current situation of Russia within the Council using the verbatim records of PACE and other documents in order to illustrate the standstill in Russian-CoE relations. *Second*, using the model presented by Andrei Tsygankov (see Figure 2), I analyze international input into national-identity creation. I argue that the unresolved and probably unresolvable riddle of Russia-West relations lies at the base of the international side of the model together with the challenge posed to traditional Russian society by the process of globalization. I believe that human rights enter the cycle of national-identity creation as an element of globalization and as such are securitized by Russian elites. *Third*, I turn to domestic inputs into the national-identity cycle. In this part, I use the description of historical determinants as put forth by Alfred J. Rieber and look at whether this description holds up in contemporary Russia. Subsequently, I analyze the coalitions rallied around the dominant view of national identity. I argue that the traditional divide of Russian elites into Atlanticists, Statists, and Eurasianists is not adequate in the case of human rights. I examine the usefulness and applicability of the win-sets proposed by Mette Skak on the basis of Putnam's model.

I close this part by discussing the general concept of securitization within Russian discourse. I argue that the mainstream discourse in Russia is securitized against the imposition of human rights, which are perceived as tools for the dissolution of Russian society. The implications of such securitization are then discussed in the last part of this chapter.

113 Dmitrii Medvedev, "Vystuplenie na 7. Vserossiiskom s"ezde sudei" (2 December 2008), available at <http://archive.kremlin.ru/text/appears/2008/12/210020.shtml>.

Russia and the CoE: Oratorical Standstill

Before the somewhat uneasy, but working, relationship between Russia and the Council of Europe could develop further, Russia began to lose a number of high-profile cases in the ECtHR. The end of 2004 and beginning of 2005 were of critical significance. *First*, in *Ilaşcu and Others v. Moldova and Russia*, the majority of the Grand Chamber of the Court found that Russia had rendered support for Transdniestria, a breakaway region of Moldova, amounting to 'effective control'.[114] The first Chechen applicants against Russia won their applications to Strasbourg in February 2005. Two months later, in *Shamayev and 12 others v. Russia and Georgia*, the Court condemned Russia for deliberately refusing to cooperate with the Court despite diplomatic assurances.[115] Moreover, around the same time, Russia suffered two major diplomatic collisions with the Council outside the Court. *First*, PACE, while monitoring preparations for the 2005 presidential election, observed that the model used for the election could be considered neither free nor fair.[116]

Second and in direct connection with the first collision, Russia unexpectedly lost the election for the new President of PACE when the done deal of electing Mikhail Margelov, a candidate with the direct support of the Russian President, was spoiled by the controversy following the Russian parliamentary elections, and the Catalan-Spanish Socialist, Lluís Maria de Puig, was elected instead.[117]

Therefore, after the first prompt reaction, the Russian relationship with the ECtHR froze and remained on the verge of breaking. Surprisingly, the relationship was not this tense even in 2000 when Russia suffered suspension of its voting privileges in PACE in April of that year.

The brief war between Russia and Georgia, the first armed conflict between Council of Europe member states in the Council's history, only aggravated the tenuous relations between Russia and the bloc. The consequences of the Georgian war came to be vigorously discussed at the PACE meeting in October 2008 after 24 members of PACE had previously submitted a request for reconsideration of the credentials of the Russian delegation on the grounds of serious violations of the basic principles of the Council of Europe. The Russian reaction was sharp and threatened that Russia would leave the CoE. In the end, the Committee of Ministers succumbed to political pressure from the Russian government, arguing that "it is better to draw former communist countries into dialogue than

114 Case of *Ilaşcu and Others v. Moldova and Russia* (8 July 2004) No.48787/99.

115 Case of *Shamayev and Others v. Georgia and Russia* (12 April 2005) No.36378/02.

116 Bill Bowring, "Tensions Multiply between Russia and Council of Europe: Could the Malaise be Terminal?", 6 *The EU-Russia Review* (2008), 4-12, at 12.

117 *Ibid.*, 9.

to isolate them"[118] and, subsequently, stopped the possible expulsion of Russia from the Council. However, the discussion showed the latent tensions that the countries of the 'New Europe' feel *vis-à-vis* Russian policies towards Georgia, in particular, and other post-Soviet countries in general.[119]

Contrary to its strategy of silent diplomacy applied during the crisis in 2000, Moscow chose to voice its opposition in full during the crisis starting in 2005. In direct response to the Court's ruling in the *Ilaşcu* case, on 20 December 2006, the Russian *Duma* refused to ratify Protocol No.14, and thus effectively blocked needed reform of the CoE. Allegedly, Russia's main concern was the perceived increase in unfair pressure on Russia by delivering an even higher number of negative judgments.[120]

The response from PACE came before long. Dick Marty, then-chairman of PACE's Committee on Legal Affairs and Human Rights (CLAHR), bluntly observed that "if the country felt that it could not comply with the principle of the independence of the Court then surely that country no longer belonged in the Council of Europe".[121] The Russian Federation was "publicly shamed at every opportunity"[122]—through media campaigns, documentaries, scholarly publications or policy papers. Protocol No.14 became the onus for Russian participation in the CoE.

Further, PACE called on the Committee of Ministers to adopt a Protocol No.14*bis* that would—without requiring the unanimous ratification of all member states—institute some of the efficiency measures within Protocol No.14 which would apply to those states adopting it. In this regard, PACE addressed the Russian position in unusually strong words:

> "[T]he Assembly strongly deplores the position taken by the Russian Federation's State Duma to refuse to provide its assent, since December 2006, to the ratification of Protocol No.14 to the Convention, which is an important amending protocol that can only enter into force when all states parties to the Convention have ratified it. By so doing, the Russian State Duma has, in effect, considerably aggravated the situation in which the Court has found itself, and has also deprived persons within its jurisdiction of the benefits of a streamlined

118 Pamela A. Jordan, "Does Membership Have Its Privileges? Entrance into the Council of Europe and Compliance with Human Rights Norms", 25 *Human Rights Quarterly* (2003), 660-688, at 684.

119 See PACE, "PACE Autumn Session: Consequences of the War between Georgia and Russia" (19 September 2008), available at <http://assembly.coe.int/ASP/Press/StopPressView.asp?ID=2081>.

120 Reiss, *op.cit.* note 107, 309.

121 PACE, Ordinary Session, "Report of the Seventh Sitting, Thursday 25 January 2007 at 10 a.m." (25 January 2007), available at <http://www.assembly.coe.int/Main.asp?link=/Documents/Records/2007/E/0701251000E.htm>.

122 Yannis S. Stivachtis, "'Civilizing' the Post-Soviet/Socialist Space: An English School Approach to State Socialization in Europe: The Cases of NATO and the Council of Europe", 18 *Perspectives* (2010), 5-32. at 25.

> case-processing procedure before the Court. The State Duma is urged, in the strongest possible terms, to recognise that the changes of the control system envisaged in Protocol No.14 (and Protocol No.14 *bis*), will permit the Court to deal with applications in a timely fashion so that it can concentrate on important cases requiring in-depth examination."[123]

Finally, after four years of blocking, Russia ratified Protocol 14 on 15 January 2010. Nevertheless, tensions have not faded. One prominent scholar noted that:

> "The Council of Europe, especially its Parliamentary Assembly, has turned into an oratorical battleground between Russian lawmakers and their European counterparts on Chechnya and other human rights issues. Moscow has even threatened to halve its contribution to the Council's budget if the criticism does not cease."[124]

One of the many critics at that time even claimed that Russia's "voluminous membership fees [were] being used for attacks on [Russia]".[125]

Russian delegates have often repeated that:

> "From the outset, the European Court of Human Rights judgement left people perplexed by its inconsistency, contradictory nature, subjective stance and flagrant political bias. That said we invariably proceed on the basis that the decisions of the Strasbourg court must be executed."[126]

In other words, even after ratification of Protocol 14, Russia sees the work of the ECtHR as biased and politicized and, thus, may not agree with its judgments; however, judgments undisputedly have to be fulfilled.

The double-faced commitment of Russian delegates to the Court's regime cannot be expressed better: it is solely the legitimacy which the regime provides that leads Russian authorities to follow the judgments. Neither coercion nor self-interest can explain this commitment, as no coercive measures exist within the regime, and self-interest has to be excluded exactly for the alleged inconsistency, contradictory nature, subjective stance and flagrant political bias of the Court. Indeed, why would any actor have a self-interest in participating in such flawed cooperation?

President Medvedev further illustrated his impression that international law and human rights were politicized and flexible in their use when he declared that:

> "It is highly symptomatic that current differences with Russia are interpreted by many in the West as a need to simply bring Russia's policies closer into line with those of the West. But we do not want to be 'embraced' in this way. [...] Sometimes we are simply told: stop being so prickly in international affairs and then democratic development and human rights issues

123 PACE, "Draft Protocol No.14 bis to the Convention for the Protection of Human Rights and Fundamental Freedoms" (30 April 2009) Opinion 271, available at <http://assembly.coe.int/Main.asp?link=/Documents/AdoptedText/ta09/EOPI271.htm>. On 12 May 2009, the Committee indeed adopted the protocol.

124 Trenin, *op.cit.* note 97.

125 Human Rights House, "The State Duma Rejected Human Rights Court Plan" (28 December 2006), available at <http://humanrightshouse.org/Articles/7680.html>.

126 PACE, "Parliamentary Questions for Oral Answer, Addendum 1" (4 October 2006), available at <http://assembly.coe.int/main.asp?Link=/documents/records/2006/e/z0610041000ad1e.htm>.

> will become secondary; that they can close their eyes to them, and they give us examples of other countries that behave in just this way and with whom they get on fine."[127]

Human rights, in Medvedev's view, became a trade-off, something the West can emphasize or downplay at will. Notice the stress Medvedev put on the division of 'us' *versus* 'them'—the personification of an almighty West which can manipulate the perception of human rights according to its own needs is mentioned three times. The alleged double standards used by the West in its relations with the outside world, together with feelings of being picked on, haunt Russian discourse.

PACE Delegate Margelov, in this regard, noted that:

> "The spread of democracy à la Europe requires not only delicacy but also deep insight into the peculiarities of cultures. [...] The intercultural dialogue is important as far as it protects from the risks that arose from the spread of democracy."[128]

In the view of the Russian delegation to PACE, culture should serve as a shield from unconditional democratization using one particular model; that is, European democracy, which is offered as a filling that fits all jars. The fear of being subjected to European supervision is strong. In the words of Aleksandr Panarin:

> "Western civilisation, politically and economically dominant in the world, works as a reductionist system, decreasing the socio-cultural and life building diversity of the world in the course of all-pervading westernisation. The very concept of Westernisation presupposes the existence of one and the only subject of history—the West [...]."[129]

Panarin's conclusion suggests that Russia perceives human rights as a tool of assimilation and reduction of the world's diversity used by Western politicians seeking fulfillment of the idea of universal justice. Doubts are consequently raised whether the 'secular liberal' concept of human rights can be accepted as universal 'without an appropriate correction' for Russian conditions.[130] The position of the Russian Orthodox Church can serve as a clear example. According to the late Patriarch Aleksei II, rights have to reflect morality; without morality, rights lose their significance and emancipatory character.[131] The dominant Russian discourse within PACE seems to hold the position that human rights need to

127 Dmitrii Medvedev, Speech at Meeting with German Political, Parliamentary and Civic Leaders (5 June 2008), available at <http://www.kremlin.ru/eng/speeches/2008/06/05/2203_type82912type82914type84779_202153.shtml>.

128 PACE, "2007 Ordinary Session Report (Second part), Addendum" (18 April 2007), available at <http://assembly.coe.int/main.asp?Link=/documents/records/2007/e/0704181500ade.htm>.

129 Aleksandr Panarin, *Revansh istorii* (Russkii mir, Moskva, 2005), quoted in Morozov, *op.cit.* note 6.

130 Masha Lipman, "Fear of the West in Russia", *The Washington Post* (2 May 2006), available at <http://www.washingtonpost.com/wp-dyn/content/article/2006/05/01/AR2006050101273.html>.

131 PACE, "2007 Ordinary Session Report (First Part): Address to the Assembly by the Patriarch Alexei II" (23 January 2007), available at <http://assembly.coe.int/main.asp?Link=/documents/records/2007/e/0701231500e.htm>.

be transformed for Russian conditions and that it is Russian culture that serves as a shield against assimilation efforts caused by the process of globalization.

In the Russian view, Russia has made some spectacular developments in the last fifteen years and is on a good path to continue. However, the West pushes for reforms too vigorously and impatiently. In the words of delegate Slutskii:

> "Why should Russia's move to full democracy be excessively fast? After all, the United Kingdom [has] a monarchy but [does not] have a written constitution. After seven decades of totalitarian rule, there was a need for patience."[132]

The notion that European values, including human rights, need to be transformed for Russian conditions is further repeated.

Thus, the conclusion to draw is the notion that human rights are not simply applicable; but that they need time to develop and to go through domestic contestation.[133] From the Russian point of view, the USSR dissolved only twenty years ago, and some authors continued predicting the dissolution of Russia itself as late as 2001.[134] Russia, in this sense, cannot be Westernized overnight and, moreover, complete Westernization is out of the question.

Russia's special sensitivity is blatantly obvious once the subject of Chechnia is touched upon. The most frequent response to the issue is that "the method for combating terrorism [is] the same around the world",[135] so why should Russia alone be criticized for following the same policies?[136] PACE in this sense comes under double fire. On the one hand, it is criticized by important NGOs for not doing enough,[137] while Russian delegates blame it for excessive politicization, bias and double standards, on the other. As one of the Russian delegates noted, she "had a feeling that [her] colleagues from Russia and [she] were in the dock

132 PACE, "2005 Ordinary Session Report (Third Part)" (22 June 2005), available at <http://assembly.coe.int/main.asp?Link=/documents/records/2005/e/0506221000e.htm>.

133 For the model of domestic contestation, see Tsygankov, *op.cit.* note 92. For its application on the perception of human rights in Russia, see Petr Preclík, "Culture Re-introduced: Contestation of Human Rights in Contemporary Russia", in European Inter-University Centre/EIUC (ed.), *E.MA Awarded Theses Collection* (Venice, Marsilio Editori, 2009), 419-510.

134 See, *inter alia*, Jeffrey Tayler, "Russia is Finished", 287 *Atlantic Monthly* (2001), 33-52.

135 PACE, "2006 Ordinary Session Report (Third Part)" (22 June 2005), available at <http://assembly.coe.int/main.asp?Link=/documents/records/2006/e/0606291000e.htm>.

136 For an interesting comparison of Russian conduct in Chechnia with US conduct in Iraq, see Chomsky, *op.cit.* note 48. For one of the latest examples, see Amnesty International, "Council of Europe Failing on Russia: Urgent Need for Vigorous Monitoring in the North Caucasus" (15 April 2008), available at <http://www.amnesty.org/en/library/info/IOR61/005/2008/en>; or Human Rights Watch, "EU-Russia Human Rights Consultations: Human Rights Watch Recommendations" (March 2008), available at <http://www.hrw.org/english/docs/2008/05/08/Rus_EU_Consult_031808.pdf>.

137 *Ibid.*

in a courtroom".[138] Another delegate vigorously objected to the "shocking paternalistic tone of the report [about honoring Russian commitments to the CoE regime]".[139] The very same delegate raised a deeply flawed, but characteristic note that "it was a paradox that the country that had liberated half of Europe from Nazism was now being criticized for not being democratic enough".[140] In other words, the savior of Europe should be praised, not criticized and taught how to become better.

From the Russian perspective, there is "no absolute freedom anywhere in the world, no perfect democracy, and no government that does not lie to its people. In essence, all are equal by virtue of sharing the same imperfections."[141] Russia then positions itself as a victim that is being picked on, a scapegoat to cover the misdeeds of others. Following a similar thread, Dmitri Trenin observed that Moscow:

> "has grown assertive and occasionally arrogant. The humility of the post-Soviet period has passed. [...] Russian leaders do not care much about acceptance by the West; even the Soviet Union worried more about its image. [...] Public relations and lobbying are simply not high on the Kremlin's agenda. [...] Russia, the Kremlin believes, will get a bad press in the West almost no matter what it does, so why bother?"[142]

Having said the above, the question necessarily arises as to why Russia remains a member of the CoE as long as it feels forced to accept rights too quickly and without question, and thus is not independent enough. In the language of William D. Jackson:

> "Governments emerging from an authoritarian past have tended to view admission to the council as a way to legitimize their claims to a democratic status that may be in question at home and internationally and also as an affirmation of their membership in political Europe."[143]

Therefore, the situation is as ambiguous as it can be. On the one hand, Russia holds on to its commitment to the European human-rights regime, while on the other hand, it refuses to accept that regime fully and immediately.

138 PACE, "2005 Ordinary Session Report (Second part), Addendum 2: Honouring of Obligations and Commitments by the Russian Federation" (22 June 2005), available at <http://assembly.coe.int/main.asp?Link=/documents/records/2005/e/0506221000eadii.htm>.

139 *Op.cit.* note 131.

140 *Ibid.*

141 Dmitri V. Trenin, "Russia Redefines Itself and Its Relations with the West", 30(2) *The Washington Quarterly* (2007), available at <http://faculty.maxwell.syr.edu/rdenever/USNatSecandForeignPol/Trenin_RussiaRedefines.pdf>.

142 Trenin, "Russia Leaves the West", *op.cit.* note 97.

143 William D. Jackson, "Russia and the Council of Europe: The Perils of Premature Admission", 51 *Problems of Post-Communism* (2004), 23-33, at 24-25.

The existence of such a thin line was proved on 15 January 2010 when the Russian *Duma*—after protracted and bitter negotiation (see above)—ratified Protocol No.14. The other branch of the legislature, the Federation Council, followed suit and the Protocol finally entered into force. Being threatened with the possibility of a Protocol No.14*bis*—with ever-worsening relations with the Council and the Court—the first deputy chairman of the *Duma* committee for international affairs, Leonid Slutskii, admitted that refusal to ratify Protocol 14 "triggered problems both for international parliamentary contacts and for the executive authority and impeded the possibility of Russian influence on the development of European institutions".[144]

Before I conclude this section, one more point should be made. Notwithstanding the impact the Court already had on the situation, there is one paramount challenge in front of it in connection with the war between Georgia and Russia in 2008.

As of October 2008, the Court had received some 2,000 applications against Georgia from people living in South Ossetia. The filing of these applications had been supported by the Russian Federation; yet in early 2011, many of these applications were dismissed by the ECtHR because the lawyers/NGOs that had filed the applications had not responded to requests for additional information by the ECtHR. In addition to the 2,000 individual applications from South Ossetians against Georgia, the European Court of Human Rights registered two outstanding interstate claims by Georgia against Russia, the first dating from 2007 and the second from the more-recent war.[145] Similarly, 32 groups of cases on behalf of 132 Georgian citizens claiming the killing or wounding of civilians, destruction of property, or illegal detention, all committed by Russian soldiers, were lodged with the Court.[146]

In any case, the Court has already taken an unprecedented step in this regard while reacting to the August 2008 war over South Ossetia. On 11 August 2008, with Russian forces heading to Tbilisi, Georgia applied to the ECtHR to the effect that Russia should refrain from taking any measures that might threaten the life of the civilian population, and allow for the creation of a humanitarian corridor to evacuate the remaining civilians and soldiers. On the following day, the Court decided to apply those measures in consideration of the risk of serious violations of the Convention. Russia, however, repeatedly ignored in its communications to the Court specific facts submitted by the Government

144 ECHR Blog, "Russian Duma Has Accepted Protocol 14 Today" (15 January 2010), available at <http://echrblog.blogspot.com/2010/01/russian-will-ratify-protocol-14-today.html>.

145 AlertNet, "S. Ossetia floods rights court with Georgia writs" (6 October 2008), available at <http://www.alertnet.org/thenews/newsdesk/L6112324.htm>.

146 Bowring, *op.cit.* note 105, 277. See, also, Arkadi Babchenko, "Voina 08.08.08. prodolzhaetsia v Strasburge", *Novaia gazeta* (23 April 2010), available at <http://www.novayagazeta.ru/data/2010/043/04.html>.

of Georgia. Moreover, the Russian Federation artificially confined the area of applicability of the measures indicated to the territory of South Ossetia, while the allegations by the Government of Georgia reached far beyond South Ossetia.[147]

International Determinants of Human-Rights Acceptance

What are the determinants of the above-illustrated discourse? What is its background? Samuel Huntington noted that the most significant feature of the world of civilizations is the relationship between the West and the others.[148] In the case of Russia, this statement seems inescapable as "the idea of [the West] is the main 'Other' in relation to which the idea of Russia [has been] defined"[149] for the last thousand years. The West became "an indispensable partner and, at the same time, the 'other' whose difference helps to clarify the distinctiveness of the identity-seeking group".[150] In this sense, I consider the relationship between the West and Russia to be the main international input into creation of the dominant view of the national identity and the biggest reservoir of historically repeated patterns and practices that designed the system of meanings of national culture. The aim of this section is to examine the impact that the Russia-West relationship has had on human-rights culture in contemporary Russia. Such a survey is relevant, as it examines the dynamics and causal powers of Russian ambivalence toward the European human-rights regime. Due to lack of space, I consciously have limited myself to analyzing only those elements of the Russia-West relationship that directly influence current Russian human-rights discourse.

For a considerable part of its history, Russia has been torn between a European and a non-European identity, whereas Europe has hesitated on whether to exclude Russia as a stranger or to accept Russia as a member of its community. As Martin Malia observed, Europe's view of Russia as a distinct civilization emerged only after the Vienna Congress in 1815, as Europe felt the fear of Russian power for the very first time.[151] Although the question is too often answered "with a checklist of negatives: Medieval Church and Empire? No. Feudalism and chivalry? No. Renaissance and Reformation? No. If one adds to this purely mechanical procedure a national history that certainly did not culminate in freedom [as

147 Organization for Security and Co-operation in Europe, "Information concerning the legal proceedings initiated by Georgia against Russia" (6 October 2008), available at <http://www.osce.org/odihr/34093?download=true>.

148 Samuel P. Huntington, *The Clash of Civilizations and the Remaking of World Order* (Simon & Schuster, New York, NY, 1996), 213.

149 Neumann, *op.cit.* note 76, 1.

150 To the contrary, Kassianova argues that, in the West, the problem of relations between the West and Russia definitely does not constitute a subject of societal self-reflection and is deliberated strictly in a pragmatic vein. See Kassianova, *op.cit.* note 16, 822.

151 Martin Malia, *Russia Under Western Eyes: From the Bronze Horseman to the Lenin Mausoleum* (The Belknap Press of Harvard University Press, London and Cambridge, MA, 2000), 91.

the history of any European state should] the verdict is clear: Russia is of non-European essence."[152] Nonetheless, Russia has never sunk to the level of Turkey, which has never been considered European. Russia's position has always been somehow different from other entities bordering on Europe due to its geography, political conjuncture with European ideas, be those of enlightened despotism of the eighteenth century or of the socialist movement later in the twentieth century, its philosophical inclinations toward the European tradition[153] or its overall audacity in proclaiming itself European.

However, one should note that there are more concepts of Europe which need to be distinguished and of which Russia has tried to become a member. As a civilization, Europe extends from its geographical core all the way to North and South America to the west and to Siberia and the Russian Pacific coast to the east. It also covers Australia, New Zealand, and Israel.[154] European civilization thus became global, encompassing a myriad of cultures, but only one civilization. Moreover, Europe as conceptualized in its institutions is marching to areas previously considered beyond Europe—in the words of Martin Malia—"turning South Caucasus into a new Southeast Europe".[155]

In order to conceptualize Europe, I argue—together with Angela Stent—that one has to differentiate at least three "Europe's [*sic*] of which Russia intends to be, is or was a part. Europe, in this sense, can serve as a mere geographical reality, a model, or an idea".[156] *First*, Europe exists as a geographical reality, as a gateway to great-power status. To put it differently, European soil is a mere theater for the projection of Russian power, one of the territories Russia can influence, can conquer or of which it can become an integral part. This view is the closest to the realist thinking in current international-relations theory. The identity of the territory is negligible; the only aspect that matters is the distribution of resources which, in turn, determines the power of the actors involved. Human rights, culture, and history have no place in this understanding.

Second, Europe works as a model of modernization. European societies have been perceived as advanced and have achieved impressive economic results even if their political systems were deemed inappropriate for Russia. From Peter the Great to Joseph Stalin, the perception of Russia being conquered by "Mongol khans, Turkish beys, Swedish feudal lords, Polish or Lithuanian pans, by English

152 *Ibid.*, 129.

153 Russian philosophy was always rooted in European philosophical trends. Consider contacts by Catherine II with Voltaire and Diderot, Hegel's impact on Russian understanding of culture and history, Marx's cardinal effect on Lenin.

154 Malia, *op.cit.* note 151, 34.

155 *Ibid.*, 32.

156 Angela Stent, "Reluctant Europeans: Three Centuries of Russian Ambivalence", in Robert Legvold (ed.), *Russian Foreign Policy in the Twenty-First Century and the Shadow of the Past* (Columbia University Press, New York, NY, 2007), 393-441, at 393.

and French capitalists, and by Japanese barons"[157] has been reproduced and dispersed in Russian national discourse over and over again. For that reason, Europe usually represented a successful model to be followed, cooperated with and observed, or at least an economic adversary that Russia needed to catch up to. Loosely, one can see this concept of Europe as a liberal notion (again, understood in terms of international-relations theory) where the important factors of analysis are economic power and mutually advantageous cooperation—or, at worst, a non-zero sum game where all can gain; the only question is how much. Again, there is no place for understanding Europe as a space with a particular identity.

Third and finally, Europe operates on the level of ideas as a loose set of notions that distinguish European from non-European. At certain times, Russia has formed a part of the European idea; at other times, it has been detached from it completely. At this point, Stent argues that only Mikhail Gorbachev managed to engage Russia on all three levels. However, this view is misleading as, at other times, Russia also has aspired to operate on all levels. Consider the rule of Catherine II, when—on the level of ideas—Russia followed the European model of enlightened despotism and tried to modernize its law based on the European model, but when it still asserted itself as a main geopolitical player in the European theater. One can reach a similar conclusion in assessing the rule of Aleksander I. Therefore, I believe Russia became European in the sense of engaging on all levels of Stent's model at multiple times in its history.

I believe the history of Europe is one of great universalistic notions.[158] We can find philosophical concepts constructing an identified Europe, not necessarily in the sense of a homogenous centralized area but, rather, of cooperation between a larger number of autonomous units based on the acknowledgement of higher, common and solid principles. One can mention the Greek polis recognizing principles of individual freedom and, in particular, the balance of powers among the members participating in the international system; the Roman Empire framed by its law,[159] Christendom as a mirror to heaven, where one God (expressed in the Pope as a spiritual leader and the Emperor as a temporal ruler) embodies the whole society; or the Enlightenment's universal human reason; and most recently, the project of the European Union or the Council of Europe—both

157 This is a paraphrase of a statement by Stalin. For the original quotation, see Neumann, *op.cit.* note 76, 123.

158 For an introductory discussion on the history of the European idea see, *inter alia*, Norman Davies, *Europe: A History* (Oxford University Press, Oxford, 1996); Peter Gowan and Perry Anderson (eds.), *The Question of Europe* (Verso, London, New York, NY, 1997); or Pagden, *op.cit.* note 59.

159 However, the phenomenal expansion of the city of Rome and the foundation of the Roman Empire were never considered European expansion; it was the Mediterranean realm. More likely, Rome meant the center of the world, so that there was no need to identify itself within one continent.

embracing the idea of a liberal, democratic common Europe. Throughout the centuries, Russia has interacted with these concepts—though not with all of them—becoming a full-fledged member at some times (Enlightenment), or being completely "thrust out into the cold of [its] Asiatic steppes"[160] at others.

In this sense, Russia tried to usurp the notion of Europe for itself at least once. During the period 1917-1939, the new progressive Europe—that is, Russia and later the USSR, based not on national boundaries, but on classes—was delineated from the old, stagnant one. The image of the Soviet Union as the true Europe, "as the young dynamic force of the future was offset against the image of an old, conflict ridden false Europe writhing on its death bed"[161] was then proselytized throughout the existence of the USSR. In that sense, Russia tried to be not only 'in', or 'of' Europe; it tried to be Europe.

However, the artificial usurpation of the notion of Europe remained only wishful thinking. Meanwhile, a different notion of Europe developed in the West, outside the Eastern bloc controlled by the Soviets. As argued by Jeremy Rifkin, a new European dream encompassing the idea of Europe emerged. In his words:

> "For Europeans, freedom is not found in autonomy, but in embeddedness. To be free is to have access to a myriad of interdependent relationships with others. The more communities one has access to, the more options and choices one has for living a full and meaningful life. With relationships come inclusion and with inclusivity comes security."[162]

In this sense, to be European means to belong to a highly symbolic community basing itself on democracy and the rule of law. In a nutshell, human rights are central to an understanding of the new European dream, which emphasizes belonging and interdependence, understands the extent to which one is civilized in terms of human-rights protection, and supports the Fukuyamist idea that history (at least, one of his ideas) has ended since there is no better concept of human order than that of a liberal democracy. Such an understanding is accepted with difficulty by an individualist, pragmatic and suspicious Russia. In this sense, the identity of the territory—that is, of Europe—presents a strong challenge to the Russian comprehension of the world and relations within it.

Let me return to the argument from part 3 of this chapter: international law is developmental; there should be a different law for liberal states, while illiberal states would be bound to develop as only liberal forms of governance would be legitimate under international law. Translated into modern discourse, human rights and democracy have become the scale used to measure the development of a society. If we accept both the democratic-norm thesis and Friedrich Martens' (1845-1909) thesis about the law of civilized nations, we have to conclude that

160 Malia, *op.cit.* note 150, 102.

161 Neumann, *op.cit.* note 76, 127.

162 Jeremy Rifkin, *The European Dream: How Europe's Vision of the Future is Quietly Eclipsing the American Dream* (Jeremy P. Tarcher/Penguin, New York, NY, 2004), 13.

Europe is somehow the most civilized region in the world and, thus, all other regions in their development head toward the West.

From a broader perspective, Europe became a part of the US-led order built around the institutional and multilateral structures created in the wake of the World War II (the UN, GATT, and the international financial institutions) and the extraordinarily dense set of transatlantic and trans-Pacific relations and alliance systems.[163] Within this framework, Europe further developed its own institutional network whose main contemporary representatives are the EU, CoE and, to a certain extent, NATO. In analyzing the attitude of Russia toward these developments, one has to realize the extent to which Russia (together with all other BRIC countries) lies outside these formations (unlike Australia, New Zealand, or Canada). Any ideational concept coming to the peripheries of the system—that is, to BRIC countries—is thus perceived as cultural imperialism.

In this sense, a significant part of Russian scholarship perceives Western interdependence and globalizing relations as a threat to Russian society. As Julia Rozanova showed, Russian scholarship perceives globalization as a process of subordination of the world to a single hyperpower, as enslaving the vast periphery to the 'golden billion', or as concealed Westernization, or even more specifically as the Americanization of the world.[164] From this perspective, Russia perceives itself as a victim of the negative impacts of Western-led globalization. Accepting the rules of globalization under these circumstances would mean the self-destruction of Russia as a nation and as a culture.

Even President Medvedev took the opportunity to criticize the negative character of the current process of globalization. In his view:

> "The crises taking place before our eyes—the financial crisis, rising prices for natural resources and food, as well as a number of global catastrophes—have clearly demonstrated that the current system of global governance is not equipped to meet the challenges it faces. [...] This has shown how illusory it is to suppose that a single country, even if it is the most powerful, can assume the role of global government."[165]

A significant number of Russian scholars then perceive the notion of self-determination to be the best formula for Russian development in the context of globalization. However, as Rozanova describes, the concept of self-determination acquires a broader significance under conditions of global civilizational transformation since it encompasses the orientation taken in the ongoing changes, the choice of place in the modern world, and the chosen strategy of how to get

163 Hurrell, *op.cit.* note 36, 4.

164 See Julia Rozanova, "Russia in the Context of Globalization", 51 *Current Sociology* (2003), 649-669.

165 Dmitrii Medvedev, Speech at the 12th Petersburg International Economic Forum (7 June 2008), available at <http://archive.kremlin.ru/eng/speeches/2008/06/07/1338_type82914type127286_202288.shtml>.

there.[166] To put it differently, self-determination means the ability and the will of a state to hold its own course and to pursue its own policies without being coerced by the outside world.

The very term 'sovereign democracy'—so often used by both elites inside and scholars outside Russia to describe the development of the Russian state—contains its own declaration of equality with the Western world view.

> "Indirectly, it also implies what the Russian Federation's role model on the world stage is: according to the logic of the Kremlin ideologists there is only one true sovereign democracy: the United States. All others are either undemocratic, like China, or not sovereign enough, like the European Union countries."[167]

In the Russian view, there is no real democracy anywhere in the world; all governments lie to their peoples, and all share the same imperfections. The falsity of Western lecturing, in Russian eyes, is then evident. Human rights, in such an international setting, are once again a tool to tie Russia to the US-led Western world. One prominent scholar has noted that "Russia's long daydream about uniting with Europe is history. [...] The new talk is [centered] on sovereignty, with the United States as the role model and China as an object of admiration and envy."[168] However, Rozanova concludes, self-determination "does not just depend on the country itself, even if it is a country as big as Russia, but is a reflection of the general world situation, the tendencies of world development".[169] In other words, Russia cannot escape the challenges imposed upon it by globalization.

Throughout its history, Russia has engaged on at least one of the levels of 'Europeanness'; however, it has never succeeded in finding its permanent place among the levels. Having become a full member of the European community, Russia too often found itself lagging behind development of the European idea, usually trying to catch up after a period of opposition. The only attempt to take the initiative in the process of creating European identity—that is, the Soviet claim to be the new Europe—failed. The question then somehow lurks in one's mind: can Russia ever become stably European? In this regard, the question is whether we understand Europeanness to be somehow genetic (as nineteenth-century nationalist thinkers believed) or whether it is a sort of an end in itself, a paramount of human development. If we understand Europe in the developmental notion—that countries do develop on the scale of protection of their own citizens and the top of the scale is the Fukuyamist liberal Western regime—human rights would become one of the universalistic conceptualizations rooted in European tradition and as such would enter the national discursive space of Russian society.

166 Rozanova, *op.cit.* note 164, 656.

167 Dmitri V. Trenin, "Russia's Foreign Policy: Self-Affirmation, or a Tool for Modernization?", *Open Democracy* (13 May 2008), available at <http://www.carnegieendowment.org/publications/index.cfm?fa=view&id=20130&prog=zru>.

168 Trenin, *op.cit.* note 141.

169 Rozanova, *op.cit.* note 164, 655.

However, human rights once again gained the connotation of being a mere "ideological smokescreen, [...] a kind of Trojan horse offered by the West in order to subvert [Russian] society".[170] In this sense, the West in Russian eyes made "an illegitimate attempt to claim the right to define what European identity should mean".[171]

A similar attitude toward notions coming from the West has traditionally been present in Russian discourse as a response to Westernizing tendencies; one can find examples even before conceptualization of the nation and nation state in the nineteenth century. The historian Nikolai Karamzin, among others, reacted to Petrine reforms by noting that:

> "Imitation became for Russia a matter of honour and pride. [...] Russia has been in existence for a thousand years as a great state. Yet we are constantly told of new institutions and of new laws, as if we had just emerged from the dark American forests."[172]

Moreover, many considered those 'new institutions and new laws' to be inescapably flawed. Aleksandr Solzhenitsyn, among many others, declared, that:

> "The West has supped more than its fill of every kind of freedom, including intellectual freedom. And has this saved it? We see it today crawling on hands and knees, its will paralyzed, uneasy about the future, spiritually racked and dejected. Unlimited external freedom in itself is quite inadequate to save us. Intellectual freedom is a gift of conditional, not intrinsic worth, only a means by which we can attain another and higher goal."[173]

As I tried to illustrate above, human rights are embedded in a European dream that emphasizes belonging and interdependence, understands the extent to which one is civilized in terms of human-rights protection and supports the Fukuyamist idea that history (at least the history of ideas) has ended since there is no better concept of human order than liberal democracy.[174] In this sense, one has to conclude that (based on the background of the European dream) human rights enter the cycle of national identity re-creation as a universal idea hostile to the historical practices of the Russian state. However, as Dmitri Trenin has observed, the Russian Empire and the USSR were "self-contained, self-sufficient, and self-sustaining. The Russian Federation is exactly the opposite".[175] Russia, therefore, has to redefine its attitude to Europe; however, the current relationship between Russia and Europe on the ideational level (thus dismissing the economic

170 Morozov, *op.cit.* note 6, 426.

171 Richard Sakwa, "Russia and Turkey: Rethinking Europe to Contest Outsider Status", 51 *Russie.Nei.Visions* (May 2010), 10.

172 Karamzin, quoted in Neumann, *op.cit.* note 76, 14.

173 Solzhenitsyn, quoted in Neumann, *op.cit.* note 76, 143.

174 See Francis Fukuyama, *The End of History and the Last Man* (Free Press, New York, NY, 1992).

175 Trenin, *op.cit.* note 97, 17.

and political level) can be characterized as a "lukewarm embrace that at times becomes a chilly estrangement".[176] A common language is often hard to find.

Domestic Determinants of Human-Rights Acceptance

Many times in its history, Russia has experienced a great state transformation period, every time changing the very structure of its political and economic system.[177] All of these revolutions bore different sets of assumptions and expectations, and valued different outcomes. One cannot effectively discuss the Russian attitude towards human rights without considering these intrinsically different notions of Russia and its identity. However, only during the last transformation period (which was unleashed by Gorbachev's and El'tsin's reforms and which—according to some[178]—ended with those of Putin) did several authors conclude that Russia "[had] arrived at a historic fork in the road", having an unparalleled chance to shake off the persistent patterns of its history and "[make] of itself something different from any Russia before".[179]

Such a chance is, on the other hand, accompanied by deep uncertainties about Russia's place in the world, its identity and purpose and has therefore resulted in several fundamental swings in Russian foreign policy during the last twenty-seven years.[180] Russia's foreign policy shifted greatly from the zealous Westernism of Gorbachev and El'tsin's first Minister of Foreign Affairs, Andrei Kozyrev, to the gradually more weary and cautious great-power-balancing policies of Evgenii Primakov, El'tsin's second Minister of Foreign Affairs and, for the time

176 Sakwa, *op.cit.* note 171, 5.

177 Legvold and his co-authors define six such periods, starting with the reforms of Ivan IV, Peter the Great, and Aleksandr II, respectively, and later in the twentieth century, first those of Lenin and Stalin and later of Gorbachev and El'tsin, thus distinguishing six regime types throughout Russian history, each of them carrying a different set of identities and assumptions: (a) the Petrine empire (1700-1825); (b) the modernizing empire (1825-1917); (c) the internationalist state of nations (1917-1932); (d) the nationalizing empire (1932-1985); (e) the transitory empire (1985-1991); and (f) the weakened multinational state with ambitions of hegemony (1991-present). See Robert Legvold (ed.), *Russian Foreign Policy in the Twenty-First Century and the Shadow of the Past* (Columbia University Press, New York, NY, 2007), 41 and 77.

178 For opposing opinions see, *first*, Medvedev, *op.cit.* note 96, ix, who claims that "the realignment in Russian foreign and security policy [in favor of Westernization] is revolutionary and has lasting value", and *second*, see Trenin's article in *Open Democracy*, where he claims that "Moscow's policies on the international front are as reactive as ever, despite the vastly greater opportunities, despite the fact that it is openly critical of the West, particularly the United States" and that Russia remains unable to create an agenda of its own. Trenin, *op.cit.* note 167.

179 Legvold, *op.cit.* note 177, 29. For similar conclusions, see Tsygankov, *op.cit.* note 74; or Trenin, *op.cit.* note 97.

180 Counted from Gorbachev's succession to the position of General Secretary of the Communist Party in 1985.

being, ended with Putin's great-power pragmatism. Whether Dmitrii Medvedev is going to influence Russia's direction remains unclear since Vladimir Putin continues to hold significant power over Russian politics.

As Stephen E. Hanson noted:

> "The central puzzle of Russian politics is that [seventeen] years after the collapse of the USSR, the country still lacks any stable and legitimate form of state order. The result is continuing pervasive political and social uncertainty—concretized in the palpable official fear that independent civil society organizations might promote additional 'colour revolutions' in Russia or other post-Soviet states."[181]

Hanson builds his argument on Max Weber's definition of the state as a set of institutions that (more or less) successfully claim a monopoly on legitimate violence in a specific territory. Attention is then drawn to three aspects: clearly defined territorial claims, control over the means of coercion, and political legitimacy. Hanson concludes that all three components remain undermined by the seventy years of Soviet rule. *First*, almost all national borders within the former USSR remain "hotly contested".[182] *Second*, the inability of Russian law enforcement to effectively control the area of the North Caucasus and to prevent terrorist attacks on Russian territory (consider the Beslan hostage tragedy, among others) suggests that Russia has "found it exceedingly difficult to maintain a monopoly of legitimate coercion within its vast territory".[183] *Third* and most significantly, Russia remains trapped within an identity crisis, as all historical means of legitimation have been discredited and the new one, popular democracy, has not yet been stabilized. As Hanson has concluded:

> "Putin's attempts to solve the problem of state identity pragmatically—mixing and matching state symbols from the tsarist, Soviet, and post-Soviet periods with little or no effort to articulate any enduring principles that such symbols might express—represents only a short-term compromise that has left the long-run definition of the Russian polity utterly unresolved."[184]

However, one thing is clear: as other forms of legitimation (such as dynastic succession or Marxist ideology) become obsolete, democratic elections are the only possible source of political legitimation and have thus become "the only game in town",[185] although the situation may resemble a "monocracy on the basis of mass consent".[186] As Robert Kagan put it: living in a predominantly liberal area,

181 Stephen E. Hanson, "The Uncertain Future of Russia's Weak State Authoritarianism", 21 *East European Politics and Societies* (2007), 67-81, at 69.

182 *Ibid.*, 70.

183 *Ibid.*, 72.

184 *Ibid.*

185 Lilia Shevtsova, "The Limits of Bureaucratic Authoritarianism", 15 *Journal of Democracy* (2004), 67-77, at 68.

186 *Ibid.*

Russia maintains the "trappings of democracy"[187] and represents itself as being democratic, however, with certain adjectives. As I have tried to show in the previous sections of this chapter, there was a stubborn Fukuyamist faith in the West that expected that "any country that is moving away from totalitarianism [to] therefore be moving towards democracy"[188] and, thus, toward the liberal Western world order. However, Russia—probably due to its ten centuries of discourse over its own uniqueness—chose the concept of self-determination and thus perceives everything that comes from the West, human rights included, with deep suspicion.

Turning to the domestic determinants of national identity, one finds oneself in a tricky position as culture is a fluid and permeable system open to constant exchange with the outside. In a traditional constructivist view, identity cannot even be formed without ideational exchange with the external 'Other'. However, in trying to search for domestic determinants, I use an article by Alfred J. Rieber as my point of departure. Rieber argues that there are four persistent factors, four unchanging sets of questions whose mix determines the political outcomes of Russian behavior. Those four are relative economic backwardness, porous frontiers, a multinational society, and cultural alienation.[189]

The fear of a weak economy led some Russian scholars to conclude that human rights are menacing the economy as such. According to Elena Lukasheva, "following Western models led to dramatic impoverishment of the people and to irreparable damage caused to the national economy".[190] The spectacular economic recovery Russia made during the 1990s makes Russians believe in their specific way. The 'declinism' of the 1990s is gone. Despite excessive dependency on oil and natural-gas exports, Russians can see that standards of living are rising. Russian cities are full of expensive boutiques, luxury cars and electronics stores. As Dmitry Trenin noted, "modernization generally happens in stages [and] since the economy is the foundation, the first stage consists in creating a middle class

187 Kagan, *op.cit.* note 5.

188 Shevtsova, *op.cit.* note 185, 69.

189 Alfred J. Rieber, "How Persistent are Persistent Factors?", in Levgold, *op.cit.* note 177, 205-278, at 206. Rieber similarly develops two dynamic, flexible factors that should explain domestic change. These are: domestic leadership and the international system. However, Rieber's explanation of change is too simplistic as the former factors overemphasize the individual level of decision-making (Gorbachev as an individual wanted to reform the USSR. However, his policies released forces beyond his individual powers, which ultimately led to dissolution of the Union) and the latter similarly overemphasize international input. As argued throughout this chapter, securitization of Russian domestic discourse is the contemporary answer to the international forces of globalization.

190 Elena A. Lukasheva, *Prava cheloveka i protsessy globalizatsii sovremennogo mira* (Institut gosudarstva i prava RAN, Moscow, 2007), 12. Unless otherwise noted, all translations in this chapter are by the author.

that will be the bedrock of social stability".[191] Only after the Russian economy manages these steps can a fully democratic system be established as a second step. To put it differently: Russia is currently driven by ruthless pragmatism and materialism as "collectivist values are in steep decline and there is no system of values that has replaced the communist one".[192] In other words, "Russia's business is business" and "what is good for Gazprom is good for Russia".[193] Human rights are then perceived as an impediment to the development of the country and as such largely derided. Trenin concludes that "citizens (in the elevated sense of members of civil society) have not arrived in Russia yet, but consumers have".[194]

The next two factors cited by Rieber are: the "ill-defined, unstable, under populated and contested frontiers"[195] and the fact that, due to expansion, the "Russian periphery acquired the characteristics of a shatter zone, inhabited by a complex mix of ethnic groups, religions and cultures".[196] The loyalty of the peoples in the shatter zone was always in question. Such a mix needed a strong state that would be able to control these unstable national mixes. The Russian state perpetually played a crucial role in stressing strategic, territorial and mobilization priorities at the expense of political and civil society, as well as the market economy. "It built roads and outposts, extended and defended borders, fought the mounted horsemen of the Great Steppe in the East and opposed regular armies that invaded from the West",[197] and thus the Russian empire was built at the expense of Russia's own sense of nationhood,[198] which then hindered the development of the notion of citizenship.

Another scholar noted that:

> "There can be no doubt that the policy of expansion and the interminable task of securing Russian rule consumed immense human and material resources over the centuries, that they diverted attention from social, economic and political developments within Russia itself, encouraged extensive at the expense of intensive growth and thus constituted one of the reasons for Russia's backwardness."[199]

In other words, the Russian state searched for total control over its vast territory and turned itself into a 'national-security state', a concept that culminated in the

191 Trenin, *op.cit.* note 167.

192 Trenin, *op.cit.* note 97, 20.

193 *Ibid.*

194 *Ibid.*, 16.

195 Rieber, *op.cit.* note 189, 208.

196 *Ibid.*, 209.

197 Medvedev, *op.cit.* note 96, x.

198 Vera Tolz, "Conflicting Homeland Myths and Nation-State Building in Postcommunist Russia", 57 *Slavic Review* (1998), 267-294, at 267.

199 Andreas Kappeler, *The Russian Empire: A Multiethnic History* (Pearson Education Limited, Harlow, UK, 2001), 323.

USSR.[200] Only a strong state organization is capable of bringing development and stability to society. In the language of Musurkul Kabylbekov, "today's Western emphasis on human rights and democracy [...] has similarities with the decay of the Roman Empire, which fell because of its softness under the blows of fierce barbarians who knew neither mercy nor hesitation".[201]

The final persistent factor distinguished by Rieber is the often-mentioned relationship with Europe. Russia "may [have been] with the West, but not of it"[202] and became culturally alienated from the West. In this sense, the idea of the Russian nation as an organic entity, where the government is the head of a popular body, needs to be mentioned. As long as there is only one body, there can be no conflict between the head and the body, only the same well-being or powerlessness are possible. As Ludmilla Selezneva has noted, all this:

> "[...] resulted in the relative weakness of individual self-consciousness, individual self-esteem and individual responsibility. On the contrary, the strong domination of a kind of 'group' or 'collective' psychology developed."[203]

Therefore, the idea of individual rights holds a different set of connotations in Russia from that in the West, as it is based on a mechanical model of human organization. In this model, the nation is schematized as a triangle where the government is on top of the triangle with society and the individual creating the base. Within such a framework, all three aspects interact with ona another and allow delimitation from one another.[204]

In this sense, one has to conclude that, based on the background of the European dream, human rights enter the cycle of national identity re-creation as universal ideas hostile to historically proven practices of the Russian state. These two paradigms seem inescapably contradictory. The current relationship between Russia and Europe on the ideational level (thus, dismissing the economic and political level) is one of misunderstanding and mutual mistrust and, therefore, looks with no favor upon the inclusion of human rights.

Let me turn my attention to the question of supportive coalitions. Several analyses have proposed a very similar breakdown of the groups present within the Russian context. The usual distinction separates the groups of Westernizers (or liberals, democrats, Atlanticists, or international institutionalists), Statists (or liberal nationalists), and Civilizationists (or Eurasianists, its more radical wings include expansionists and ultra-nationalists).[205]

200 Medvedev, *op.cit.* note 96, x.

201 Cited in Müllerson, *op.cit.* note 33, 1629.

202 Rieber, *op.cit.* note 189, 257.

203 Ludmilla Selezneva, "Post-Soviet Russian Foreign Policy: Between Doctrine and Pragmatism", 11 *European Security* (2002), 10-28, at 2, 12.

204 Neumann, *op.cit.* note 76, 196.

205 See, *inter alia*, Neumann, *op.cit.* note 76, 159; Kassianova, *op.cit.* note 16, 824-825; Jackson,

However, as Viatcheslav Morozov argued:

> "The almost universally accepted classification of the foreign policy elite into 'Atlanticists' and 'Eurasianists' (or 'Westernizers' and 'Nationalists') does not really work in the case of human rights: a great majority of those usually described as 'Atlanticists' seem to share the basic [perception] of human rights as a foreign policy instrument, not as a goal."[206]

As I have tried to illustrate, Russian discourse tends "to interpret Russia as a unique civilization combining genuine native values with some elements of the West and the East".[207]

In this sense, the use of Mette Skak's observation model seems to be more appropriate. Building on Putnam's two-level-game model, Skak proposed two hypotheses suiting the Russian context. For the domestic-level game board, she claims that the hegemonic win-set in Russia tends to be an "illiberal one of *derzhavnik* anti-Americanism and neo-imperialism, but not extremist".[208] As for the foreign-policy game board, the relevant win-set is one of "liberalism that accepts the unique power of the USA and hence implies bandwaggoning, not balancing".[209] Applying this ideational framework to Russian foreign policy, Skak analyzed the shortcomings of different notions of Russian identity and policy orientation. She noted that both Gorbachev and El'tsin had failed in playing the domestic level successfully and gradually had lost the support of domestic groupings. Both presidents had hoped to counterbalance domestic weaknesses by gaining support in the West, which had proved fatal as support did not come to the desired extent.

President Putin behaved more carefully. As Jeffrey Mankoff argued, Putin was "agile enough to come across as a liberal [...], a statist, or a Russian nationalist as the situation demand[ed]".[210] Putin managed to create a fairly homogenous view of the Russian national character, which "increasingly identif[ies] with traditional Russian values of centralization, a strong state, and an emphasis on Russia's uniqueness",[211] but which, however, perceives human rights as outside values that are strange to Russian culture.

This view is further supported by some other societal groupings, with the Russian Orthodox Church being among the strongest. In April 2006, during the Tenth World Council of the Russian People, the Russian Orthodox Church

op.cit. note 69, 33 and 36; or Tsygankov, *op.cit.* note 74, 61. The classification of groups may slightly differ from author to author; however, the main sets of ideas presented remain the same in all of these analyses.

206 Morozov, *op.cit.* note 6, 413.

207 *Ibid.*

208 Skak, *op.cit.* note 101, 87.

209 *Ibid.*

210 Jeffrey Mankoff, "Russia and the West: Taking the Longer View", 30 *The Washington Quarterly* (2007), 123-135, at 126.

211 *Ibid.*, 129.

adopted its own declaration of human rights and dignity in which it declared that there are values holding the same level as human rights—faith, morality, sanctuary, and the fatherland—and that no other rights should have precedence over these values. The declaration similarly condemned abuse of rights for political or ideological purposes.[212] From the point of view of the late Patriarch Aleksei II, a break had occurred

> "[...] between human rights and morality, and this break [threatened] European civilization. We can see it in a new generation of rights that contradict morality and in how human rights are used to justify immoral behavior."[213]

Similar views have also been supported and independently declared by the Russian delegates to PACE. As delegate Korobeinkov asked:

> "Why, for example, does Russia need such an extravagant value as homosexual marriage? We do not need this European lapse from virtue at all."[214]

Moreover, during the very same World Council, the Church criticized Western human-rights views, as doubts were raised whether the 'secular liberal' concept of human rights could be accepted as universal 'without an appropriate correction'.[215] As Masha Lipman reported:

> "The council was broadly publicized by the government-controlled media, and a television talk show a couple of days later had an audience that showed its strong support for the view that the Western concept of human rights was inherently alien to the Russian people."[216]

One can conclude that the Russian Orthodox Church seems to support and enforce the securitization policies promoted by the state authorities within domestic discursive space and upholds the notion that human rights are alien to the Russian people, and are in need of adjustment for Russian conditions.

Securitization of Domestic Discourse

In order to conclude the examination of the current human-rights discourse in Russia, I argue that what happens in the Russian context is a securitization of identity. As Viatcheslav Morozov put it, when one portrays Westernization as a threat:

> "Societal identity plays the role of the referential object of a security discourse, and thus the danger of entropy is perceived as an existential threat to society itself. If the West is allowed to succeed in its universalizing project, society will cease to exist. From this point of view it

212 Moscow Patriarchate, "Deklaratsiia o pravakh i dostoinstve cheloveka 10. Vsemirnogo Russkogo Narodnogo Sobora" (14 April 2006), available at <http://www.patriarchia.ru/db/text/103235.html>.

213 PACE, *op.cit.* note 131.

214 PACE, "Memorandum of Understanding between the Council of Europe and the European Union, Addendum 2" (13 April 2006), available at <http://assembly.coe.int/main.asp?Link=/documents/records/2006/e/0604131000ead2.htm>.

215 Lipman, *op.cit.* note 130.

216 *Ibid.*

> does not matter that 'entropy' brings no physical threat to individual human beings—every one of us may be alive and well, but we will no longer be us."[217]

I argue, along the lines of Morozov's article, that the practice of securitization of human-rights discourse continues to function.

Perceived as tools of globalization, hampering the development of the Russian economy and threatening to assimilate Russian culture, human rights are seen as often hostile semantic variables challenging dominant practices, systems of legitimization and the overall system of meanings in society. In other words, rights are being securitized, as they are perceived as being imposed from outside with the aim of dissolving and assimilating Russian society into the emerging 'global West'. Viewed in this light, the above-mentioned fear of entropy is nothing less than a threat to the identity of the Russian nation, as "the meaning of history [lies] in preserving the identity of a given subject—of a people".[218] For human rights, to be successfully contested in such an environment is extremely difficult.

How can one understand the concept of securitization? As Thierry Balzacq argued, securitization should be understood as a strategic-pragmatic practice that occurs "within, and as part of, a configuration of circumstances, including the context, the psycho-cultural disposition of the audience, and the power that both speaker and listener bring to the interaction".[219] The domestic discursive space closes itself, and by using "various artefacts (metaphors, emotions, stereotypes, gestures, silence, and even lies)",[220] it attempts to discredit or exclude some variables from the contestation cycle. As I illustrated above, Russian delegates to PACE, on the one hand, recognize Russia's commitment to the European regime of human-rights protection, including the authority of the ECtHR but, on the other hand, blame the West for bending the original meaning of rights, unlimited broadening of the understanding of the ECtHR[221] or for alleged use of double standards in assessing the situation in different CoE member states. Human rights seem to be the case of variables being securitized by state elites and, simply put, by the state itself.[222]

In the case of such negative identification between the self and contested variables entering semantic space, "interactions between self and other make self's identity more insecure; hence there is a greater need to reproduce and re-inscribe self's identity in relation to the other, strengthening the tendency to represent

217 Morozov, *op.cit.* note 6, 19.

218 Aleksandr Panarin, quoted in Morozov, *op.cit.* note 6.

219 Thierry Balzacq, "The Three Faces of Securitization: Political Agency, Audience and Context", 11 *European Journal of International Relations* (2005), 171-201, at 172.

220 *Ibid.*

221 See Clare Ovey and Robin White, *The European Convention on Human Rights* (Oxford University Press, Oxford, 2006), 241-299.

222 Kassianova, *op.cit.* note 16, 825.

the differences".[223] At the same time the perceived external threat "increases the national cohesion and centralization, in fact foreign policy elitism".[224] I believe that I have managed to illustrate such dynamisms—that is, the perpetual ardent reproduction of the discourse and its even more ardent defense *vis-à-vis* external challengers.

However, as Sjöstedt puts it, "the securitizing act is 'not simply a realm of instrumental rationality and rhetorical manipulation' but obligates and enables a certain subsequent behavior to handle the securitized threat".[225] In this sense, the political leader not only needs to rhetorically manipulate the discourse; the securitization process allows him to behave in a certain way in his future actions. In other words, successful securitization of human-rights discourse permits a bolder stand *vis-à-vis* the contested other.

Three basic assumptions need to be fulfilled for effective securitization. Such securitization needs to be audience-centered, context-dependent, and power-laden. As Balzacq explained:

> "The first of these has three components—(i) the audience's frame of reference; (ii) its readiness to be convinced, which depends on whether it perceives the securitizing actor as knowing the issue and as trustworthy; and (iii) its ability to grant or deny a formal mandate to public officials. The second set of factors concerns contextual effects on the audience's responsiveness to the securitizing actor's arguments—relevant aspects of the Zeitgeist that influence the listener, and the impact of the immediate situation on the way the securitizing author's sentences are interpreted by the listener. The third set involves the capacity of the securitizing actor to use appropriate words and cogent frames of reference in a given context, in order to win the support of the target audience for political purposes."[226]

The importance of the attention given to the role of the audience is pivotal. As Anderson put it, "individuals decide what sources of information to use, how much information to receive/consume, and what conclusions to draw from this information".[227] In this sense, people and politics are not detached from each other. Using Putnam's model of a two-level board game and Tsygankov's explanation of how foreign policy is formed, I argue that arguments based on the individual level of decision making—such as Jeremy Shestack's—are insufficient, as they overlook the need of any political leader, including world dictators, to

223 Bahar Rumelili, "Constructing Identity and Relating to Difference: Understanding the EU's Mode of Differentiation", 30 *Review of International Studies* (2004), 27-47, at 36.

224 Hans Mouritzen and Mikkel Runge Olesen, "The Interplay of Geopolitics and Historical Lessons in Foreign Policy: Denmark Facing German Post-War Rearmament", 45 *Cooperation and Conflict* (2010), 406-427, at 410.

225 Roxanna Sjöstedt, "Exploring the Construction of Threats: The Securitization of HIV/AIDS in Russia", 39 *Security Dialogue* (2008), 7-29, at 9.

226 Balzacq, *op.cit.* note 219, 192.

227 Christopher J. Anderson *et al.*, "In the Eye of the Beholder? The Foundations of Subjective Human Rights Conditions in East-Central Europe", 38 *Comparative Political Studies* (2005), 771-798, at 777.

be backed up by a supportive national coalition. The successful use of discourse is then needed in order to gather and maintain national support, which later presents itself through the system of elections, public polls, or domestic political negotiations.

The Russian public, *first of all*, is indeed able to grant a formal mandate for state officials, as election has become the only means of legitimization within the state. In that sense, a successful exertion of influence over domestic discourse has proved necessary for domestic political conduct. The authoritarian practices of the regime provided the means for effective control over the dominant discourse; however, they did not prove to be cardinal for securitization of discourse. As Mankoff argued, the Russian public "increasingly identif[ies] with traditional Russian values of centralization, a strong state, and emphasis on Russia's uniqueness",[228] so that the arguments used by the securitizing agent correspond with the *Zeitgeist* of the audience. Therefore, the need to exercise strict control over the dissemination of information decreases as the Russian audience finds public officials and their version of the world more trustworthy and knowledgeable of the issue.

Second, the securitizing agent indeed maintains the capacity to use appropriate words and sentences to uphold its case, and the West gives enough examples to build it on: unclear conduct in the theater of Afghanistan, Iraq, and Kosovo are the most visible cases. The economic shock from the 1990s and the inability of international financial organizations to prevent it only further deepened distrust in the Western liberal worldview.

Thus, I argue that the conditions for successful discourse securitization are fulfilled and indeed used by Russian political elites. The Russian state, in this sense, effectively securitizes human rights by using a myriad of national myths, constructing the image of negative Western-led globalization and of the danger of assimilation and loss of Russian culture. Such a defense is offered in the form of rejecting human rights and other liberal principles as being of secondary importance in comparison with societal identity. Rights need to be accepted progressively, respecting the level of development of Russian society, its institutions and overall state of economy, and translated into the Russian context. Thus, what Russia demands is a much wider margin of appreciation due to its special nature.

Coming back to Tsygankov's model (see Figure 1), the Russian identity-creation cycle, in its relation to human rights, is stuck somewhere in the second stage. On the one hand, Russia signed on to the European human-rights regime, introduced new laws catering to human-rights concepts, and has been following the judgments of the ECtHR at least at the level of individual reparations. Thus, conducive institutional arrangements—as foreseen by Tsygankov—have been created. However, repetitive historical practices have created a hostile environment toward human rights.

228 Mankoff, *op.cit.* note 211, 129.

Third, the activities of political entrepreneurs actively follow the thread of securitization and create a hostile discourse, applying a vast reservoir of historical practices going against the notion of human rights. All this combined with Mette Skak's hypotheses built on Putnam's model—*i.e.*, with the notion that state authorities find the strongest support on the domestic board while acting in illiberal, but not extremist, ways, leads one to conclude that conditions for securitization of Russian human-rights discourse are significantly propitious.

However, the stronger securitizing policies are, the stronger is the clash with the much "deeper discursive structures within Russian society that have to do with Russia's self-perception as a European nation".[229] Centuries of balancing between Europe and non-Europe resurface again as securitization of Russian discourse may proceed only up to a certain point in order not to cross the line and turn its back on Europe completely. To that extent, Russian domestic discursive space has to redefine itself so that currently highly disputed and challenged ideas may become more and more accepted and slowly embedded in national institutions.

Conclusions: Implications for the Council

Humankind is a societal creature and organizes itself into communities—families, tribes, clans and, above all, nations. Human rights, in this regard, tend to overlook these societal groupings, as rights present human beings as atomized individuals. Throughout this chapter, I have argued against such an understanding and have further argued that an analysis examining the interaction of human rights with the societal identity of people is needed. My research, therefore, has tried to outline a framework for such an analysis within the scope of the discipline of international relations. To put it differently: human rights, in their aspiration for universal recognition, encounter local cultures, enter their sovereign space and influence their inner dynamics. The system of distribution of power and resources, of legitimization of rulers and the legitimacy of their ways of ruling may all be rebuilt from the ground. The interaction between local culture and global human rights needs to be studied as a discursive construction. This chapter has been a first effort to do so.

The initial assumption was that human rights read purely on the level of law—regulating relations between the state and individuals within the state's power—is insufficient in explaining why some non-Western cultures find it difficult to incorporate the notion of human rights into their social orders. In other words, the legal understanding of human rights fails to explain the resistance of some cultures to the idea of universal human rights and traps itself in a vicious circle of an oratorical stalemate. Human-rights lawyers then find themselves, as Martti Koskenniemi observed, trapped within:

229 Morozov, *op.cit.* note 6, 422.

> "an unreflective pragmatism, with the implicit assumption that the problems of theory are non-problems and that the sociological and normative issues of the world order can be treated by closely sticking to one's doctrinal task of analysing valid law."[230]

I have tried to posit my research in between the 'naïve universalism' of the former and the 'lazy relativism'[231] of the latter. I have proposed that human-rights scholarship should re-introduce the concept of culture into its research designs in order to be able to explain the interaction between cultural groupings and globally dominant discourses, such as human rights. Only a reconceptualization of culture can bring about an exhaustive analysis explaining the process of embedding rights into national institutions and overall national orders. As Christen Pursiainen has argued, if there is a long-term interest in maintaining a legally based international community, the law should not be based on external sanctions but, rather, on "shared interests, common values and patterned expectations".[232] All these interests, values and expectations are culturally bound and defined variables that a legal understanding of rights cannot incorporate into its scope nor can it explain the process through which they are shaped. In other words, the legal models downplay the traditionally significant role of the community and its collective understanding of justice and morality.[233]

In order to re-introduce culture into human-rights research conducted within the scope of international relations—that is, in order to understand the interaction between global human-rights discourse and the local discourse of a particular culture—I have proposed conceptualizing culture on the level of national identity. National identity works as a localized subsystem of human culture, which allows its operationalization for the purpose of research; it is a concept through which a state understands its goals and, at the same time, it is a rhetorical space within which action taken is legitimized and support gathered.[234] I have further argued that human rights ought to be conceptualized as symbolic technologies[235] and studied as discursive variables that enter the cycle of national-identity formation. Human rights, in that sense, possess a creational power to establish or influence the idiographic understanding of who one is and what one wants, and thus to change the nature of the individual national identity.

The necessary external framework for such an analysis is provided by the theory of transnational discursive democracy, the model for which rests "on the notion that discourses and their interactions are consequential in producing international outcomes through their influence upon and constitution of

230 Koskenniemi, *op.cit.* note 10, 3.

231 Francois Jullien, quoted in Leben, *op.cit.* note 63, 79.

232 Pursiainen, *op.cit.* note 75, 157.

233 *Ibid.*

234 Paraphrasing Weldes, *op.cit.* note 73, 276.

235 Laffey and Weldes, *op.cit.* note 89, 195.

actors".[236] In this sense, as soon as one accepts the constraining and enabling power of external dominant discourses such as liberal economy, human rights, or sustainable development, one has to ask how these discourses actually influence domestic discursive spaces. How can one operationalize the alleged power of these dominant discourses while entering national space? How can one describe the functioning or resistance of alternative discourses?

For that reason, I proposed that the contestation thesis introduced by Andrei P. Tsygankov should also be used for the case of human rights.[237] According to Tsygankov, when new ideas enter the process of national-identity formation, they are highly contested, challenged and questioned. Only as they acquire some support—be it political or societal—and consolidate their position within the cycle of constant recreation of shared meanings do they become embedded in the societal order and its institutions and thus are less, or hardly, challenged. I argue that human rights cannot escape the contestation cycle. In other words, human rights are not somewhere 'out there' waiting to be discovered and directly applied from point zero. They have to be contested against competing legitimizing projects so that, through contestation, human rights become embedded in a society's institutions and bound with national identity.

Having examined the theoretical model of how to understand the interaction between human rights and local identities, I ventured into applying the model to a case study of the Russian Federation, which I chose for its never-solved dilemma of whether to be in Europe, of Europe, or simply outside Europe. I offered a discourse analysis examining the myths and connotations connected with notions of human rights.

Russia, in search of a new identity, became a member of the Council of Europe, ratified the European Convention for the Protection of Human Rights and Fundamental Freedoms with several of its additional Protocols, and acknowledged the jurisdiction of the European Court of Human Rights. However, as verbatim records showed, Russian human-rights-related discourse within the Council—and, especially, within its Parliamentary Assembly—is securitized against any further introduction of human rights into the Russian context, as rights allegedly challenge Russian sovereignty and its internal consolidation. Following Russian discourse within PACE, human rights gained the connotation of being a tool for assimilation of non-Western cultures in the course of global Westernization and are suspected of posing a threat to Russian sovereignty. Human rights are further seen as hampering the state's power, economy, and the identity of its society. Russian discourse assigns the West the characteristics of an unbidden and self-appointed mentor who uses and bends human rights flexibly according to his will and who is biased against newcomers. The criticism Russia receives for administrative

236 Dryzek, *op.cit.* note 17, 102.

237 Tsygankov, *op.cit.* note 92, 17.

control over its media, political and non-governmental organizations, unfinished legal reform, unsatisfactory liberalization of its internal market, and for a variety of its foreign-policy decisions is seen as unsubstantiated, using double standards, or even poorly grounded. The general recommendations made by the ECtHR are largely dismissed for their alleged bias and politicized nature.

I have concluded that Russian discourse is currently undergoing a stage of securitization against newly introduced meanings. Translated into Tsygankov's model (see Figure 1), human rights have reached the second stage of the model: they are embedded in the institutional order of the Russian Federation. However, political entrepreneurs basing their actions on historical practices actively, and to a significant extent successfully, securitized against further extension of human rights within the Russian societal order. The hypotheses proposed by Mette Skak thus seem to be holding for the case of human rights as the broadest supportive coalition—that is, the biggest win-set, is concentrated around the ideas that human rights are mere tools of the West, not goals of any sort.

On the other hand, it should remain clear that the process described is mutual. In no way do the OSCE, CoE or Europe in general possess the only true understanding of human rights. Indeed, it is the nature of culture that it is an open, permeable system, and the same contestation runs in every such system. I have used Russia as an example of how the contestation process may influence the formation of foreign policy.

One should see this struggle within the bigger picture: Russia—together with many other aspiring powers—lies outside the dominant world order created since the end of the World War II. A country that finds itself in the midst of the re-creation of its identity perceives the gravitational force of the dominant worldview challenging, if not threatening, its own historically proven practices. Russia, in this sense, stakes a claim to the right to self-determination. However, the concept of self-determination in this context is understood much more broadly, as it "encompasses the orientation taken in the ongoing changes, the choice of place in the modern world, and the chosen strategy how to get there".[238] Human rights, in that sense, may decrease the perceived level of autonomy and allegedly threaten Russian sovereignty. Therefore, this chapter has sought to show that the process of embedding human rights in future Russian society inescapably includes their contestation within the national-identity re-creation cycle. With Russian discourse securitized against the Western one, the possibility of overcoming the stalemate described is negligible.

What are the implications of such a state for the Council of Europe? *First*, it is important to acknowledge that, to a significant extent, Russia's membership in the CoE has brought about a positive effect—Russia has accepted the judgments of the ECtHR and has pursued partial legal reform; membership generally has

238 Rozanova, *op.cit.* note 164, 656.

offered Russia's "nascent civil society [the possibility] to seek support in Strasbourg for legal and political reforms at home".[239]

However, the approximation of Russian political culture to European values is far from being either complete or even straightforward. The missing ratification of Protocol No.6, lacking follow-up to ECtHR decisions and to pledges made in front of PACE in the year of Russia's accession to the Council—as well as continuing concerns over the situation in the Northern Caucasus—all remain to embarrass relations between the Council and Russia. As I have illustrated, the situation in PACE resembles an oratorical battleground between Russian delegates and their European counterparts. Moreover, as Pamela Jordan has observed:

> "[Russian] compliance [with the demands of the CoE] tends to occur largely for instrumentalist reasons, and arguably the Council of Europe has been forced to adjust its expectations to justify keeping these members on board."[240]

Only as long as the Council's negotiators keep on board all national delegations can any pressure put on Russia be effective.

However, while examining Russia's human-rights record, the analysis conducted by human-rights scholars or directly by the CoE usually lacks recognition of the creational power of human rights to influence the identity of the state being investigated. Quite to the contrary, as I have sought to demonstrate, Russia emphasizes the challenge that human rights pose to its identity. The Russian perception—that it faces a threat of assimilation into a fully Westernized world and that any further introduction of human rights may hamper Russian culture, as it helps the above-mentioned assimilation—should be taken into account within the CoE.

What can the Council do to enhance the chances of human rights overcoming the state of securitization put upon them? The Council of Europe needs to acknowledge the creational power of human rights and its influence on the national identity of its members. Socially constructed connotations of human rights—that is, their alleged hostility, exteriority and truculence—should be addressed. In this sense, it is indeed better—in my view—to draw new members in than to isolate them by criticizing, or even by excluding them. The transformative nature of Russian domestic space, its energy, and intractability create a unique occasion for embedding human rights in Russia. However, "Western leaders [should] disabuse themselves of the notion that by preaching values one can actually plant them".[241] In that sense, as Richard Sakwa has aptly noted:

239 Jackson, *op.cit.* note 143, 32.

240 Jordan, *op.cit.* note 118, 688.

241 Trenin, *op.cit.* note 97.

> "Russia's main critique of the universalistic agenda of human rights and democratic standards is not that they were inappropriate, but that they have been appropriated [...] and applied selectively."[242]

"We want to return to Europe!" was the motto of the states formerly included in the Warsaw Pact after its collapse in 1990. Western Europe faced a demand from the former Soviet bloc to regain European status as if, during the Cold War, it had been moved to Asia.[243] For Russia, the return has been painful—the economic and mainly the ideational shock badly wounded the national pride of Russians. The transformation period is far from over, and glaring, and somehow even showy support for marginalized opposition groupings in the vain hope of a fully Westernized, liberal democratic Russia only further alienates the ruling elites and deepens their securitization efforts. The Council should rethink the fundamentals of its approach to Russia. As Dmitri Trenin has bluntly summarized:

> "Russia's domestic transformation will not follow the course of, say, Poland's: modernizing Russia by means of EU integration will not be an option. Nor will Russia adopt the French approach: an occasionally dissenting but solidly Euro-Atlantic foreign and security policy."[244]

To ostracize Russia for not following the way of Central European countries is futile. Once admitted, Russia—similarly to Turkey—would inescapably remain somehow on the margins of the organization and, thus, the margins of appreciation should be set wider.

The dilemma is clearly already visible in the Preamble to the 1993 Russian Constitution. On the one hand, it declares "establishing [of] human rights and freedoms, civil peace and accord" while "revering the memory of ancestors who have passed on to us their love for the Fatherland [and] reviving the sovereign statehood of Russia".[245] Russia signed up to the human-rights regime, acknowledging its universality, while reserving the right of sovereign statehood and keeping the historical concept of the Fatherland at the same time. The ambivalence of these pledges illustrates the Russian striving to be acknowledged as civilized but being left to do the civilizing itself. As Viatscheslav Morozov has remarked, the stronger the securitizing policies are the stronger is the clash with much deeper discursive structures within Russian society that have to do with Russia's self-perception as a European nation.[246] In other words, Russia is neither willing to accept the Western view (and, thus, securitizes its discourse against dissemination of Western meanings), nor is it able to ignore it. Securitization may continue only to a certain point. Therefore, the Council of Europe should

242 Sakwa, *op.cit.* note 171, 10.

243 Pagden, *op.cit.* note 59, 47.

244 *Ibid.*

245 For both quotes, see the RF Constitution of 25 December 1993, Preamble, *Rossiiskaia gazeta* (25 December 1993), as amended at *id.* (21 January 2009).

246 Morozov, *op.cit.* note 6, 422.

find a balance between ostracizing Russia from Europe and turning a blind eye to the Russian situation in fear of the former. Russia has always balanced on the edge of Europe, and this situation is likely to continue. To put it differently, the more successful securitization is, the more Russia alienates itself from the European system and proves itself to be non-European.

Russia is neither leaving the West, nor is it running into its embrace. The Council of Europe's organs should be aware of the course of securitization being pursued in Russia; however, in reality, the onus is on Russia to decide to what degree it wishes to participate in the existing European regimes and institutions.

Tilting at Windmills? The European Response to Violations of Media Freedom in Russia

Dorothea Schönfeld

Introduction

The gunshot that so suddenly finished the life of the famous journalist and human-rights defender Anna Politkovskaia, on 7 October 2006, was not only a disastrous event for the journalistic community in Russia but, also, an alarming shot for many European organizations. Although her murder was not nearly the first crime committed against journalists in Russia, it resulted in much more media attention and public action than ever before. Next to the activities of NGOs that had been fighting for media freedom for several years, in 2006 governmental organizations were also finally woken up. Immediately after the murder, the European Union (EU), the Organization for Security and Cooperation in Europe (OSCE) and the Council of Europe (CoE) sent letters of appeal to the Russian government asking for a thorough investigation of the murder and reminding the Russian authorities of their obligation to promote freedom of expression. The response of the Russian authorities is remarkable: instead of mourning the death of a critical journalist and promising to improve the situation of the press in Russia, President Vladimir Putin tried to downplay the importance of Anna Politkovskaia. In a confrontation with German Chancellor Angela Merkel, he said that "the journalist was proving more influential dead than alive".[1] Far from accepting European criticism, the Russian government emphasized that the media were free in Russia and that Europe simply had a wrong perception of the current state of affairs.[2] More than five years later, the flawed Politkovskaia investigation is still ongoing and no one yet has been convicted of her murder.[3] Generally, it seems that the overall situation of the media has even changed for the worse. Are all the actions and letters written by European organizations without effect?

The case of Anna Politkovskaia is not an isolated incident but, rather, a symptom of the current situation of the media in Russia, the measures that European organizations take, and apparent ignorance by the Russian government. In this study, I will examine why European organizations are not more successful in promoting freedom of expression in Russia. It is suggested that one can only

1 "Politkovskaya Mourned as 'Last Hope'", *Radio Free Europe/Radio Liberty* (16 October 2006), available at <http://www.rferl.org/content/article/1071958.html>.

2 Margareta Mommsen and Angelika Nussberger, *Das System Putin: Gelenkte Demokratie und politische Justiz in Russland* (C.H. Beck, Munich, 2007), 170.

3 "Politkovskaya Murder: Russian Ex-policeman Arrested", *BBC News* (23 August 2011), available at <http://www.bbc.co.uk/news/world-europe-14640457>.

Lauri Mälksoo, ed.
Russia and European Human-Rights Law: The Rise of the Civilizational Argument 91-149

overcome the current blockade of the European human-rights system when the patterns and the reasons are clearly identified. Therefore, all further actions by European organizations depend on a proper analysis of the problem.

The first part of this analysis is a kind of 'inventory'; it provides a solid empirical foundation for subsequent speculation. Apparently, there is a deep gap between European ideals of freedom of expression, which have been codified in different national and international treaties, and the current situation of the media in Russia. Fewer and fewer independent media are tolerated by the suppressive state authorities. According to the Committee to Protect Journalists (CPJ), Russia is one of the most dangerous countries in the world for journalists. The main European organizations in charge of promoting human rights in Europe by their very mandate attempt to bridge the gap. In pursuing this aim, they apply different methods, yet predominantly they appeal directly to the Russian government. Although some minor progress has been achieved—most notably in the field of legal reforms initiated by the European Court of Human Rights (ECtHR)—realistically these official declarations, recommendations, and letters of appeal are often mere paperwork with little impact. With some exceptions, European organizations are often seen as tilting at windmills.

In the second part of this work, I will analyze the reasons for the apparent failure of European measures and possible ways out. Can the gap between aspiration and reality be explained by different interpretations of freedom of expression and its limits in the Western and in the Russian context? I will argue that insistence on an 'ideological' clash between Europe and Russia is a mere rhetorical trick by the ruling political forces to hide a lack of democratic commitment in Russia and to avoid criticism from the West. Instead of indirectly supporting the Russian idea of a 'sovereign democracy', one should rather maintain a universal understanding of freedom of expression and its limits. Otherwise, interference by European organizations in Russian domestic politics would be unjustified. Whereas these 'ideological' reasons—or, at least, their historical necessity—can be rejected, 'practical' reasons for the insignificant impact of European measures cannot be denied; thus, the inefficiency of European organizations will be treated as a problem of implementation.

The European Standard

Without doubt, freedom of expression[4] is an idea cherished by mankind, if not from the very beginning, then at the latest when philosophers in antiquity first expressed their ideas about the relationship between the individual and society. It is the ideal of a genuine free society where everybody can express their thoughts,

4 In this chapter, I will use the term 'freedom of expression' instead of 'freedom of speech' or 'freedom of opinion'; terms that are mostly used synonymously. The first term evokes the broadest associations and is used in the relevant legal literature.

opinions, and ideas, share information without interference and enter into public discourse. Indeed, this has always been the point of reference for free thinkers, political philosophers, and utopians such as Socrates (who had to pay with his life for his uncompromising struggle for his own ideas), the philosophers of the age of Enlightenment such as Immanuel Kant, and liberal thinkers such as John Stuart Mill. There are mainly two perspectives on freedom of expression that repeat themselves throughout history: theories with a focus on the individual regard freedom of expression first and foremost as an *individual* right—being the *conditio sine qua non* for unhampered self-development and self-fulfillment. Political theories, by contrast, stress the *political or societal* relevance of freedom of expression. Without a free flow of information between citizens and governmental representatives, society will no longer be a functioning entity, hence losing all means of coordination. Freedom of expression is even more important in democratic societies. Given the translation of the word democracy as 'governance of the people', only a society where individuals and different groups have the possibility to express their political opinions and contribute to political discussions can be regarded as truly democratic. In that sense, the concepts of freedom of expression and a pluralistic democracy imply one another. In this work, I will stress the political function of freedom of expression—with media freedom being nothing other than a societal specification of the underlying right to freedom of expression.

When human rights were eventually formulated at the time of the American and French revolutions and codified in legal treaties, freedom of expression was put in a very prominent place among the most important civil and political rights. Until today, it has been able to maintain its status as one of the core human rights. Starting with the 1948 Universal Declaration of Human Rights (UDHR) and the 1966 International Covenant on Civil and Political Rights (ICCPR) through to regional human-rights treaties such as the 1950 European Convention on Human Rights (ECHR), the right to express one's opinion, thoughts, and ideas in different media has been consistently protected by the relevant treaties—for the most part, in similar expressions as Article 19 UDHR:

> "Everyone has the right to freedom of opinion and expression; this right includes freedom to hold opinions without interference and to seek, receive and impart information and ideas through any media and regardless of frontiers."[5]

The fundamental importance of freedom of expression is confirmed in the case law of domestic and international courts, in legal commentaries and academic writing.

Under the surface of a universal recognition of this right, however, several disputes occur regarding the scope of the right. Almost all these treaties added limitations to the purely affirmative formulation in the UDHR. Whenever a right is not absolute, there is more than one interpretation as to how much

5 UDHR, GA Res. 217 A (III), adopted 10 December 1948, Art.19.

freedom of expression weighs when balanced against rights or interests of other individuals or states. *Prima facie* freedom of expression is different in different legal systems: In the United States (US), freedom of expression is interpreted very strongly according to the First Amendment of the US Constitution, where it is guaranteed without restriction. Most European courts and the ECtHR, by contrast, prefer a narrower interpretation. This is probably due to the tragic historical experiences of genocide and totalitarianism in the twentieth century having shown that uncontrolled freedom of speech and opinion can entail the total subversion of democracy.[6] Upon closer examination, however, it turns out that the core of the right does not vary between states that legitimately call themselves 'democratic'. The very concept of freedom of expression—defined as individual self-expression even though it is not always convenient for others—calls for a threshold model or a so-called minimum standard: negatively, overly broad restrictions on freedom of expression would undermine the concept and infringe on the human right of freedom of expression, as will be seen in the case of Russia. Positively, countries such as the US are entitled to affirm freedom of expression even more and to prioritize it over other rights. This threshold model has the advantage of maintaining a universal understanding of human rights without losing sight of certain cultural differences.

Due to its philosophical and historical influences, the European interpretation of freedom of expression is certainly one of the most famous in the world. The European legal norm reflects the threshold model in a convincing way: scope and legitimate restrictions are very well defined and have proven successful in practice. In the following part of this chapter, I will outline the basic understanding of freedom of expression as established in the case law of the ECtHR, which authoritatively represents the European 'way of thinking'. Even the structure of Article 10 ECHR reflects the European idea of a prudent weighing of the individual right to self-expression and other important rights and social requirements. Article 10(1) affirms the high esteem that Europeans give to freedom of expression, which is constantly repeated in ECtHR case law. In the 1976 *Handyside* case, the Court held that freedom of expression is inherent in the concept of a democratic and pluralistic society and indispensable for the "development of every man"[7]. Article 10(2), by contrast, lists legitimate restrictions: all these criteria have to be interpreted by the Court in the light of the "duties and responsibilities" of every citizen using their right to freedom of expression. In addition to the specific limitation in Article 10, a possible violation

6 Anthony Lester, "Freedom of Expression", in R.St.J. Macdonald, F. Matscher and H. Petzhold (eds.), *The European System for the Protection of Human Rights* (Martinus Nijhoff Publishers, Dordrecht, Boston, London, 2003), 465-491, at 467ff, 473ff; and F.M. Rudinsky (ed.), *Civil Human Rights in Russia: Modern Problems of Theory and Practice* (Transaction Publishers, New Brunswick, NJ, London, 2008), 50.

7 Case of *Handyside v. The United Kingdom* (7 December 1976) No.5493/72, para. 49.

of the human rights of other persons can limit the exercise of freedom of expression as indicated in the provision "the protection of the reputation or rights of others". It is further restricted by provisions such as Article 15 (Derogation in times of emergency), Article 16 (Restrictions on political activity of aliens) and Article 17 (Prohibition of abuse of rights).

Yet limitations are not a universal excuse for states in pursuing their own interests. When evoking Article 10(2) in a legitimate way, they have to satisfy the following three tests, which are common to Articles 8-11 ECHR: state interference has to be prescribed by law, in pursuance of at least one of the legitimate aims formulated in Article 10(2) and necessary in a democratic society. In most cases, the first condition is fulfilled, as all states to which the ECHR applies are states in which the rule of law is established—at least, on paper. More controversies occur with regard to application of the second test: only over the course of time could the Court clarify the exact meaning of the legitimate aims given in Article 10(2). The most difficult test is the third one. In a political context, it is very difficult to define when a specific measure is necessary, thus stronger than being only reasonable or desirable, but weaker than being indispensable. In *Handyside*, the Court developed the notion of a 'pressing social need';[8] but this definition also remains rather unclear from a philosophical point of view. The doctrine of 'margin of appreciation', established in the same case, tries to solve that problem by giving domestic courts, which are familiar with the situation in their countries, more responsibility in judging a case.[9] However, this provision is very much contested, as the ECtHR plays with the risk of losing its authority as a supranational court. States should use their power to restrict freedom of expression carefully, proportionately, and in good faith. Therefore, the breadth of the restriction has to be taken into account. In addition, all the rules have to be adapted to the special circumstances of each case—a nontrivial task the ECtHR has had to fulfill right from the beginning.

To carry out this task, the ECtHR has developed certain principles in its multifaceted case law,[10] principles that will become relevant also when analyzing Russian cases concerning freedom of expression:

1) Already in 1976, the Court held in *Handyside* that freedom of expression does not apply only to moderate and liberal information and ideas but, also, to those that "offend, shock or disturb",[11] an expression constantly repeated in

8 *Ibid.*, para. 48.

9 *Ibid.*, para. 48ff.

10 Lester, *op.cit.* note 6, 465ff; and Anton Burkov, *The Impact of the European Convention on Human Rights on Russian Law: Legislation and Application in 1996-2006* (Ibidem-Verlag, Stuttgart, 2007), 65.

11 Case of *Handyside v. The United Kingdom*, *op.cit.* note 7, para. 49.

the Court's case law—thus rejecting a too narrow interpretation of freedom of expression.

2) The press and other media are in need of special protection as they are the only means of imparting "information and ideas concerning matters [...] of public interest". This principle was established in the first 1979 *Sunday Times* case.[12] The 1985 case of *Barthold v. Germany* confirms the estimation of the press as a "purveyor of information and public watchdog".[13] However, one cannot hastily deduce that the state also has a positive obligation to promote media pluralism. So far, this has only been stated in a political context.

3) Because freedom of expression is the *conditio sine qua non* of any political debate, tolerance of offending statements has to be wider when they refer to the government and to particular politicians, as stated in 1986 in the case of *Lingens*.[14] In accepting a public position in the government, a politician has to be aware of the possibility of media scrutiny and even has to allow a certain degree of exaggeration.

4) In assessing whether freedom of expression exceeds its limits, a distinction also has to be drawn between facts and value-judgments as developed in the *Lingens* case.[15]

All these principles suggest that freedom of expression has a higher priority than other rights or interests and that the given restrictions have to be narrowly interpreted. In the special circumstances, however, the Court has not always been very eager to apply the broadest interpretation of freedom of expression. There are several cases such as *Handyside* and *Glasenapp v. Germany* (1976 and 1968 respectively)[16] where the Court decided either against the then-existing Commission or the dissenting judges within the Court and argued that interference by the government was justified—stirring up discontent by several academic writers. Anthony Lester claims an overly loose interpretation of the limitations can seriously endanger freedom of expression and has already done so. He also questions the "elastic and elusive" doctrine of margin of appreciation, substantiating the allegation that, in practice, the Court does not always strengthen the principle of freedom of expression against national interests. I would agree with his conclusion that freedom of expression cannot be limited exceedingly without jeopardizing the whole concept. It is an ongoing challenge of the Court to follow its own principles in practice, as there are many judges within the ECtHR who do not want (or do not dare) to interpret freedom of expression

12 Case of *The Sunday Times v. The United Kingdom* (26 April 1979) No.6538/74, para. 65.

13 Case of *Barthold v. Germany* (25 March 1985) No.8734/79, para. 58.

14 Case of *Lingens v. Austria* (8 July 1986) No.9815/82, para. 42.

15 *Ibid.*, para. 46.

16 Case of *Glasenapp v. Germany* (28 August 1986) No.9228/80.

more strictly.[17] However, the principles themselves are quite well founded and consistently recognize the fundamental importance of freedom of expression for a democratic society.

Yet, freedom of expression should not only be a philosophical or a legal idea, it has to be put into practice. Article 10 and the established principles have to be applied by the ECtHR, but this is not sufficient for broad implementation: it also has to be integrated in each European constitution to make it fruitful at the domestic level. Indeed, in all European countries, freedom of expression is an integral part of their constitutions. This is also the case in the Russian Federation, where freedom of expression is protected twofold. *First*, Article 10 ECHR can be directly evoked according to Article 15(4) of the 1993 Russian Constitution, providing for direct applicability of international treaties to which Russia is a party. In theory, it can be enforced not only before the Constitutional Court and the Supreme Court but, also, before every lower-level court. The monistic principle is even integrated in the first chapter of the Constitution entitled "The Fundamentals of the Constitutional System", as one of the basic provisions of the whole Constitution, which is extremely difficult to withdraw. *Second*, freedom of expression is incorporated in national legislation. It can be found in Chapter 2 of the Russian Constitution named "Rights and Freedoms of Man and Citizen". Article 29, which guarantees "freedom of ideas and speech", interpreted in the light of other constitutional provisions, fully complies with the established standard and principles; Article 29(5) even bans censorship to protect the freedom of mass communication.[18] Russian politicians have to respect and to promote freedom of expression in their political activities as required by the democratic nature of their country.

In theory, human rights are protected all over Europe—including Russia, which undeniably takes part in the European human-rights system. In practice, however, things look different ...

Russian Reality: The Situation of the Media

The question of whether freedom of expression is respected in a country can be assessed in different contexts. It becomes visible during election campaigns, at political demonstrations, and in the art scene. The best indicator for the level of freedom of expression, however, is the media being the main transmitter of information and opinions. In this chapter, media freedom is understood as the independent and critical activity of different media unhampered by governmental bodies or other authorities. Governmental control and concentrated ownership

17 Lester, *op.cit.* note 6, 470 ff., 485, 490ff.

18 RF Constitution (12 December 1993), *Rossiiskaia gazeta* (25 December 1993).

are incompatible with media freedom. Media freedom includes the possibility of citizens to receive media content without interference.[19]

Does a European observer have enough insight to decide whether media freedom exists in Russia today? What are the appropriate means of evaluating the level of media freedom in such a huge country with thousands of media outlets and different levels of control in the regions? Obviously, media freedom is not as easy to quantify as the number of murdered or missing persons, for example. There are attempts to measure the current state of affairs, nevertheless. Having analyzed existing quantitative research on media freedom, it became obvious that every questionnaire that rankings are based on had to make a choice of who to ask. In the end, every quantitative result can be deduced from qualitative investigations. Due to these considerations, I have chosen to follow the qualitative track. But who should we listen to? It is inevitable that the perceptions of a normal inhabitant of a small and destitute town, a civil-society activist in Moscow, and an exiled journalist from Russia living in the EU differ considerably. In this chapter, I assume that professionals working either in the press or in civil-society organizations with a focus on media freedom have the best insight into the current situation. Certainly, they do not represent the majority of the people in Russia but can decide on a daily basis whether the state exerts legal, political, or economic pressure on the media. It is cautiously submitted that sometimes a few, highly educated and dedicated people have a better overview of the situation in Russia than the majority of people who do not care whether the information they receive in the public news is reliable or not. It is in the interest of Russian media professionals to be heard abroad; so, any interested European observer can easily listen to their voices. The more difficult the situation has become, the more literature on media freedom has been published—first and foremost, from Russian authors themselves. This work is based on statements of the focus group: diverse articles from Russian scholars and activists and findings of interviews that I conducted in Tartu, St. Petersburg and in Moscow with media professionals and human-rights activists.

Indices of Media Freedom

Out of numerous organizations in the world engaged in assessing media freedom, three prominent indices are chosen to give a preliminary idea of the state of affairs. It is interesting to see that all these organizations agree in classifying Russia as a country with serious problems, even if they apply different indicators.

19 Different concepts of press freedom are depicted in Lee B. Becker, Tudor Vlad and Nancy Nusser, "An Evaluation of Press Freedom Indicators", 69(1), *International Communication Gazette* (2007), 5-28, at 5ff; and Greg Simons and Dmitry Strovsky, "Censorship in Contemporary Russian Journalism in the Age of the War Against Terrorism: A Historical Perspective", 21(2) *European Journal of Communication* (2006), 189-211, at 191.

The index most often cited is the Freedom of the Press Index published by the US-based Freedom House. This annually ranks 195 countries/territories and categorizes them as 'free' (0-30 points), 'partly free' (31-60 points) or 'not free' (61-100 points out of 100). The organization uses a 23-item questionnaire that is given to the same relevant people as envisaged above: journalists, media workers and national and international civil-society activists. The ranking of a country is determined on the basis of the points the country receives in the three categories of Laws and Administration, Political Influences, and Economic Pressures.[20] Due to the broad scope of questions taking into account not only direct interference by state authorities but, also, legal provisions and the economic situation and due to the accuracy with which data are collected, the index has managed to become the common point of reference for many media professionals all over the world. Furthermore, it is an excellent source to learn about major changes in societies, as Freedom House has been collecting data since 1980. For example, Freedom of the Press Index 2010, which covers the year 2009, categorizes Russia as 'Not Free', with 81 points, and ranks it in 175th place out of 196.[21] In the 2009 country report, Russia is described as "one of the most dangerous countries in the world for the media due to widespread lawlessness that allows politicians, security agents, and criminals to silence journalists by any means", ranking even lower than in previous years.[22] There are some rumors that the index is sponsored by the US government and, therefore, biased—an argument that was also brought forward by the Russian authorities in reaction to the downgrading of Russia from 'Partly Free' to 'Not Free' in 2004.[23] Even if no direct funding was detected, the doubt could not be eliminated that the questionnaire reflects a certain preconception of media freedom and pluralism and maybe a Western or American point of view. The neutrality or objectivity of quantitative research should be questioned at a general level. Surveys are mere collections of personal

20 One could object that three categories are perhaps not enough to come to a differentiated assessment of the situation of the media throughout the world, but for this purpose it is always possible to take the rankings and the country reports into account. See Freedom House, Methodology, available at <http://www.freedomhouse.org/template.cfm?page=350&ana_page=359&year=2009>.

21 Freedom House, Freedom of the Press 2010, Table of Global Press Freedom Rankings, available at <http://www.freedomhouse.org/sites/default/files/FOTP%202011%20Tables%20and%20Graphs_0.pdf>. In the 2012 Freedom House ranking for example, Russia remains categorized as 'Not Free' with 80 points and ties for 180th place with Azerbaijan and Zimbabwe, available at <http://www.freedomhouse.org/sites/default/files/FOTP%202012%20Booklet.pdf>.

22 Freedom House, Country Reports, Russia (2010), available at <http://www.freedomhouse.org/template.cfm?page=251&country=7689&year=2010>.

23 Ministry of Foreign Affairs of the Russian Federation, "Information and Press Department, Russian MFA Information and Press Department commentary regarding the report of Freedom House on democracy in Russia" (20 June 2006).

perceptions and conclusions that are transformed into numbers—as objective as they might appear. Accordingly, the Freedom of the Press Index is not the ultimate truth that Russia is not free but, rather, an adequate visualization of qualitative research from a certain perspective. The whole questionnaire presumes a comprehensive concept of media freedom, claiming that the media have to be embedded in a democratic society. The question whether this concept is only 'Western' or universally applicable has to be decided in the course of this work.

Reflections on the objectivity of surveys also apply to the annual World Press Freedom Index which is issued by Reporters without Borders (RSF), a French NGO with a focus on press freedom. In 2002, the organization published its first media-freedom survey, which is now based on a 40-item questionnaire. Overall, the questions are less vaguely formulated than in the Freedom of the Press Index but are similar in content. According to Becker *et al.*, the organization contents itself with three or four completed questionnaires per country to the same target group, which would not be very representative. This number, however, is not confirmed by the organization itself. Be that as it may, this survey is also based on a subjective evaluation by an elite group. For example, in the World Press Freedom Index 2011-2012 (covering the time span from 1 December 2010 to 30 November 2011), Russia ranks very low: 142nd place out of 179 countries: it received a score of 60.00 (whereas Finland and Norway were the 'best' states with 10.00 points while Eritrea was the 'worst' with 142.00 points). In addition, in the 2011-2012 survey, Russia scored worse than in previous years.[24] The conformity between these two indices is not astonishing, as the underlying concept of media freedom, methodology, and the target group are nearly the same.

The third important index is the list of journalists killed, published by another media-rights organization: the Committee to Protect Journalists (CPJ). In distinction from the other surveys, the CPJ focuses only on murders of journalists and subsequent investigations. Taking the total number of 912 journalists killed from January 1992 to May 2012, the organization issues a ranking of life-threatening countries for journalists and provides a detailed database of cases. Russia, with 53 murders,[25] is often cited in the relevant literature as the fourth most dangerous country in the world after Iraq, the Philippines, and Algeria. One has to be quite careful to assess the current situation in Russia only on the basis of the CPJ survey. The findings of the two other surveys are deduced from very broad questions in different sectors of society, whereas the CPJ index is purely negative. For good reasons, there have been objections that the mere number of journalists murdered is not sufficient to determine the situation in a

24 RSF, World Press Freedom Index, "How the 2011-12 Index Was Compiled" (20 January 2012), available at <http://en.rsf.org/IMG/pdf/how_the_2011-2012_index_was_compiled.pdf>; and RSF, World Press Freedom Index 2011-12, available at <http://en.rsf.org/IMG/CLASSEMENT_2012/C_GENERAL_ANG.pdf >.

25 CPJ, "Journalists Killed since 1992", available at <http://cpj.org/killed/>.

particular country. Even if no murders occur, as in North Korea, for instance, the situation of the media is not necessarily free. The CPJ index provides interesting insights, as it measures one aspect that has not been dealt with sufficiently in the other indices, but it has to be read in context. Arguably, the assumed concept of freedom of the press as the mere absence of fear or reprisal is too negative; hence, it has to merge in a broader concept of freedom of expression within a democratic society.

Examination of the three surveys has shown that Russia is a country where journalists have to cope with increased difficulties in pursuing their profession. The degree of repression, the methods by which journalists are put under pressure and the root causes, however, can only be identified when the current situation is analyzed in a qualitative manner. In this chapter, I will apply a very broad and comprehensive concept of freedom of expression, presupposing (together with European organizations) that freedom of expression and democracy are intrinsically linked.

Historical Influences

The past matters. This general sentence proves true especially in Russia, where historical events, developments, and ideologies have always been points of reference. As it is not possible to analyze the development of the press in Russia from the very beginning, which has been described as a continuous struggle of censorship and freedom of the press,[26] I will focus on developments in the twentieth century. The Soviet period and the 1990s strongly influenced the current situation of the media and public perceptions.

As is commonly known, in the USSR only one opinion was broadcast and tolerated: the official doctrine of the Communist Party. Rigid censorship was part of the daily life of Russian citizens from 1922 onwards. Alternative opinions could only be expressed and heard in 'kitchen debates' with family and friends and in some underground editions (*samizdat*) run by the so-called intelligentsia.[27] With the announcement of *glasnost'* by Mikhail Gorbachev, a new period of freedom started in Russia, as did a time of confusion. When the few marginalized papers could finally free themselves from ideological control in the course of the USSR's collapse, the media resembled a swarm flying out in different directions without a proper idea of media plurality.[28] In 1992, for instance, in the year prior to promulgation of the new Russian Constitution guaranteeing the right to freedom of expression, a new law on the press was

26 Simons and Strovsky, *op.cit.* note 19, 196ff.

27 Yekaterina Parkhomenko, "Blog Talk: Virtual Kitchen Debates", 37(1) *Index on Censorship* (2008), 174-178, at 175.

28 Interview with Elena Leonidovna Grishina, Director of the regional NGO Center for Public Information, editor of the information bulletin Moscow Helsinki Group Chronicle, Moscow (20 May 2008).

enacted triggering the registration of more than 400 new publications and media companies; very few of them still exist.[29] Many journalists had a highly romantic idea of free, liberal and democratic societies in mind, which could not fully be realized. Few journalists would have expected that not only politics but also economics could exercise immense pressure; so within a short time many media outlets went bankrupt or fell into the hands of oligarchs, most prominently to Media-Most, owned by Vladimir Gusinskii. Only because the 1990s appear free from today's perspective, one should be careful not to follow this evaluation without further consideration.[30] Certainly, different opinions were expressed in the oligarch-dominated media—sometimes so vividly that people were talking about a war of information[31]—but independent reporting was not sufficiently consolidated. Probably the transition was too fast to establish truly independent TV channels, radio stations, and newspapers and to put into practice the corresponding institutional change. The years after 1991 were challenging for Russian citizens in many respects and other pressing problems had to be solved. It is understandable that freedom of the press was not so much appreciated or, even worse, that people often associated media freedom with the unhampered economic power of the few in the economic elite. It is of the utmost importance to keep this in mind. Even today, the words 'democracy' and 'media plurality' evoke very bad associations,[32] which make it extremely difficult for the media to defend their own importance.

Looking back, it is hard to tell when the first enthusiasm evaporated and when media workers submitted themselves again to the control of economic elites or politicians. Control of the media became tight again if not under Boris El'tsin, who himself sponsored biased media coverage before elections, then certainly under Vladimir Putin.[33] For many analysts, the beginning of the second Chechen

29 Nadezhda Azhgikhina, "The Struggle for Press Freedom in Russia: Reflections of a Russian Journalist", 59(8) *Europe-Asia Studies* (2007), 1245-1262, at 1252. The legislation is: RF Zakon "O sredstvakh massovoi informatsii" (27 December 1991) No.2124-1 (as amended), *Rossiiskaia gazeta* (8 February 1992).

30 *Ibid.*, 1253; Alexander Tscherkassow, "Ein schleichendes Gift: Der Tschetschenienkrieg und die russische Gesellschaft", in *Russland auf dem Weg zum Rechtstaat? Antworten aus der Zivilgesellschaft* (German Institute for Human Rights, Berlin, 2003), 96-110, at 98; Alexej Simonow, "Wer braucht in Russland die Freiheit des Wortes? Zur Lage der Medien", in *ibid.*, 80-87, at 84; and Jonathan Becker, "Lessons from Russia: A Neo-Authoritarian Media System", 19(2) *European Journal of Communication* (2004), 139-163, at 148, 156.

31 Joint session of students of the St. Petersburg State University Faculty of Law and students from Tartu University, St. Petersburg (16 May 2008).

32 Interview with Nataliia Rostova, Head of the Mass Media Division, *Novaia gazeta*, Moscow (19 May 2008).

33 Simonow, *op.cit.* note 30, 84; Edward Lucas, "The Big Squeeze: The Message to Journalists is Clear: Keep Quiet", 37(1) *Index on Censorship* (2008), 26-34, at 27; and Becker, *op.cit.* note 30, 140.

War marked the beginning of biased news coverage, partly due to the decision of many editors-in-chief to adopt the official position.[34] Because of the widespread self-censorship of journalists at that time, it was very easy for the authorities to guide the scattered swarm of journalists. The squeeze on the media became more visible with Media-Most's forced change of ownership from Gusinskii to the state-controlled energy giant Gazprom in 2001 after he had been imprisoned for alleged tax violations. For many observers, this was a pretext to gain control over the defiant channel *NTV*, which had been under pressure for some time. In the following month, the news became more and more biased, the popular satirical puppet show *Kukly* of Victor Shenderovich, which had mocked Vladimir Putin several times, was closed down, and journalists were dismissed when they refused to adopt the official position. In the same year, *ORT* (now Channel One), the TV station of another oligarch, Boris Berezovsii, which reported critically about the government's measures in the *Kursk* tragedy and other events, was also handed over to Gazprom under duress. Within a couple of years, all TV channels that employed journalists from the former channels and that reported critically about political events were shut down: TV-S and TV-6, for instance. There was not much protest in society following these events, however. The estimated 10,000 people who assembled in front of Media-Most were by far not enough to reverse the decision of the administration. Many citizens were even gloating, holding the oligarchs responsible for their current economic situation. Apparently, the few years after the dissolution of the USSR could not build enough confidence in the media. Each submission of journalists to state control was perceived as evidence that the mass media would always remain in the hands of power.[35]

The Media Landscape of Russia

Sadly enough, this evaluation seems to be true when having a closer look at the different players in the Russian media market and at recent trends. All analysts agree that the media are controlled by the political authorities and by government-directed companies such as Gazprom; they only disagree with regard to the exact percentages. But mostly the numbers are quite high: some Russian scholars assess that more than 80% of the broadcast media and up to 70% of newspapers are subject to direct or indirect governmental control.[36]

34 Mommsen and Nussberger, *op.cit.* note 2, 54; and Mascha Gessen, "Am Rande der Öffentlichkeit: Die Medien und der Krieg in Tschetschenien", in *Russland auf dem Weg zum Rechtstaat? Antworten aus der Zivilgesellschaft*, *op.cit.* note 30, 102-107, at 105.

35 Alexei Bessudnov, "Media Map: A Survey of Outlets and Trends", 37(1) *Index on Censorship* (2008), 183-189, at 183; Lucas, *op.cit.* note 33, 28ff.; Nataliia Rostova, "Cult Fiction: The Making of a Russian Hero", 37(1) *Index on Censorship* (2008), 155-163, at 158; and Victor Shenderovich, "Tales From Hoffmann: Putin Fails to See the Funny Side", 37(1) *Index on Censorship* (2008), 48-57, at 49ff.

36 Shenderovich, *op.cit.* note 35, 57; and Azhgikhina, *op.cit.* note 29, 1253.

According to a 2007 poll, 90% of Russian citizens regard television as their main source of information—also due to financial considerations, as a subscription to a newspaper is quite expensive—and around half of them believe in the objectivity of the news.[37] Therefore, the Kremlin has been very keen to keep the TV channels under control from the very beginning. As Vladimir Putin's popularity is somehow the 'merit' of television campaigns, he is very well aware of the power of the broadcast media to influence public opinion.[38] Since *NTV* and *ORT*/Channel One have been brought into line, there are nearly no independent TV channels left. Only Ren-TV, a minor channel with limited reach, and foreign channels can maintain some independent reporting. The vast majority of people, however, stick to the main pro-Kremlin channels Channel One, *Rossiia* Channel, *NTV*, TV-Center, *STS* and Channel Five.[39]

The radio situation is slightly better, albeit far from being pluralistic. The two main channels, Radio *Rossii* and Radio *Maiak*, are owned by the state media company *VGTRK* (All-Russia State Television and Broadcasting Company). Even if they claim to be neutral, they are increasingly adopting the state position or are being transformed into mere life-coaching stations.[40] Listeners with an interest in Russia's social and political situation have the option of switching to *Ekho Moskvy*, a radio station that is famous all over Russia for its independent reporting. The journalists often broadcast interviews with opposition politicians and discuss pressing social questions. *Ekho Moskvy* is a very interesting case. Many workers in the media field wonder how the station can maintain its independence, even after it was taken over by Gazprom. Probably the state regards the station as 'official opposition', which can be kept under control if desired. Alternatively, it can be explained by the strong personalities of journalists who do not submit themselves to state control.[41] Apart from *Ekho Moskvy*, foreign broadcasters such as Radio Liberty and the BBC disseminate liberal-democratic views. Occasionally, they are subject to government intrusion.[42]

The same trends can be observed in the Russian print media. The most widely circulated newspapers and magazines are tabloids such as the popular newspaper *Argumenty i fakty*, which is read by around 7 million people, and *Komsomol'skaia pravda*. Most of these tabloids are in the hands of big media holding companies

37 Quoted in Lucas, *op.cit.* note 33, 29.

38 Interview with Igor Aleksandrovich Iakovenko, Head of the Union of Journalists in Russia, Moscow (20 May 2008).

39 Lucas, *op.cit.* note 33, 28, 30; and Bessudnov, *op.cit.* note 35, 184ff.

40 Interview with Svetlana Svistunova, TV and radio journalist with Radio *Maiak*, and Nadezhda Azhgikhina, Secretary of the Union of Journalists of Russia (Center for Creative Programs), Moscow (20 May 2008).

41 *Ibid.*; and Mommsen and Nussberger, *op.cit.* note 2, 49.

42 Bessudnov, *op.cit.* note 35, 188; and Lucas, *op.cit.* note 33, 30.

(Profmedia, Sviazinvestbank and Gazprom), thus formally independent of the government, but nearly all of them align with the Kremlin. As an alternative, interested readers can purchase more serious broadsheets and weekly magazines with different political orientations and a wide range of topics. They have a much smaller circulation than tabloids and are mainly available in the big cities. Pro-Kremlin newspapers such as *Rossiiskaia gazeta* are counterbalanced by more or less independent newspapers such as *Izvestiia* with a mixed staff of pro-Kremlin and more liberal journalists and by the forthright liberal newspaper *Novaia gazeta*. The latter is probably the most famous independent newspaper due to its open oppositional stance and its high-quality investigations, especially in Chechnia. Throughout Russia, however, no more than 170,000 copies are sold—mainly to intellectuals—and the total readership has never gone beyond one million.[43] Other newspapers with a focus on business such as *Vedomosti* and *Kommersant*, with a similar low circulation of some 225,000 copies, regularly express critical opinions.[44] One should not forget to mention the regional press: some one hundred independent newspapers—such as the one with the telling name *Moi gorod bez tsenzury* (My Town Without Censorship) in Khanti-Mansiisk, for instance—have been able to hold their ground against the economic and political powers. Regarding the situation throughout the country, however, the situation in the regions is worse than in the cities, as most local papers are directly or indirectly controlled by regional authorities. But even if independent national newspapers or magazines are available, people in the regions—who are on average poorer than people from the cities—are often unable to afford them.[45]

The only source of information that is not under governmental control is the Internet. Though some websites disseminate the official version of events, all other web pages can be consulted nearly without interference. In contrast to Soviet times and to other authoritarian regimes with total control over the media, any willing researcher in Russia can find virtually all types of independent information.[46] To get reliable information, anyone with Internet access can consult the websites of national and international newspapers and other news agencies or can actively take part in discussions about social and political problems in

43 Rostova, interview, *op.cit.* note 32.

44 Bessudnov, *op.cit.* note 35,185ff.

45 Maria Eismont, "Towns Without Censorship: Local Journalists are Standing up to Threats", 37(1) *Index on Censorship* (2008), 121-130, at 124ff., 128; and Sergei Bachinin, "Under Pressure: The Regional Press is Often the Only Source of Reliable News", 37(1) *Index on Censorship* (2008), 131-138, at 132. For more information, see RSF, "Russia, Heroes and Henchmen: The Work of Journalists and the Media in the Russian Regions" (September 2009), available at <http://www.reporter-ohne-grenzen.de/fileadmin/pdf/Atlas_engl.pdf>. *Moi gorod bez tsenzury* remains accessible, in early 2012, at <http://bezcenzura.ru/>.

46 Maxim Trudolyubov, "Words or Deeds: Why Isn't Free Speech Valued More Highly?", 37(1) *Index on Censorship* (2008), 97-104, at 101.

different blogs. This so-called 'do-it-yourself journalism' has become more and more popular in recent years, and often newspapers such as *Novaia gazeta* quote topical blogs in their publications. Even if government-linked groups such as the youth movement *Nashi* or pro-government companies could gain control over single blogs as happened with the popular blog <LiveJournal.com>, they have never been able to suppress the entire community of bloggers. For many intellectuals, journalists, and other activists, the Internet is the last refuge of independent reporting and a possibility to exchange first-hand knowledge and to organize social protest.[47] Until now, only some 45.25 million citizens (or 32%) of the population have access to this medium,[48] but it can be expected that the exponential growth of Internet facilities will continue in the coming decades.

It follows that the Russian authorities have nearly managed to bring all media under control (excluding the Internet and its future potential). If the presidential administration wants to manipulate public opinion, it has all the levers in its hands to do so.

Media Content

The news and other political programs of the state-controlled media are clearly biased towards the ruling political forces. The dominance of the United Russia party of President Vladimir Putin and his predecessor Dmitrii Medvedev was especially apparent before the elections for the State *Duma* in December 2007 and the presidential election in March 2008. Election observers—such as those from the OSCE—often have criticized the fact that other parties had virtually no opportunity to campaign alternative political programs. At times, they were not able to access more than 4% of airtime to present themselves to the wider public. The content of the media seems to be a huge election campaign in favor of Putin, which started in 1999 and did not even change after Medvedev became president.[49]

Severe criticism has been banned from the screens: nearly no public discussion took place after disastrous events such as the sinking of the submarine *Kursk*, the hostage-taking and storming of the musical theater Nord-Ost, or the Beslan school siege. Apparently, the main channels were put under pressure to report only the official version of events. For example, Raf Shakirov, the editor-in-chief

47 Parkhomenko, *op.cit.* note 27, 175ff.; and interview with Anna Zherdeva, Youth Human Rights Movement, Moscow Helsinki Group, Moscow (20 May 2008).

48 ITU, ICT Statistics Database, available at <http://www.itu.int/ict/statistics>.

49 Rostova, *op.cit.* note 35, 155ff.; Mommsen and Nussberger, *op.cit.* note 2, 48ff.; and Paul J. Saunders and Dimitri K. Simes, "Who Controls Russia?", *The International Herald Tribune* (9 November 2009), available at <http://www.nytimes.com/2009/11/10/opinion/10iht-edsimes.html?_r=2>. Equally, in the 2012 presidential election campaign, the omnipresence of Putin in most media channels—with little scope for opposition parties—was painfully obvious.

of the then-independent newspaper *Izvestiia*, was fired after publishing pictures of Beslan without official approval of the government.[50] Evidence suggests that the media receive regular instructions from the presidential administration or from the security forces on permitted themes and topics.[51] The taboo topic *par excellence* is the armed conflict in the Caucasus region, especially in Chechnia. Anyone investigating current violations of human rights in the region and not praising the current governor puts themselves at risk. In addition to forbidden topics, a rumor of a blacklist with forbidden names is propagated among the journalistic community. This blacklist includes human-rights activists and opposition politicians.[52] Russian people live in an information vacuum. Often, daily social and political events are completely ignored. The miners' strike in Kuzbass, for instance, or demonstrations such as the '*Marsh Nesoglasnykh*' ('Dissenters' March') in spring 2007, simply did not have any news coverage. If opponents are mentioned, they are presented as "marginal individuals, manipulated by enemies or foreign intelligence services" illegitimately attacking the Russian state and its people.[53] This indirect pressure on editors and journalists has the same result as direct censorship: several topics are simply not dealt with in today's Russia.

However, for the sake of plausibility, the government cannot exclude criticism altogether; so, sometimes, 'official opposition' is tolerated. Its only function is to emphasize the effectiveness of state measures dealing immediately with the concerns of Russian citizens. In some talk shows, Putin has presented himself as the wise king giving promises and advice to his subjects, confirming the assessment of Babchenko that the media are nothing more than a fairy tale.

> "[Television] does not lie: it simply presents imaginary tales that have nothing whatsoever to do with reality. Watching television, you get the impression that Russia is an advanced state with a stable and flourishing economy, a functioning legal system and a democratic leadership that is constantly concerned with the wellbeing of its people."[54]

The political programs analyzed, though, are not at the center of attention of the mass media, they are rather embedded in a huge entertainment wave. The trend of closing down analytical programs and intellectual debate in favor of entertainment, life-counseling programs and sports cannot be neglected. Radio

50 Azhgikhina, *op.cit.* note 29, 1256; and Lucas, *op.cit.* note 33, 31.

51 Bessudnov, *op.cit.* note 35, 184; Arkady Babchenko, "Information Vacuum: The New Censorship is More Damaging than the Old", 37(1) *Index on Censorship* (2008), 116-120, at 119ff.; Fatima Tlisova, "Nothing Personal: A Journalist's Account of Intimidation Tactics", 37(1) *Index on Censorship* (2008), 35-46, at 36; and interview with Nataliia Rostova, *op.cit.* note 32.

52 "Journalists Union Head Laments State of Media", *Radio Free Europe/Radio Liberty* (23 May 2007), available at <http://www.rferl.org/featuresarticle/2007/05/ecd96fc3-4927-47f6-b233-df343d29a793.html>.

53 Azhgikhina, *op.cit.* note 29, 1246; and Babchenko, *op.cit.* note 51, 117.

54 Babchenko, *op.cit.* note 51, 117.

Maiak, for example—in former times known for a high standard of journalism—has closed all its scientific features despite protests from listeners and journalists.[55] Tabloid journalism is booming in Russia—in TV, on the radio, and in the newspapers. The Russian media are in a paradoxical situation. On the one hand, political topics and individuals are excluded; on the other hand, everything seems to be allowed. One has to be extremely careful not to be misled by the apparent freedom and liberalization of the Russian media. The media today are a combination of political propaganda and very cheap journalism: a quite dangerous mixture. Overwhelmed by consumer goods and fairy tales about the political situation, critical thoughts vanish, and without noticing, people turn into supporters of United Russia. Pursuing her profession as an observer of the mass media, Nataliia Rostova is sometimes afraid of being influenced herself by the incessant propaganda broadcast in the media.[56]

Various Methods of Pressure

As most Russian citizens are exposed to to these programs in the mass media, the few existing independent channels and newspapers do not have much resonance in society. It has been sarcastically noted that "repression is simply unnecessary. Control over central television channels [...] is sufficient for the ruling party to close its eyes to a few dissident newspapers".[57] Ignoring, indeed, is one of the means that the Russian authorities use regularly when confronted with defiant media workers. When journalists publish stories about topics that are less taboo than Chechnia, *e.g.*, corruption, they often receive no response at all. Being ignored has an immense effect on the morale of independent media workers. Many journalists suffer from isolation, the feeling of inefficacy, or general tiredness. Not seeing any prospects in the media field any more, some journalists change their jobs to get a better reputation.[58] The method of ignoring is sinister: often journalists are lulled into a false sense of security. Probably, the Kremlin is observing every single move of the media, even if there is no immediate reaction:

> "It would be unwise to underestimate the lengths the authorities, both federal and regional, go to in monitoring and identifying 'unreliable' journalists. Russian journalists deemed unreliable are most likely to have measures taken against them by the regional authorities."[59]

It is one feature of authoritarian or even totalitarian regimes that control by the state is omnipresent, but mostly invisible. As the case arises, however, its

55 Svistunova and Azhgikhina, interview, *op.cit.* note 40.

56 Rostova, interview, *op.cit.* note 32.

57 Eismont, *op.cit.* note 45, 123.

58 Rostova, interview, *op.cit.* note 32; and Eismont, *op.cit.* note 45, 128.

59 Timur Aliev, "Reporting Chechnya: Chechens No Longer Trust Russian Journalism", 37(1) *Index on Censorship* (2008), 140-145, at 143.

onslaughts are even harder. They range from raids of offices to murder, as will be seen in the following.

In most cases, they use relatively 'harmless' measures such as raiding editorial offices in search of documents or bills that can prove illegal acts.[60] In recent years, it has become common practice to look for pirated software. As 90-95% of the software used in media stations and offices of NGOs is not licensed, it is relatively easy for law-enforcement bodies to confiscate computers, to sanction the CEO, and to close the outlet under the (legal) provision of combating IT crime. The Russian Union of Journalists (RUJ) is conducting an interesting project in cooperation with Microsoft to install legal software in editorial offices at lower prices; but, until now, they have not been able to solve the problem entirely.[61] Another example is the forced change of ownership of *NTV* and *ORT*/Channel One because of alleged tax evasion. Even if a misdemeanor is minor, the consequences can be very serious. In most cases, the strictest sanction, closure of the media outlet, is applied. As only critical media are affected by these actions,[62] pirated software or tax issues are obviously only pretexts to get rid of inconvenient channels or newspapers.

State authorities use not only tax and Internet legislation but also other legal means to suppress independent reporting—in spite of constitutional guarantees. The best example is the 2002 law "On Combating Extremist Activity" (later amended in 2007). Whereas the law has rarely been used to shut down extremist or fascist newspapers, it has had a huge impact on civil society in general. The vague expressions "public justification of terrorism", "mass distribution of knowingly extremist materials" and "arousing social, racial, national or religious discord" and its broad field of application makes it a useful tool to silence independent media and NGOs. Seemingly, the law was deliberately formulated as vaguely as possible to "encompass all ideologically unacceptable activity".[63] State officials frequently send warnings to inconvenient media outlets: in the first two months after adoption of the amendments, *Ekho Moskvy* received fifteen letters invoking the law on extremism in reaction to interviews that the radio conducted with the Estonian president and the opposition Russian politician Gary Kasparov.[64] In light of the law on extremism, several laws such as the federal law on mass media and the federal law on public associations were amended as well.[65] Similarly, legislation

60 Becker, *op.cit.* note 30, 151; and Mommsen and Nussberger, *op.cit.* note 2, 48.

61 Iakovenko, interview, *op.cit.* note 38.

62 Eismont, *op.cit.* note 45, 122; and Alexander Verkhovsky, "Extreme Measures: How the Law is Being Used to Stifle the Media", 37(1) *Index on Censorship* (2008), 164-172, at 166.

63 Verkhovsky, *op.cit.* note 62, 165.

64 Lucas, *op.cit.* note 33, 31.

65 Amnesty International, "Freedom limited: The Right to Freedom of Expression in the Russian Federation", AI Index: EUR 46/008/2008 (Public) (26 February 2008), 17ff.

concerning anti-terror measures is misused to stifle criticism. The worldwide 'war on terror'—which in itself has entailed many human-rights violations in the US and elsewhere—also has reverberations in Russia. The Doctrine of Information Security, which restricts freedom of speech in the coverage of anti-terror operations, and the Convention on Counter-Terrorism are convenient excuses to circumvent constitutional guarantees and well-established legal principles.[66] Similar to the law on extremism, it is often used to suppress independent reporting under the banner of the 'patriotic duty' of journalists—especially after terrorist incidents such as the siege of the school in Beslan. In addition to the laws on extremism and terrorism, there have been several attempts by the President, the *Duma*, and the Federation Council to sharpen the relatively liberal 1991 Mass Media Law. The amendments of 2003 entail stricter regulation of the media in times of elections and there have even been proposals to reintroduce 'official' censorship.[67]

The arbitrary use of the law concerns not only editorial offices but also individual journalists, who are the main victims of suppression of the media. In some regions with a strict governor, lawsuits against journalists have become common practice, with up to ten complaints a year.[68] It is impossible to name all the cases where journalists, bloggers, and civil-society activists were found guilty because of violations of one of the above-mentioned legal provisions or of the law protecting reputation, honor and dignity. In fact, most cases are so-called defamation cases. Whenever a public official feels libeled by journalistic activity—even when the facts the journalist reveals were right—s/he can demand compensation. Often, journalists and editorial houses have to pay exorbitant sums in compensation when they lose (unfair) trials or can even be sent to prison (for up to five years).[69] Russia is one of the last countries in Europe where libel entails custodial sentences under Articles 129 and 130 of the Russian Criminal Code. If one journalist is held responsible for defamation, the whole publication is endangered, as media outlets can lose their broadcasting license.[70] A few defamation cases ended up before the ECtHR, which nearly without

66 Simons and Strovsky, *op.cit.* note 19, 189, 202ff.

67 Trudolyubov, *op.cit.* note 46, 100; Alexei Simonov, "Crime without Punishment: A Culture of Impunity Rules in Russia", 37(1) *Index on Censorship* (2008), 60-73, at 85; and Gessen, *op.cit.* note 34, 106. There were, in fact, two sets of amendments in 2003: 4 July and 8 December (No.94-FZ and No.169-FZ respectively).

68 Simonow, *op.cit.* note 30, 81; and Bachinin, *op.cit.* note 45, 133.

69 Azhgikhina, *op.cit.* note 29, 1259; Trudolyubov, *op.cit.* note 46, 100; OSCE, "OSCE Media Watchdog concerned about Prison Sentence for Journalist in Russia" (23 June 2005); and Amnesty International, "UA in Focus: Mightier than the Sword: The Struggle for Press Freedom", AI Index: ACT 60/010/2007 (Public) (May 2007), 3.

70 CoE, "PACE Rapporteur concerned about the Russian State Duma initiative to shut down media for defamatory reports" (29 April 2008) Press release 072.

exception ruled in favor of the journalist (as will be seen, below, in "Enforcement Mechanisms: Legal Means: The ECtHR and Russia").

In addition to these legal and semi-legal measures, the Russian authorities with the assistance of the security service, the *FSB*, exert much more pressure on editorial houses and journalists through extra-legal means. Due to the secret nature of these measures, they are not as easy to prove as lawsuits for instance, but that does not mean that they are not used—probably quite the opposite. With due care, I have decided to take seriously the reports of journalists who have received threats in some form or another. It is unlikely that all of them are inventing the same stories. Regularly, independent newspapers have been experiencing a sudden rent increase for their premises, withdrawal of significant advertisers, and printing problems of certain editions—which are likely to be caused by activities of state officials. Very often, offices and private houses are unlawfully raided (mainly during the night) with papers, disks and computers stolen.[71] Even if journalists complain later on and get their items back, the crucial material was already reviewed by the respective intruders. These raids fulfill two functions: *first*, they provide the security service with necessary information; *second*, they issue warnings to journalists not to continue investigating certain events. Other means of warnings are 'confidential' talks, telephone tapping, which is sometimes not even clandestine, and tracking of editors-in-chief and journalists.[72]

These measures are mild compared with serious human-rights violations such as the abduction, beating, and murder of journalists. The more censored a topic, the more serious the consequences for 'defiant' journalists. It has often been said that anyone writing about human-rights violations in Chechnia puts their own life at risk. Therefore, it is not surprising that journalists have been beaten up mostly in the Caucasus region. Fatima Tlisova, a Caucasus correspondent with the newspaper *Obshchaia gazeta*, who later fled from Russia, had to spend one month in hospital to recover from a beating.[73] Sometimes, journalists are abducted without their families and friends knowing anything—as was the case with Elina Ersenoeva, a journalist with the Chechen Society newspaper.[74] These acts are serious warnings as to what could happen next and what does happen

71 Aliev, *op.cit.* note 59, 144; Eismont, *op.cit.* note 45, 123; Verkhovsky, *op.cit.* note 62, 167; and Simonow, *op.cit.* note 30, 64.

72 Babchenko, *op.cit.* note 51, 117; Eismont, *op.cit.* note 45, 123; Bachinin, *op.cit.* note 45, 133; and Tlisova, *op.cit.* note 51, 42.

73 Tlisova, *op.cit.* note 51, 39.

74 See United Nations, Human Rights Council, Report of the Special Rapporteur, Ambeyi Ligabo, Addendum, Summary of Cases Transmitted to Governments and Replies Received, UN Index: A/HRC/4/27/Add.1 (26 March 2007), 200. (The report is reproduced only in English, French and Spanish and does not contain the original Russian-language name of the Chechen society newspaper.)

in fact: sadly, the journalistic community and human-rights defenders mourn a large number of dead journalists, not only in the Caucasus context. The number of journalists killed differs from index to index. Whereas CPJ reports 53 murders (1992-2012), the Russian organization Glasnost Defense Foundation (GDF) lists 209 cases of journalist killings in almost the same time span (1992-2010).[75] This result can be explained by the different measurements applied: CPJ counts only cases where the causal link between the journalist's profession and the murder is clearly established. GDF, however, counts all cases of injury to, or murder of, journalists and do not count only those that were undoubtedly caused by reasons other than professional activities, thus reversing the burden of proof. In my opinion, the second method is more appropriate, as there are many 'accidents' explicable by deliberate acts of others, for example car accidents caused by large trucks.[76] Who can explain the case of Ivan Safronov, who worked for the newspaper *Kommersant*, who surprisingly committed suicide before he was able to publish an article on Russian arms deals with Arab states?[77] Or the case of the journalist Ol'ga Kotovskaia, who fell from the fourteenth storey of a building one day after winning a major legal case?[78] Even if the figure of more than 200 murders is too high, as it also includes journalists killed in war zones, it is certainly higher than 52. But it should not be only about numbers: every single journalist killed in pursuing their task as a public watchdog tells a lot about the deteriorating conditions for journalists in Russia. The murder on 7 October 2006 of the journalist and human-rights defender Anna Politkovskaia—who was working for the newspaper *Novaia gazeta*—is probably the most famous. All over the world, journalists and human-rights organizations organized marches in memory of her courageous investigations in the North Caucasus.[79] As mentioned above, European organizations sent thousands of letters to the government.[80]

75 GDF, Murdered Journalists, available at <http://www.gdf.ru/murdered_journalists/list/2010>. According to GDF, two-thirds of the victims (140 journalists) died in peacetime and almost a quarter of journalists died in Moscow, where most TV channels, radio stations and newspapers are situated.

76 Azhgikhina, *op.cit.* note 29, 1247; John Crowfoot, "Barometers of Freedom: the Difficulties of Measuring the Media Climate", 37(1) *Index on Censorship* (2008), 75-81, at 79; and Simonov, *op.cit.* note 67, 61ff.

77 Crowfoot, *op.cit.* note 76, 79; and Azhgikhina, *op.cit.* note 29, 1247.

78 Luke Harding, "Colleagues Urge Investigation into Russian Journalist's Death", *The Guardian* (1 December 2009), available at <http://www.guardian.co.uk/world/2009/dec/01/olga-kotovskaya-journalist-death-kaliningrad>.

79 Crowfoot, *op.cit.* note 76, 79; Aliev, *op.cit.* note 59, 142; Azhgikhina, *op.cit.* note 29, 1247; and Radio Free Europe/Radio Liberty, *op.cit.* note 1.

80 See, *inter alia*, CoE, "Murder of Anna Politkovskaya: Time to Know the Truth, Says PACE President" (6 October 2007) Press release 660; CoE, PACE, "Murder of Anna Politkovskaya: PACE Calls for Parliamentary Investigations into the Unresolved Murders of Journalists and Announces a Specific Monitoring Mechanism" (25 January 2007); and OSCE, "OSCE Chairman Shocked by Murder of Russian Journalist Anna Politkovskaya" (7 October 2006).

The editorial house of *Novaia gazeta* was nearly overrun by foreign journalists after the murder occurred.[81] However, this justifiable media attention should not make us forget all the other cases of journalists killed. *Novaia gazeta* lost not only Anna Politkovskaia but, also, Iurii Shchekochikhin, Igor Domnikov, and Anastasiia Baburova. Unfortunately, the series of murders did not stop in 2006. The murder of Nataliia Estemirova—who also was associated with *Novaia gazeta*—is one of the rare cases that attracted international attention anew. In most cases, it is very difficult to prove that the state itself or the security forces are the causes of these murders. In any case, the Russian authorities were indirectly responsible if they failed to investigate them properly. According to a speech by the then-OSCE Representative on Freedom of the Media (RFOM), Miklos Haraszti:

> "There is only one thing more intimidating for free speech than harassment, physical attacks and murder of media workers; and that is when governments tolerate harassment, attacks, and murders."[82]

Without thorough investigation of the murders, the chilling effect on other journalists becomes even stronger. Seldom are the perpetrators identified—whereas those who ordered the murder remain unknown—but mostly investigations are closed with the standard expression: no suspects have been identified.[83] Based on information received from the office of the Russian Federation Prosecutor-General, the GDF conducted very interesting research with regard to the investigation of crimes. Whereas the "rate of disclosure for murder and attempted murder" is as high as 80% in Russia, the disclosure rate of "serious crimes against journalists" from 2004-2006 is only 9%.[84] Reluctance to investigate permits only one conclusion: the state is deliberately violating its positive obligation to protect journalists.

These dangerous conditions have made many journalists flee the country. Most prominent is the case of Elena Tregubova, who published two books about the Kremlin. After nearly being murdered, she was forced to move to London

81 Rostova, interview, *op.cit.* note 32.

82 OSCE, RFOM, Keynote speech by Miklos Haraszti to the International Federation of Journalists, World Congress, World Trade Center, Moscow (28 May 2007).

83 Lucas, *op.cit.* note 33, 33; Simonov, *op.cit.* note 67, 65ff.; Crowfoot, *op.cit.* note 76, 79; and CPJ, "Anatomy of Injustice: The Unsolved Killings of Journalists in Russia" (September 2009), 9.

84 Simonov, *op.cit.* note 67, 70.

in 2007. In an interview, she says that she would be in 'mortal danger' if she went back.[85]

A Free Society or an Authoritarian State?

Regarding the overall situation of the media in Russia, it is difficult to believe Putin's high esteem of the mass media as "one of the cornerstones of democracy" announced at the beginning of his first term of office[86] or Medvedev's 2008 comment in Germany that "television is fully independent".[87] Seemingly, these statements are mere attempts to conceal the real state of affairs. According to prominent human-rights activists, Medvedev's meeting with journalists from *Novaia gazeta* and NGOs in 2009 and his solemn assertions to investigate the murders of well-known Russian journalists on different occasions also does not show a real appreciation of their work but, rather, the aspiration to present Russia to the West as a free and democratic country.[88] These diverse perceptions point to the general problem of categorizing the current situation of the media in Russia.

Russia's media are placed somewhere between the unhampered media of a free and pluralist democracy and the controlled media of a totalitarian regime. Even if it is clear that the media are not as free and democratic as Putin and Medvedev would like to suggest, there can be considerable dispute about the seriousness of the situation. With certain free media outlets, the current situation is certainly not as fatal as in the USSR. In contrast to those times, willing Russian citizens can express their own ideas without immediate interference by state authorities, have unhampered access to independent information on the Internet and public discussion seems to be tolerated to a certain degree in some radio channels and in various internet blogs. But these are exceptions. Today, we should not deceive ourselves and prove Putin and Medvedev right in their evaluations that the media are (still) free. Nearly unnoticeably, more and more freedom has been taken away from media outlets in recent years. Whereas 'normal' Russian citizens are perhaps not yet affected, civil-society activists and especially journalists come increasingly under pressure. In accordance with the indices of

85 "Ex-Kremlin Journalist Talks From UK Asylum", *Radio Free Europe/Radio Liberty* (8 April 2008), available at <http://www.rferl.org/featuresarticle/2008/04/22035904-7986-4176-b919-23f062624f9d.html>; Bachinin, *op.cit.* note 45,132; and Lucas, *op.cit.* note 33, 32.

86 Quoted in Becker, *op.cit.* note 30, 148.

87 Judy Dempsey, "Medvedev, in Germany, Revisits Russia's Tensions with the West", *The New York Times* (5 June 2008), available at <http://www.nytimes.com/2008/06/05/world/europe/05iht-germany.4.13505869.html>.

88 Interview with Dmitri Medvedev, *Der Spiegel* (9 November 2009), available at <http://www.spiegel.de/spiegel/print/d-67682716.html>; Clifford J. Levy, "A Puzzle over Intentions of Russia's President", *The New York Times* (2 May 2009), available at <http://www.nytimes.com/2009/05/03/world/europe/03medvedev.html>; and Ellen Barry, "Medvedev Meets Editor of Newspaper Where Slain Journalists Worked", *The New York Times* (30 January 2009), available at <http://www.nytimes.com/2009/01/31/world/europe/31medvedev.html>.

Freedom House and RSF, most people working in the media field clearly see a negative trend toward authoritarianism.[89] Most radically, Igor Iakovenko, head of the RUJ, compares the situation in Russia with Hitler's coming to power in Germany and the establishment of the first state-controlled radio programs under the banner of joy and national unity.[90] Even if Iakovenko also admits that "the level of lack of freedom and censorship in Russia is categorically different from what we had in the Soviet Union",[91] he warns with harsh words not to underestimate the dangers. Whether Russia is still a democracy or already an authoritarian regime cannot be decided without further consideration of other sectors of society and a thorough analysis of all relevant institutions. But for the media sector, at least, one can reach the well-founded conclusion that Russia has departed from democratic practices and has installed a media system with strong tendencies towards authoritarianism.

Bridging the Gap: European Enforcement Mechanisms

The gap between the noble idea of a free society where freedom of expression has to be protected, even when statements offend, shock, or disturb, and the actual state of affairs in Russia is becoming more and more visible. It is a truism that standard setting alone is not sufficient for freedom of expression to be protected on every sublevel of the European human-rights system. In addition, there also have to be working mechanisms to implement the agreed legal standards in practice against reluctant governments. In the following part of this chapter, I will present the measures the main European organizations have taken to promote freedom of expression in Russia and answer the question whether they have been influential enough to make a real difference for media workers in Russia. After having sketched Russia's relations with the EU, I will focus on the two other European organizations with a stronger human-rights mandate. In detail, the Russian position in the OSCE will be analyzed, and special attention will be given to promotion of freedom of expression through the RFOM. But before anything else, I will focus on the CoE and its legal mechanism, the ECtHR.

The EU: Human-Rights Rhetoric

When analyzing European-Russian relations, most scholars focus on the EU and its ambivalent contacts with the Russian neighbor. There is plenty of literature in the field of international relations and foreign policy examining the power struggle between the EU and Russia, with most of them coming to similar

89 Arch Puddington, "The 2006 Freedom House Survey: The Pushback against Democracy", 18(2) *Journal of Democracy* (2007), 125-137, at 125; Becker, *op.cit.* note 30, 157; and interview with Elena Leonidovna Grishina, *op.cit.* note 28.

90 Iakovenko, interview, *op.cit.* note 38.

91 Radio Free Europe/Radio Liberty, *op.cit.* note 52.

conclusions: whereas the 1990s were dominated by a rhetoric of equal partnership, shared principles and common objectives, as is manifested in treaties and agreements such as the 1994 Partnership and Cooperation Agreement (PCA) and the 2003 four 'common spaces',[92] today the rosy picture of EU-Russian relations has to be overcome—even if "impressive symbolic activity, including heady summits, strategies, roadmaps and the ritual invocation of a 'strategic partnership'"[93] continues. With Russia regaining trust in its own economic and political capabilities in recent years, European-Russian relations have often been nothing more than a huge political and strategic contest, where economic power is going to win in the end.

On the evidence of economic interaction, which is probably the lowest common denominator in EU-Russian relations, human rights have to step back. This is obvious in the above-mentioned treaties, where cooperation in the human-rights sector and other steps for promotion of democracy are always presented in second place after close economic ties are stressed. Given this prioritization, it is not surprising that criticism of the human-rights situation in Russia, which is sometimes expressed by heads of state at numerous summits, is not taken seriously. Even if some battles appear on the surface of daily politics, the underlying economic dependence puts the importance of these confrontations into perspective. Without reproaching hypocrisy, one has to be realistic that the EU will never sacrifice its economic and strategic interests to the benefit of human rights, or at least not in every case. This is even explicitly stated in a 2007 EU policy paper:

> "Our cooperation, carried out on the basis of common values such as democracy, respect for human rights and fundamental freedoms, must reflect the necessary balance between security, on the one hand, and justice and freedom, on the other."[94]

Respect for human rights is a guiding principle for external affairs, but that does not transform the EU into a human-rights organization.

With regard to media freedom, the situation is similar. In fact, the EU pays attention to the situation of the media in Russia and addresses the issue in mutual negotiations. But, mostly, the criticism is too specific when only directed at single events—such as the murder of Anna Politkovskaia. It is easily imaginable

92 EU, European Commission, External Relations, "The European Union and Russia: Close Neighbours, Global Players, Strategic Partners" (2007), 3; and EU, European Commission, External Relations, "Country Strategy Paper 2007-2013: Russian Federation" (2007), 6, 21. The extension or replacement of the PCA has been under discussion for some time; see, *e.g.*, the EU's note at <http://ec.europa.eu/trade/creating-opportunities/bilateral-relations/countries/russia/>.

93 Sergei Medvedev, *EU-Russian Relations: Alternative Futures* (The Finnish Institute of International Affairs, Helsinki, 2006), 9ff.; and Mark Leonard and Nicu Popescu, *A Power Audit of EU-Russia Relations* (European Council on Foreign Relations, London, 2007), 25.

94 "The European Union and Russia", *op.cit.* note 92, 14.

that political appeals can help in some cases, but they can never replace effective mechanisms of implementation. Even inaugurated consultations on human-rights matters, which include a regular invocation of media freedom, are still exposed to political considerations and human-rights rhetoric.[95] Hence, any ambitious expectations that the EU could force Russia to respect an independent media should be withdrawn.

The OSCE

A Consensus-Based Organization

In contrast to the EU, the OSCE has the advantage of speaking to Russia as an equal member next to traditional European states. Founded in 1975 as the Conference for Security and Cooperation in Europe (CSCE) after two years of negotiations between two opposing political blocs, it was a forum for "discussion, dialogue, verbal confrontation and adoption of documents" right from the beginning.[96] Moreover, institutionalization after 1990 did not change the main characteristic of the OSCE: the consensus decision-making process. The consensus principle was often called into question, as it slows down the decision-making process and leads only to insignificant outcomes. Against this, there are strong arguments for maintaining it. States such as Russia—which react with displeasure to criticism from the outside—would probably never accept any decisions taken against their will. In theory, any declaration, institution or mechanism agreed upon is supported by each member; one can therefore expect better compliance by particular states. The impact of the OSCE has nevertheless been discussed. Can an organization force it members to comply with their 'political commitments', which are not 'legal obligations'?[97] The answer to this question depends on the perception of the power of law in international relations. Sometimes, it is probably better to achieve an amelioration of a situation in using soft political means and mutual agreements rather than winning *de jure* even if the situation does not change at all.

From the very beginning, the OSCE acted according to the concept of comprehensive security, thus including a so-called 'human dimension' in mutual negotiations.[98] It was a key experience of the Cold War that human security is more than the absence of armed conflict. After the collapse of the USSR, the OSCE committed itself even more strongly to promotion of human rights and

95 *Ibid.*, 15.

96 Rachel Brett, "Human Rights and the OSCE", 18(3) *Human Rights Quarterly* (1996), 668-693, at 670.

97 *Ibid.*, 671, 673ff.

98 Manfred Nowak, *Introduction to the International Human Rights Regime* (Martinus Nijhoff Publishers, Leiden, 2003), 222; and Brett, *op.cit.* note 96, 677.

democratization with the establishment of human dimension mechanisms, long-duration missions and with the creation of human-rights institutions such as the RFOM.[99] Even if the OSCE is still a 'security' organization and not a human-rights organization, it also strongly supports the ideas of human rights, democracy, and the rule of law in public discourse. Unfortunately, insistence on human rights is not at all welcomed by Russia. Whereas "the OSCE had traditionally been one of the most favoured organisations for Russian foreign policy makers as it so clearly represented the institution of sovereignty and equality of its members, and diplomacy", nowadays "frustration with the OSCE's concerns over human rights and democratic elections within the Commonwealth of Independent States (CIS) had altered this perception considerably".[100] This has even led Russia to temporarily cease its payments to the organization.[101] The harsh critique of the previous parliamentary and presidential elections by the OSCE's election-monitoring body has deepened the distrust between Russia and the OSCE.

The RFOM

The OSCE's high esteem of media rights is reflected in the establishment of the RFOM in 1997—the first and "only intergovernmental media freedom watchdog in the world".[102] Acknowledging the important role the media play in free and democratic societies, the RFOM's main task is to monitor media developments in the 56 participating states of the OSCE to prevent any undue interference (early-warning function). In the case of assaults against journalists, it is supposed to remind governments of their obligation to investigate incidents without undue delay and to put forward positive measures (rapid-response function). In performing this task, the RFOM composes letters to the respective ministries of foreign affairs, produces reports to the Permanent Council of the OSCE, addresses human-rights violations in public and cooperates with national and international media organizations and NGOs.[103] However, in his report to the Permanent Council of 13 March 2008, the former RFOM, Miklos Haraszti, was quite critical about the cooperation of member states with his institution:

> "Unfortunately, today we see a certain 'meltdown' of OSCE commitments. Their universality is being questioned. Ten years ago, the establishment of this office marked a moment when all participating States committed themselves to the universal values of democracy, including the protection of free expression and media pluralism. Today, just as in the days before the formation of the OSCE, different interpretations of democracy are being cultivated again,

99 Brett, *op.cit.* note 96, 669, 679.

100 Pami Aalto, "Russia's Quest for International Society and the Prospects for Regional-Level International Societies", 21(4) *International Relations* (2007), 463.

101 Leonard and Popescu, *op.cit.* note 93, 20.

102 OSCE, Representative on Freedom of the Media Miklós Haraszti, Regular Report to the Permanent Council, OSCE Index: FOM.GAL/2/08/Rev.2 (Public) (13 March 2008), 1.

103 OSCE, RFOM, Freedom of Expression, Free Flow of Information, Freedom of Media: CSCE/OSCE Main Provisions 1975-2007 (26 March 2008).

> also with regards to speech rights. The requests for co-operation from the OSCE Institutions mandated to care for the fulfilment of the human rights commitments again are sometimes regarded as 'intrusion into internal affairs'."[104]

The reaction of the Russian authorities shows that his evaluation is correct. Responding to a letter of appeal by Miklos Haraszti regarding the State *Duma* election in December 2007 and alleged violation of freedom of the press, Minister of Foreign Affairs Sergei Lavrov reacted as rather affronted by 'accusations'. He blamed Haraszti for not having founded his observations on facts and having erroneously taken the "media coverage of the work of the President of Russia" for 'electioneering'. In the end, Lavrov reproached him for "non-professionalism and a desire to see the negative in all that concerns Russia". For him:

> "It is crystal clear that the message of Haraszti is a part of the propagandist attempts to discredit the Russian parliamentary elections being undertaken by certain forces in the West. In addition, his demarche obviously goes beyond the scope of the mandate of the OSCE Representative on Freedom of the Media."[105]

Two main conclusions can be drawn from this correspondence. *First*, Lavrov seems to be concerned that the OSCE (and the West in general) could question whether Russia is a democratic state. His answer is symptomatic of the general defensiveness of the Russian government when confronted with (probably well-founded) criticism by European organizations. *Second*, the harsh response demonstrates that the RFOM's letter is taken seriously by the Russian government. Generally, the Russian government responds to the RFOM's letters and justifies its actions instead of ignoring them completely. Sometimes, Russia even promises to investigate specific assaults and to take different (legal) action.[106]

Do these letters prove successful in practice? In the case of media coverage in election campaigns, Haraszti notes that "the trend of a lack of equal access in the broadcast media seemed to continue"—also in the presidential election campaign in March 2008.[107] Or to give another example: despite constant appeals to protect journalists by the office of the RFOM in letters to the government and in the (foreign) media, especially after the death of Anna Politkovskaia,[108] more journalists were killed. Does that mean that the institution of the RFOM is pointless? Would the RFOM's letters ever have the power to change the actual

104 OSCE, *op.cit.* note 102, 1.

105 Ministry of Foreign Affairs of the Russian Federation, Information and Press Department, MFA Information and Press Department Commentary Regarding Letter from OSCE Representative on Freedom of the Media Miklos Haraszti to Russian Minister of Foreign Affairs Sergei Lavrov (10 December 2007). For a similar comment, see OSCE, RFOM Miklós Haraszti, Regular Report to the Permanent Council (2 April 2009), 10.

106 OSCE, RFOM Miklós Haraszti, Regular Report to the Permanent Council, OSCE Index: FOM.GAL/4/09/Rev.1 (Public) (29 October 2009), 7ff., 12ff.

107 OSCE, RFOM Miklós Haraszti, Regular Report to the Permanent Council, OSCE Index: FOM.GAL/2/08/Rev.2 (Public) (13 March 2008), 8ff.

108 OSCE, "OSCE Chairman Shocked…", *op.cit.* note 80.

situation? It is a question of belief whether relatively 'soft' political institutions make a difference at all. It is very hard to estimate the factual consequences of appeal letters, correspondence and public discussion, as many different factors determine events in a country. In any case, it is impossible to know what would have happened without any criticism.

The CoE

Accession of Russia to the CoE

Whereas the human-rights work of the EU is 'corrupted' by other interests and whereas the OSCE's commitment to democracy and human rights is embedded in the ultimate aim of security, the CoE is the only European organization with a pure mandate for human rights, democracy, and the rule of law. In this respect, the organization is unique in Europe. On 28 February 1996, Russia became the thirty-ninth member state of the CoE. Consequently it had to ratify the ECHR and accept the jurisdiction of the ECtHR (which happened on 5 May 1998). The relatively rapid accession of Russia to the CoE—a decision that is still highly contested within the CoE—cannot be studied irrespective of overall European development. The years after the velvet revolutions in Eastern Europe—at the end of the 1980s and the final collapse of the communist bloc in 1991—were probably one of the most challenging periods for the CoE. On the one hand, it meant a great success for much vaunted European values. It is still hard to believe that the ideas of human rights, democracy and the rule of law possessed such a revolutionary potential at that time. Few would have thought how fast quasi-democratic governments were established in Eastern European countries and in Russia. In that sense, the CoE could not reject any of these countries without deceiving the hopes of so many people for free and democratic societies.[109] This is especially true of some influential liberal-democratic forces in Russia with an open pro-Western approach, for which accession to this 'moral' European organization seemed to be motivated by a strong belief in the values promoted.[110] On the other hand, it also threatened the strict criteria of the CoE by accepting states too early even if they did not fully comply with the norms agreed upon in the ECHR.

Despite some reforms—such as adoption of the new 1993 Russian Constitution—Russia had also not fulfilled most criteria of membership: as a legacy of the communist regime, the legal culture remained extremely weak, the

109 Pamela A. Jordan, "Does Membership Have Its Privileges?: Entrance into the Council of Europe and Compliance with Human Rights Norms", 25 *Human Rights Quarterly* (2003), 660-668, at 661.

110 Timofei Bordachev, "Russia's European Problem: Eastward Enlargement of the EU and Moscow's Policy 1993-2003", in O. Antonenko and K. Pinnick (eds.), *Russia and the European Union* (Routledge, London, 2005), 51-66, at 55ff.

situation of the army was disastrous and there was only a very frail civil society. Most problematic, though, was the situation in Chechnia. Thus, the CoE faced an important dilemma in the years following the breakdown of communism. In the end, the integrationist party prevailed, claiming that it was better to include the Eastern European countries, the former Soviet republics and Russia. Optimistically, CoE membership was seen as the best means to integrate Russia and other countries into 'political' Europe and its human-rights regime and to support domestic liberal forces.[111]

> "Once a state has been granted admission without having met the council's formal standards, it often faces less pressure to complete the array of reforms necessary to substantively achieve the standards. The implications of Russia's premature admission to the council have been especially apparent."[112]

The missing ratification of Protocol 6 concerning abolition of the death penalty, desultory reforms of civil and criminal proceedings, and lack of reforms in other areas since 1996 confirm this statement.[113] One has to be quite dewy-eyed not to see that Russia lags very much behind in fulfilling its obligations to the CoE.

Enforcement Mechanisms: Political Means

It seems that in addressing Russia, the CoE primarily uses political pressure, which is limited and rather weak. Of course, the reputation of Russia in international relations suffers when blamed for human-rights violations in public, and the method of shaming has a certain power in particular events, but, probably, structural change cannot be achieved only through public discourse. The stronger a state becomes, the more reluctant it is in implementing external proposals. As a last resort, the Parliamentary Assembly of the Council of Europe (PACE) could suspend the voting rights of the Russian representatives and ask the Committee of Ministers to expel Russia from the CoE under Article 8 of the Treaty of London; but in the whole history of the CoE, this has happened only once: after the military coup in Greece in 1967.[114] It is not in the interest of the CoE—and of some of its powerful members such as France, Germany, and Italy—to lose its influence on Russia. The same dilemma that has already been discussed in the

111 Jordan, *op.cit.* note 109, 662ff., 680; Nuala Mole, "European Human Rights Law in National and International Practice: Common Experiences and Differences", Report of the Seminar 'Implementation of Human Rights: The Efficiency of Justice in the Council of Europe and its Member States', Netherlands Ministry of Foreign Affairs, NCJM, Dutch section the International Commission of Jurists (19-20 April 2004), The Hague, Leiden, 72ff.; and Mommsen and Nussberger, *op.cit.* note 2, 163ff.

112 William D. Jackson, "Russia and the Council of Europe: The Perils of Premature Admission", 51(5) *Problems of Post-Communism* (2004), 23-33, at 24ff.

113 Leonard and Popescu, *op.cit.* note 93, 24; Jackson, *op.cit.* note 112, 26ff.; and Jordan, *op.cit.* note 109, 680ff.

114 Jackson, *op.cit.* note 112, 32.

previous paragraph arises again. One cannot blame the CoE for not sanctioning Russia more strictly, if there are no real levers to do so.

The lack of powerful means to exert pressure becomes apparent at the sight of the different political measures concerning media freedom in Russia. Being one of the most outstanding values of democracy, freedom of expression is taken seriously by an organization that defines itself as a watchdog of democratic societies.[115] Therefore, it attentively follows developments in Russia and observes the current situation of the media. Every major political event that has to do with the precarious situation of the media, leads the CoE to speak out in public.[116] In addition, pressing questions of daily politics concerning freedom of expression are very often discussed at regular meetings of PACE with Russian officials. On special occasions, *e.g.*, at the Forum for the Future of Democracy in Moscow, PACE meets journalists and representatives of civil society.[117] All press releases and meetings since autumn 2006 have persistently mentioned the case of Anna Politkovskaia and appealed for criminal investigations. In addition to these occasional reactions, the CoE promotes media pluralism in a more systematic way by producing regular reports on Russia that include the worrisome state of affairs of the media and produces declarations, recommendations, and guidelines.[118] This growing paperwork is similarly 'successful' as the measures of the RFOM. Russian representatives are in fact answering to the different bodies of the CoE, but that does not make them follow the proposals in practice.[119] Certainly, it is better to have a small impact than no influence at all, but one should look out for other measures to make the work of the CoE more effective in the future.

115 See, for instance, CoE, Declaration of the Committee of Ministers on measures to promote respect of Article 10 of the European Convention on Human Rights (13 January 2010).

116 CoE, "Russia's parliamentary elections: political stability and economic growth should go hand in hand with strengthening democracy" (9 November 2007) Press release 767; CoE, "PACE President to visit Russia with 2008 presidential election and the ratification of Protocols 6 and 14 on the agenda" (18 December 2007) Press release 931; and CoE, "Russian Presidential election: for an election to be good it takes a good process, not just a good election day" (3 March 2008) Press release 150.

117 CoE, "Democracy needs freedom, says PACE President at the Forum for the Future of Democracy in Moscow" (18 October 2006) Press release 607; and CoE, "PACE President on working visit to Moscow" (9 January 2007) Press release 010.

118 Examples are: CoE, "Declaration by the Committee of Ministers on the protection and promotion of investigative journalism" (26 September 2007); CoE, "Declaration of the Committee of Ministers on protecting the role of the media in democracy in the context of media concentration" (31 January 2007); CoE, "Recommendation CM/Rec(2007)2 of the Committee of Ministers to member states on media pluralism and diversity of media content" (31 January 2007); and CoE, "Guidelines of the Committee of Ministers of the Council of Europe on protecting freedom of expression and information in times of crisis" (26 September 2007).

119 Jordan, *op.cit.* note 109, 680; and Jackson, *op.cit.* note 112, 31.

Enforcement Mechanisms: Legal Means: The ECtHR and Russia

But the CoE does not have to confine itself to mere political pressure. It is one of the most outstanding and distinctive characteristics of this organization that it also has a judicial mechanism at its disposal: the ECtHR. Is the Court's authority strong enough to be taken seriously even in the Russian Federation? Does its jurisprudence reach every single district court and ordinary court within this immense country? On paper, there is no doubt at all that Russia respects the ECHR and its legal body, the ECtHR. According to the already-mentioned provisions of direct applicability of international law, Article 46(3) of the Russian Constitution and the ratification of Protocol 11, each and every Russian citizen can invoke the ECHR before ordinary courts and apply to the Court in Strasbourg after having exhausted all domestic remedies.[120] Russian citizens immediately made use of these legal possibilities: already by the beginning of 2009, 70,513 applications had reached the ECtHR, and every year the number of petitions increases as exponentially as the overall flood of cases to the Court. Since most petitions (36,083) were rejected as inadmissible, gradually Russian lawyers, NGOs and legal advisory organizations have learned to use the method of individual complaints to the Court in pursuing their respective objective.[121]

The Russian Federation, in fact, accepts the Court. Since 1996, Russia has been sending judges to the Court, defending itself in proceedings like any other state and accepting the jurisprudence of the Court, even if it disagrees with specific decisions. There has not been a single case where Russia has not paid compensation.[122] It is more difficult to assess whether Russia is also complying with general measures and putting forward reforms that would change the overall situation in the country. There is not an easy answer to this question, as some measures have been taken only half-heartedly, while other measures are difficult to monitor.

In his instructive 2007 volume *The Impact of the European Convention on Human Rights on Russian Law: Legislation and Application in 1996-2006*, Anton Burkov examined in detail whether and to what extent the Russian courts on different levels are using the ECHR and the case-law of the ECtHR. He comes to the conclusion that despite "normative provisions", the degree of

120 Jackson, *op.cit.* note 112, 23; and Manja Hussner, "The Incorporation of International Human Rights Treaties into the Russian System of Law", in Andreas Umland (ed.), *The Implementation of the European Convention on Human Rights in Russia: Philosophical, Legal and Empirical Studies, Proceedings of an International Conference Held at Yekaterinburg on 6-7 April 2001* (Stuttgart, 2004), 91-104, at 97.

121 Jackson, *op.cit.* note 112, 23ff.; Jordan, *op.cit.* note 109, 681ff.; and ECtHR, Country Fact Sheets, 1959-2009.

122 Jordan, *op.cit.* note 109, 682, 685ff; and CoE, "Respect for Court Decisions in Russia: Round Table at the Council of Europe" (31 October 2006) Press release 652.

factual implementation by domestic courts is "unsatisfactory".[123] On paper and in rhetoric, the ECHR is regarded as one of the most important instruments for the protection of human rights; but, in practice, courts seldom refer to the ECHR and even less often to its case law. Often, Russian officials ignore that the ratification of the ECHR implies more than just 'the right to write to Strasbourg' but, rather, the systematic integration of its provisions into the legal system of Russia.[124] There is, however, a variety of approaches among different courts. Whereas the Supreme Court and the Higher Arbitrazh Court almost seem to ignore the ECHR, the Constitutional Court and the subordinate district and high courts refer much more often to the different articles of the ECHR—albeit in a very general manner. In many cases, a competent usage of the ECHR and its case law was prompted by the arguments of the applicant,[125] which shows that the situation is not hopeless: well-trained lawyers and legal advisory institutions can truly make a difference in implementing European standards in Russian law. In academia, the impact of ECtHR jurisprudence is already noticeable, but there is still much to be done to make a difference in practice as well. The more the ECHR is invoked in domestic proceedings, the better the prospect of a true impact of the agreed human-rights standards.

Enforcement Mechanisms: Case Law Concerning Article 10

Since Russia's accession to the CoE, the ECtHR has decided twenty-one relevant cases alleging a violation of Article 10 by the Russian Federation. As the time between the application and the final decision of a case amounts to six years, the events that current cases are dealing with happened mostly in 2001-2006. Therefore, the case law is not representative of the actual situation but, rather, for the years when the situation worsened since Putin's first term of office. Nevertheless, they show tendencies as to how the Russian domestic courts normally decide when confronted with a 'defiant' press. Already in the past, the number of cases increased exponentially; it is likely that this trend will continue in the future. In almost all cases, the ECtHR found Russia in violation of Article 10—except in the cases of *Shabanov and Tren v. Russia*[126] and *Pasko v. Russia*[127] where the Court held in favor of the state (2006 and 2009 respectively).

123 Burkov, *op.cit.* note 10, 33, 83; Burkov's book is one of the rare sources in English analyzing implementation of the ECHR in Russia. But occasionally his assessment is too quantitative. Even if the ECHR were not mentioned in specific cases, its provisions nevertheless could have significant influence upon the development of Russian law.

124 *Ibid.*, 20.

125 *Ibid.*, 56ff., 84.

126 Case of *Shabanov and Tren v. Russia* (14 December 2006) No.5433/02.

127 Case of *Pasko v. Russia* (22 October 2009) No.69519/01.

Apart from the 2007 case of *Dzhavodov v. Russia,*[128] the case of *Pasko v. Russia* and another 2009 case of (*Kudeshkina v. Russia*),[129] all the other cases against Russia have been so-called 'defamation' cases: evoking Article 152 of the RF 1994 Civil Code, which states that "an individual shall be entitled to claim, before a court, a rectification of information damaging his honor, dignity and professional reputation, unless the person who disseminated the information proves that it was true",[130] state authorities or individuals started lawsuits in response to articles in the media. As all freedom-of-expression cases against Russia are so-called 'clone' cases, it is sufficient to analyze one case in detail: the 2007 *Krasulya v. Russia* case[131] is representative of the reasoning of both the domestic courts and the ECtHR. In his position as editor-in-chief of the regional newspaper *Novyi grazhdanskii mir*, the applicant was sentenced to a year (!) imprisonment by a domestic court for defamation of the governor after publishing an article in his newspaper. In that work, he had alleged bribery and had given a critical judgment of the governor's abilities as a politician and manager using the expression "loud and ambitious, but completely incapable governor".[132] Appealing to the ECtHR, the applicant invoked Article 10 and the principles of the court's case law, most notably the idea that politicians are public figures who have to tolerate more severe criticism than private individuals. He also argued that value judgments are not susceptible of proof as statements of fact, as such allowing a certain degree of exaggeration. Thus, the sanctions imposed by the state were disproportionate.[133] After having assessed the facts, the ECtHR agreed with most of the arguments of the applicant. The court held that the state had failed to balance the legitimate aim of the reputation and the right of others against freedom of expression of the journalist; hence, it had not fulfilled the test of necessity.[134] Furthermore, the state had overstepped the narrow margin of appreciation. Even if the sentence of one year's imprisonment was suspended, the reaction of the state was held to be inadequate. In the end, Russia was found to have violated Article 10.

128 Case of *Dzhavadov v. Russia* (27 September 2007) No.30160/04.

129 Case of *Kudeshkina v. Russia* (26 February 2009) No.29492/05.

130 RF Civil Code, promulgated by RF Federal Laws of 30 November 1994, 26 January 1996, 26 November 2001 and 18 December 2006, *Rossiiskaia gazeta* (8 December 1994, 6/7/8 February 1996, 3 December 2001 and 22 December 2006 respectively).

131 Case of *Krasulya v. Russia* (22 February 2007) No.12365/03; compare especially the very similar case ECtHR, *Chemodurov v. Russia* (31 July 2007) No.72683/01, which also deals with corruption.

132 Case of *Krasulya v. Russia, op.cit.* note 131, paras. 7-9, 21.

133 *Ibid.*, paras. 22, 32, 37; see, also, case of *Karman v. Russia* (14 December 2006) No.29372/02, 35ff.

134 Case of *Krasulya v. Russia, op.cit.* note 131, paras. 34ff., 45; see, also, case of *Filatenko v. Russia* (6 December 2007) No.73219/01, para. 48.

Consistently, the ECtHR expresses its high regard for freedom of expression as constituting "one of the essential foundations of a democratic society and one of the basic conditions for its progress and for each individual's self-fulfilment"—a formulation that is reiterated on every possible occasion.[135] The twenty-one cases are good examples as to how the established principles of the court's case law can be applied in practice—especially the second principle, which asserts the "essential role of the press in ensuring the proper functioning of political democracy" and its contribution to ongoing political debate.[136] This is particularly apparent in the 2007 case of *Dyuldin and Kislov v. Russia*, which problematizes the current state of affairs of the media in Russia.[137] Here, journalists, trade-union leaders and civil-society activists were successfully sued by the Penza regional government for having published an open letter to the president and other officials. For the ECtHR, it is indisputable that the open letter—which alleged corruption, monopolies, and intimidation of the independent media—is part of the political debate on an important matter of general concern and as such protected by Article 10.[138] Explicitly, the ECtHR confirmed the linkages of the independence of the media, on the one hand, and a pluralistic, tolerant, broadminded and—first and foremost—democratic society, on the other hand:

> "Freedom of the press [...] enables everyone to participate in the free political debate which is at the very core of the concept of a democratic society."[139]

Especially in election times, the media has to be protected, as was validated by the court in *Grinberg v. Russia*[140] and in *Filatenko v. Russia* (2005 and 2007 respectively).[141] Because of the fundamental importance of media freedom, weighty reasons are required to justify restrictions on political expression in the media.[142]

The case law of the ECtHR concerning Russia and Article 10 says a lot about the Russian understanding in antecedent domestic proceedings. In (nearly) all cases, Russian courts gave priority to other rights—especially to the right of the reputation of others, mainly politicians—than to freedom of expression. The frequent use of defamation proceedings—which is not only the case in Russia—shows that freedom of expression is a provision in the 1993 RF Constitution with weak legal standing before domestic courts. Or to put it more drastically: the law on defamation is used to stifle criticism more than to protect the human rights of others. The court states accordingly:

135 See, for example, case of *Dzhavadov v. Russia*, *op.cit.* note 128, para. 31.

136 Case of *Krasulya v. Russia*, *op.cit.* note 131, paras. 36, 38.

137 Case of *Dyuldin and Kislov v. Russia* (31 July 2007) No.25968/02.

138 *Ibid.*, paras. 7, 9ff.

139 *Ibid.*, paras. 37ff.

140 Case of *Grinberg v. Russia* (21 July 2005) No.23472/03.

141 Case of *Filatenko v. Russia*, *op.cit.* note 134.

142 See, *inter alia*, the case of *Dyuldin and Kislov v. Russia*, *op.cit.* note 137, para. 41.

> "If all State officials were allowed to sue in defamation in connection with any statement critical of administration of State affairs [...] journalists would be inundated with lawsuits. Not only would that result in an excessive and disproportionate burden being placed on the media, straining their resources and involving them in endless litigation, it would also inevitably have a chilling effect on the press in the performance of its task of purveyor of information and public watchdog."[143]

The ECtHR, by contrast, is very clear in its standards. It uses the individual complaint procedure as a means to promote its own ideas of freedom of expression and to show Russian courts that freedom of expression cannot be interpreted arbitrarily. On the contrary: the value of freedom of expression has to be protected against an authoritarian interpretation.

The Russian authorities are also accepting the ECtHR's jurisdiction in these cases, albeit grudgingly.

A General Assessment of European Measures

To sum up, it can be said that the three European organizations analyzed have dissimilar mandates and fields of attention, so each of them can address Russia with miscellaneous means, but all of them are only partly successful. They seem to tilt at windmills. Pessimistically, one could come to the sad conclusion that a strong organization (EU) is not willing to put more pressure on Russia for not threatening mutual relations even more and that the willing organizations (OSCE, CoE) are not strong enough to exercise any meaningful influence on Russia. Especially political means such as letters of appeal, meetings and negotiations are often nothing more than rhetoric and solemn asseverations. It is a matter of principle whether the small steps taken by the Russian authorities in response to political pressure are nevertheless appreciated. Naturally, one can never prove if the situation would not have been worse without constant European supervision.

Nevertheless, as the situation is right now, legal means seem to be the most promising way, as Russia is respecting the ECtHR more than any other such institution. The court, though, is dependent on cases brought by citizens of Russia, sometimes concerning very detailed questions. All the same, the court tries to address questions on a very general level. Unfavorably, the court is only concerned with breaches of the negative obligations of states and not with the positive obligation of Russia to ensure media plurality[144]—a task the court cannot fulfill. To date, however, legal pressure is the best way to promote freedom of expression in Russia. It is not impossible to slowly convince Russian courts to adopt the same standards as the ECtHR and to harmonize human-rights law

143 Case of *Dyuldin and Kislov v. Russia, op.cit.* note 137, para. 43; see, also, CoE PACE, "Towards decriminalisation of defamation" (4 October 2007) Resolution 1577.

144 Christian Jacq and Francis Teitgen, "The Press", in Mireille Delmas-Marty (ed.), *The European Convention for the Protection of Human Rights: International Protection versus National Restrictions* (Martinus Nijhoff Publishers, Dordrecht, Boston, London, 1992), 59-81, at 62, 64.

and domestic law subsequently. The more often Russia loses defamation cases, the more it should internalize the reasoning of the Court.

Why Are European Organizations Not More Successful?

What are the reasons for the constant rejections of European ideas and proposals by the Russian authorities and Russian society? As the immense literature on European-Russian relations testifies, which we shall analyze in part below, there is no easy answer to this question. To overcome the tangle of sometimes contradictory historical, sociological, philosophical and mere pragmatic explanations, one has to draw a distinction between obstacles at the conceptual level and at the level of implementation. Rebutting the 'ideological' arguments will pave the way for further pragmatic considerations. It will be demonstrated that none of the obstacles on both levels are insurmountable.

Some arguments—especially those focusing on a specific Russian national tradition and mentality—have to be read very carefully, as they tend to oversimplify historical and sociological processes. History is never linear and easy to grasp; rather, it is a row of achievements, regressions, eruptions and unexpected events. Accordingly, historical and modern societies are never monolithic but, rather, composed of competing groups and actors with different preferences and ideas. Hence the 'Russian mentality' applies probably only to a dominant social group at a specific time, but it does not necessarily also determine the course of events in the future. In other word, identifying the dominant historical and societal forces helps us to explain the current behavior of the Russian authorities, journalists, and broader society—but they do not dictate them once and for all.

Even if now the mass of people stands behind the regime, the situation could change if a critical mass changed their position. According to American political scientist John Zaller, society is composed of the elite (1-2%), a maximum of 5-10% of people who have an interest in politics and 90% of people who can be influenced in one direction or another.[145] Even if these numbers are contestable, the theory is probably right that the mass of people does not determine the political direction of a state but, rather, only some more or less influential minority groups. In that sense, it is feasible to change public opinion. Instead of convincing every single Russian citizen (out of approximately 142 million), 'only' some leading figures and groups in public life have to adopt another position and their message will probably spread. In that sense, it is still not decided whether Russia will develop in an authoritarian direction or whether liberal forces will prevail in the end.

Generally, human-rights work needs the prospect of social change, otherwise all its efforts to address governments and civil society would be in vain.

[145] Quoted in Trudolyubov, *op.cit.* note 46, 101; and see John R. Zaller, *The Nature and Origins of Mass Opinion* (Cambridge University Press, Cambridge, 1992).

A Clash of Ideas?

Confronted with criticism from European organizations, Russian politicians, scholars, and other public figures mainly use two counterarguments that are closely interconnected. *First*, they claim the West has no right to interfere in Russia's affairs. *Second*, they emphasize a different understanding of statehood, democracy, and human rights, including freedom of expression in the Russian context. Both arguments have been used as long as Russian-European relations have existed, and they have never been uncontested. Instead of uncritically maintaining the position of cultural relativism, which is supported by the ruling forces in Russia, one should rather look out for alternatives. It will be shown below that the idea of the universal applicability of human rights has also been influential in Russia.

The Never-Ceasing Debate Between Slavophiles and Westernizers

The mutual influence of European and Russian history should not be ignored. A short outline of modern history shows that nothing can be done in either Europe or Russia without being noticed by the 'Other'.[146] In the eighteenth century, Russia was a guarantor of the European balance of power and an important partner for most European states. This 'friendship of monarchs' was challenged by the constitutional movement all over Europe and the eruption of revolutions in Europe at the end of the eighteenth and in the nineteenth century, and eventually by the October Revolution in Russia. Much mistrust and skepticism could be found on both sides following these events. The twentieth century was often nothing other than an open confrontation between two different models of society: communism and capitalism. After the collapse of the communist bloc, European-Russian 'friendship' has intensified once again. With common membership in organizations such as the CoE and the OSCE, linkages between both were more and more formalized, if not legalized. In recent years, there seems to be a worsening of mutual relations, however, as the previous chapter tells. Overall, the relationship between Russia and Europe has never been constant and uncontroversial, but it always existed in one form or another.

The same applies to debates about European-Russian relations that went hand-in-hand with historical changes. As in all other historical contexts, there was never only a single position—even if one prevailed in the end. In his opus *Russia and the Idea of Europe*, Iver Neumann analyzes the history of ideas in Russia with a focus on the perception of Europe in detail. For Neumann, Russian history has always been dominated by two positions, which he—as many others—has termed 'Slavophiles' and 'Westernizers' and which later transformed into 'Romantic Nationalists' and 'Liberals'.[147] Even if they were marginalized at

146 Iver B. Neumann, *Russia and the Idea of Europe: A Study in Identity and International Relations* (Routledge, London, New York, NY, 1996), 1.

147 *Ibid.*, 28ff., 41ff., 158ff.

certain times, especially during the time of Soviet ideology, they never ceased to exist. For Neumann, the period after 1991 is a continuation of the struggle between both groups.

It is the very relation with Europe that makes the difference between the two positions. Slavophiles/Romantic Nationalists emphasize the uniqueness of Russia and its people, pointing at its incomparable history, its own religious traditions, or the Russian mentality. The proposition that identity is always dependent on differences—which was formulated by none other than Georg Wilhelm Friedrich Hegel—is confirmed by the fact that Slavophiles/Romantic Nationals always contrast Russia with Europe. Generally, Europe is perceived as morally inferior—even if it might be stronger in the economic or military sphere. It is an ongoing challenge for Russia to resist its temptations and to stick to its own traditions. Accordingly, any interference by Europe in Russian affairs is seen as a threat or even as an attack.

The Westernizers, by contrast, do not perceive European ideas and behavior as a threat but, rather, as an example to follow. Westernizers—such as Friedrich F. von Martens (1845-1909), the diplomat and legal scholar who taught in St. Petersburg—claim that European models are the best means of civilization.[148] Only in following this path will Russia become a truly modern country. For that reason, European interference is seen as a necessary help. Today, most Westernizers would rather call themselves liberals so as to not indirectly support the idea of Slavophiles that Russia and Europe are completely different societies.

The primary problem of Neumann's analysis is that he does not seem to be aware of this problem. In the end, I would not draw the line between Slavophiles and Westernizers but, rather, between Nationalists and Liberals in the sense that both have a totally different understanding of history and society. The former maintain a kind of cultural exceptionalism, whereas the latter would claim that certain patterns repeat themselves in different societies. In human-rights terminology, this is nothing other than the famous discussion about cultural relativism and universalism.

However, even if the description of the Russian history of ideas as a continuous battle between two forces runs the danger of simplifying the debate—as next to these two positions, there are not only communist forces but, certainly, many others as well—it is a valuable tool for examining the debate in Russia about the West in recent times. Again, one can discern the very same positions. The state-controlled media usually use the language of the Nationalists in their endeavor to show Russia as a unique country. In a 2008 article, Irina Maryniak scrutinizes the grand narrative of the Putin-Medvedev regime:

148 Lauri Mälksoo, "The History of International Legal Theory in Russia: A Civilizational Dialogue with Europe", 19(1) *European Journal of International Law* (2008), 211-232, at 221.

> "To the outside world, Putin has presented a Russia that is talented, tough, with a vigorous tradition, and determined to continue developing in a way wholly its own, undistorted by the insipid superficialities of western culture and ambition. Russia is different, and will not be patronised into a false sense that is merely a peripheral and under-civilised annexe to Western Europe."[149]

An opposing position is hardly audible in the media; thus, most Russians are constantly exposed to these ideas. Critical journalists and human-rights activists resisting the current regime, however, would define themselves as 'liberals' or 'democrats'.[150]

The clear distinction between Nationalists and Liberals, however, becomes blurred when Russian authorities address European powers or when they have to react to their reproaches. To not destroy the good economic relations and other cooperation in the sphere of security and the war on terror, interstate rhetoric is cooperative and friendly. But one can read between the lines that the old mistrust has not disappeared. One example is the 2005 statement of Foreign Minister Lavrov in an interview with the Russian newspaper *Izvestiia*:

> "Many Western capitals are already wondering about the ultimate results of the building up of suspicion and hostility toward Russia [...] The casualties may be mutual understanding and confidence in our relations that have been built up with such difficulty in the years since the end of the cold war. To prevent that happening mutual efforts are needed. Russia is trying to cover its part of the way, demonstrating openness and readiness for dialogue, constantly seeking mutually acceptable solutions of issues that divide us. But our partners would be well advised to renounce some stereotypes that damage mutual confidence."[151]

On some occasions, however, especially when it comes to criticism of the democratic behavior of Russia during elections or its human-rights record, the Russian government uses exactly the same arguments that were used already hundreds of years ago by Slavophiles. In reaction to OSCE criticism for refusing international election observers, Putin said that Russia—as a sovereign state—does not permit a foreign adjustment of its elections.[152] Another example is the already-mentioned letter to the RFOM, where Lavrov explicitly calls the criticism "propagandist attempts to discredit the Russian parliamentary elections being undertaken by certain forces in the West".[153] Often, criticism by NGOs or by Russian opposi-

149 Irina Maryniak, "Phoenix Rising: A Grand Narrative is Being Written", 37(1) *Index on Censorship* (2008), 105-115, at 108.

150 Rostova, interview, *op.cit.* note 32; and Zherdeva, interview, *op.cit.* note 47.

151 Ministry of Foreign Affairs of the Russian Federation, Information and Press Department, Interview with Russian Foreign Minister Sergei Lavrov, originally published in *Izvestiia* (10 February 2005).

152 Elke Windisch, "Präsidentschaftswahlen: OSZE sagt Mission in Russland ab: Wahlbeobachter unerwünscht: Die russischen Präsidentschaftswahlen im März werden von der OSZE nicht vor Ort unter die Lupe genommen", *Der Tagesspiegel* (8 February 2008).

153 Ministry of Foreign Affairs of the Russian Federation, *op.cit.* note 105.

tion politicians prompts the reproach that they are stooges of the West.[154] When Putin was asked why Garry Kasparov had been put in jail, he answered:

> "Why did Mr. Kasparov, when arrested, speak out in English rather than Russian? When a politician works the crowd of other nations rather than the Russian nation, it tells you something."[155]

To sum up, one can say that the argument of Western intruders can still be found in Russian discourse; but, mostly, it is not expressed openly to avoid an open confrontation with Europe. For pragmatic reasons, the Russian authorities chose the way of cooperation and dialogue—at least rhetorically—instead of maintaining old patterns. Historical arguments are still used, but they are not the only determinants any more.

This also is a chance for European organizations. As long as they have other means of persuasion—such as economic benefits or the prospect of a democratic reputation—Russia will not react openly against them. These short-term tactical considerations, however, are not sufficient to rebut the idea of non-interference once and for all. Without a positive answer to the question of whether European organizations have authorization to interfere in Russia, all action taken by European organizations would be unjustified. But there are good arguments on the conceptual level as well; *first and foremost*, the legal principle of *pacta sunt servanda*. In joining an organization such as the OSCE and in signing and ratifying the ECHR, Russia voluntarily submitted itself to the scrutiny of these organizations. Even if Russia's accession to the CoE was accomplished at a time when Russian-European relations were more harmonious, obligations under international law are not temporary or dependent on the actual political situation. Otherwise, legal treaties would be reduced to mere politics. As long as the Russian Federation does not withdraw from its treaties, it is bound by them. *Second*, Russia itself is very fond of being 'part of international society'.[156] Otherwise, it would not have joined the different organizations and would not attend their meetings. It frequently makes use of the international mechanism on its own—in questioning the way Estonia and Latvia treat the Russian minority,[157] for instance. One can even observe an increase of invocations of international law by Russia—most exemplary, before and after Kosovo's declaration of independence. It is a question of fairness that other states can approach Russia as well. *Third*, apart from the EU,

154 United Nations, Human Rights Council, Report of the Special Rapporteur, Amebyi Ligabo, Addendum, Summary of cases transmitted to Governments and replies received, UN Index: A/HRC/4/27/Add.1 (26 March 2007), 2ff.

155 "The Time Interview: Putin Opens a Window on His Life", 170(26/27) *Time Magazine* (2007), 42ff.

156 Aalto, *op.cit.* note 100, 459ff.; and "Wir waren naiv" (interview with Dmitrii Medvedev), *Der Spiegel* (9 November 2009), available at <http://www.spiegel.de/spiegel/print/d-67682716.html>.

157 Aalto, *op.cit.* note 100, 468.

European organizations do not criticize Russia from outside. Instead of upholding the facile distinction between one European community and their values and organizations and the Russian 'Other', it would be more appropriate to speak about internal quarrels *within* these organizations. Accordingly, all the means described are internal control mechanisms. *Last but not least*, one can submit that European organizations are obliged to interfere in Russian domestic politics by their very mandate. It is their objective to monitor the human-rights situation, the status of democracy and the rule of law in its member states. Human rights are today no longer the internal affair of individual countries, however powerful. In the end, the question of whether they have authorization to interfere in Russia can be affirmed without any doubt.

Another Idea of Freedom of Expression?

But even if Russia were keen to cooperate with the West, it would not necessarily accept the European understanding of human rights and implement all proposals in its domestic system. Quite the opposite: the Russian authorities claim that the idea of human rights should not be understood in a European—hence individualist—sense. Europeans like to see them as personal guarantees against the state whereas, in Russia, individualism has never been very influential. From the very beginning, the unity of the Russian people and a collective Russian spirit are considered to be more important than individual self-fulfillment. Accordingly, it is not advisable to endanger the functioning of the whole society if only some people benefit from it.[158] This is especially true with regard to political rights and freedom of expression in particular—those human rights that are intrinsically linked with 'individualism'.

Thinking in these terms, the Russian authorities often stress journalists' 'duties and responsibilities' toward national unity and security. This is noticeable especially in the context of terrorism, where freedom of expression is always outbalanced by national security.[159] But also in other contexts, the reputation of others, public interest, national security and the functioning of the political regime seem to be legitimate reasons to restrict freedom of expression, as has been analyzed before. This touches the very substance of the notion of freedom of expression. Does freedom of expression really have a different status in the Russian Federation than in some other smaller, well-consolidated European democracies?

Arguably, collectivism—being different from totalitarianism—does not imply a total neglect of individuals and their legitimate rights. Instead of maintaining a different notion of freedom of expression in the European and in the Russian context, I would assent to a universal understanding of freedom of

158 Maryniak, *op.cit.* note 149, 112; Rudinsky, *op.cit.* note 6, 58; and Sergej Kowaljow, "War Isaac Newton ein Westler? Russlands Weg zur Geltung der Menschenrechte", in *Russland auf dem Weg zum Rechtstaat? Antworten aus der Zivilgesellschaft*, *op.cit.* note 30, 42-51, at 42.

159 Simons and Strovsky, *op.cit.* note 19, 193, 205.

expression. It should be stressed that it is not possible to limit freedom of expression excessively, as it will undermine the whole concept. There is an internal logic in Article 10. If the provisions of Article 10(2) always win over affirmation of the right, the provision loses its meaning and could all the same be abandoned. Or in less legal terms: if no one dares to criticize the state anymore as this could threaten national security and unity, freedom of expression has simply ceased to exist.

In that sense, the Russian concept of freedom of expression is only a concealment of the authoritarian tendencies of its media system. Russia is permanently violating the right to freedom of expression, and all its excuses, that it has simply balanced it differently, are sheer rhetorical tricks—obscuring the fact of a controlled media and stifled criticism. Those responsible are very clever indeed: while controlling the most important medium in Russia, the television, and while excluding the most explosive topics, they allow a few relatively independent media outlets and public discussion on less restricted topics. Asked by domestic organizations or by European human-rights defenders, they would always point to them—thereby showing that media freedom exists in Russia. With good reason, this has been described as 'cardboard imitations' of press freedom by RSF.[160] Probably the Russian authorities are aware that total censorship would provoke overwhelming counter-reactions from both civil society and European organizations.

European organizations, especially their strong member states, should not be satisfied with Russian excuses but, rather, should force Russian authorities to make a decision. Either they abandon the right to freedom of expression officially—so that Europe would know what kind of regime it is confronted with and could take appropriate measures, an option that is not very likely at the moment—or they should take the concept of freedom of expression more seriously. In the end, it is not the ECtHR approaching Russia with the pledge to protect freedom of expression according to its standards but, rather, Russia should decide if it wants at all to maintain the value of freedom of expression, which is intrinsically linked with a pluralistic, tolerant and broadminded democracy. Or to put it more bluntly: Russia should decide whether its membership in the CoE, with its affirmation of democracy, human rights, and the rule of law, is still compatible with its own practice. Therefore, the question how freedom of expression is interpreted in Russia is rather a question of whether Russia is still a democracy. If and only if Russia wants to maintain freedom of expression in its Constitution and in other legal provisions, it should apply it according to the European (or even universal) standard. That does not mean that the scope of the right has to be exactly the same as in Europe, where it also varies from country to country, but it cannot be restricted endlessly. Under a certain threshold, that is, when the limitation always prevails over the right to express one's own opinion, it makes no sense to talk of a right to freedom of expression any longer. European organizations only

160 Becker, *op.cit.* note 30, 157.

want Russia to keep its word. Mere asseverations that 'freedom of the press is one of the basic conditions for developing democracy in the country' and that Russia will 'listen to criticism' are not enough.[161] The Russian authorities should match their actions with their words.

Today, many Russian citizens working in the field of journalism or human rights would affirm this assessment that the high esteem of media freedom is only a façade. Instead of supporting the position of the government, they maintain a universal understanding of human rights and freedom of expression, respectively.[162] When asked whether there are different standards in Russia and in Europe, Igor Iakovenko, head of the RUJ, replies cynically:

> "Yes there are: The government would like to protect its own right to steal, to be independent from its own people, the right to violate human rights—and at the same time using all profits of the European civilisation. Their children have good education in Britain, and they keep their money in Swiss banks, in France or in some other countries. It's clear. I would like to highlight something: There are not two freedoms or two democracies; there is one right and one freedom and one quality: good or bad. Freedom either exists or not."[163]

Alexei Simonov also remarks sarcastically:

> "We remain a country where you can murder disloyal journalists with impunity, but which reacts over sensitively when international organisations place it at the bottom of their press freedom rankings. Evidently the 'sovereignty' in our democracy means that we want to be, if not top in the rankings, then in a league of our own."[164]

Not only civil-society activists but, also, Russian legal scholars presume a universal understanding of human rights. Introducing his book about civil rights in Russia, Rudinsky gives a true panegyric for the universal character of human rights:

> "In Western Europe and America there is a tendency to identify human rights with values of the western Atlantic civilisation, but it is an erroneous representation. [...] Russia has contributed to the formation and recognition of the [...] universal concept of human rights."[165]

The whole debate cannot be reduced to an 'ideological' clash between Europe and Russia. It is rather the continuous struggle of different positions within Russia. Although the position of cultural exceptionalism prevails at the moment, Russian citizens will not necessarily also support its propositions in the future. It is possible that more and more people will see the contradiction in the term 'sovereign democracy' and will try to change a *pro forma* democracy into real public participation.

161 Ministry of Foreign Affairs of the Russian Federation, Information and Press Department, Interview with correspondents from the Dutch television channel *Nederland 1* and the daily newspaper *NRC Handelsblad* (31 October 2005).

162 Zherdeva, interview, *op.cit.* note 47; and Grishina, interview, *op.cit.* note 28.

163 Iakovenko, interview, *op.cit.* note 38.

164 Simonov, *op.cit.* note 67, 73.

165 Rudinsky, *op.cit.* note 6, 12ff.

A Complex Task

Having rebutted all conceptual arguments, it seems to be less difficult to break through the other obstacles. Yet it is not an easy task to overcome the difficulties arising at a 'mere' pragmatic level. Currently, implementation of legal standards at every sublevel of society is even a major challenge for European organizations. In pursuing this task, they are actually faced with a complex web of responsibilities and competences. I will show that it is not sufficient to convince the governmental authorities—which is a difficult task in itself—although they have the main responsibility and the greatest power to turn the situation of the media for the worse or for the better.[166] Without functioning institutions directly or indirectly linked with the media system and without sufficient support in civil society, the situation will not change—even if governmental authorities are willing.[167] At the end of this chapter, some initiatives from civil-society organizations, which are partly supported by European organizations, will be presented and discussed.

Lack of Political Will

First and foremost, implementation of European proposals founder on the constant reluctance of the governmental authorities. In states with authoritarian tendencies such as Russia, an independent media is often perceived as the main enemy to the power consolidation of political forces.[168] In that sense, it is the first sector of society that has to be brought under control to guarantee the integrity and stability of the Russian state.[169] The media are certainly not an innocent democratic means but, rather, a powerful tool to gain or lose power; therefore, particularly 'dangerous' topics such as terrorist incidents and opposition parties are banned from public discourse. At the sight of the enormous size of the Russian state and its constant struggles with separatist groups close to its borders, one can understand the ruling political forces: somehow, they 'have' to suppress the media for their very survival. European organizations often underestimate the power dimension of the media, as their formal appeals to respect media freedom for the sake of democratization testify. But even if they noticed it, they were in

166 Becker, *op.cit.* note 30, 140, 146ff., 158.

167 Crowfoot, *op.cit.* note 76, 78; Becker, *op.cit.* note 30, 140ff.; and Simonow, *op.cit.* note 30, 82.

168 Mommsen and Nussberger, *op.cit.* note 2, 47; and interview with Igor Aleksandrovich Iakovenko, *op.cit.* note 38: When asked why the government is so afraid of an independent media, Iakovenko answered:

> "I think it [the media] is more dangerous than you could expect. Try to look around the world from Putin's and his colleagues viewpoint. Try to catch Yukos when there is an independent media around you. How to experience such a disaster like the Beslan tragedy, the Nord Ost hostage case and the Kursk submarine disaster?"

169 Simonow, *op.cit.* note 30, 82, 84; Azhgikhina, *op.cit.* note 29, 1256; and Tscherkassow, *op.cit.* note 30, 100.

a difficult situation. How can they expect the Russian government to allow an independent media that threatens that government's very existence?

It is obvious that appeals to governments that have already departed from the democratic way and where the media are already under state control can no longer be effective. There are not many options left. Next to continuing appeals to the government—which could be harsher than at the moment—they can only try to circumvent the ruling elites and address other political actors within Russia, which have to question the legitimacy of their government themselves.

The Institutional Blockade: Overcoming Self-Censorship

To understand the relatively rapid shift of most media outlets towards the governmental position, one has also to take into account the decisions of managers and journalists themselves, whose responsibilities have not been discussed sufficiently so far. It is undeniable that next to governmental pressure, 'voluntary' cooperation between journalists and the state is the main reason for current state control over the media. It seems that after the troublesome 1990s—with their fierce competition between media outlets—many managers welcomed the help of the state. For a small change of reporting, they could gain a lot of support—not only financially. After the forced change of ownership of *NTV* and *ORT*/Channel One, many journalists decided to support the new line of the channel.[170] Self-censorship was visible especially after terrorist incidents such as Beslan, where most TV channels "followed a strict routine of 'self-imposed' guidelines in their coverage of the events".[171] In the regions, too, self-censorship is an enormous problem, as most regional journalists are much more dependent on the benevolence of local governors. During the election campaign for the State *Duma*, for example, newspapers in Kirov *Oblast'* were offered large amounts of 'charitable aid' from local governors if they stopped disseminating negative information about United Russia. Sadly enough, it worked out: only one newspaper, *Viatskii nabliudatel'*, continued writing in a critical style.[172] Throughout the country, managers and journalists submitted themselves to the control of the state, thereby accepting the limited scope of topics for their own personal benefit. With a carrot and a stick, it was very easy to bring nearly the entire community of journalists under control. It is mere speculation what would have happened if journalists had resisted more in the 1990s.

Today, most critical journalists become very angry when talking about this lack of professional ethics of their colleagues.[173] Even if it can be explained by

170 Azhgikhina, *op.cit.* note 29, 1260; Simons and Strovsky, *op.cit.* note 19, 189, 193ff.; and Simonow, *op.cit.* note 30, 86.

171 Simons and Strovsky, *op.cit.* note 19, 206.

172 Bachinin, *op.cit.* note 45, 132ff.; Aliev, *op.cit.* note 59, 144; and Eismont, *op.cit.* note 45, 124.

173 Simonov, *op.cit.* note 67, 71, 86; Azhgikhina, *op.cit.* note 29, 1248; "Journalists Union

the lack of democratic experience among most journalists who grew up during the Soviet era or by the demanding economic circumstances in the 1990s, it is not justifiable. Self-censorship is illegitimate, as it undermines belief in the independence and impartiality of the media and leads to its total control. The more a media system is influenced, the more difficult it is for editors and for journalists to resist the pressure of the state. They increasingly have to fear for the existence of media outlets or their jobs or even for their physical integrity. That is why journalists who maintain a strong position against state authorities are even more admirable. As Simonov, head of the GDF, formulates it: "Reporters have been growing ever more reluctant to do their job honestly. In fact, this creates a system where the simple fulfillment of one's professional duty is seen almost as heroism."[174] It is a sign of hope that many known or unknown journalists are still fighting against the governmental authorities—convinced that the journalistic community will rediscover their social and moral responsibility one day.

The Institutional Blockade: Partiality of the Judiciary

As Russian authorities often forward journalistic 'offenses' to the courts, the judiciary is in a prominent position to either protect journalists and media outlets against state pressure or to compromise media freedom by legal means. The latter is the case in most Russian courts.[175] The ECtHR defamation cases discussed earlier illustrate that judicial bodies are often misusing their power. The dependence of the judiciary on executive and legislative power—and, as such, the abandoning of checks and balances—is an immense problem. It calls into question whether Russia is still a state under the rule of law and a functioning democracy. Here, it has to suffice to cite the problem in general terms as a further discussion of the features of the legal system in Russia, in any meaningful detail, would go beyond the scope of this discussion.[176]

Arguably, one cannot change the situation of the media in Russia without also taking the judiciary into consideration. There are some journalistic, quasi-legal organizations in Russia, most prominently the GDF, but also Jurists for Constitutional Rights and Freedoms (JURIX) and the NGO Sutyajnik, which openly address the link between violations of media freedom and the judiciary. To this effect, they assist journalists in their defense when sued for libel or other 'misdemeanors'. Due to their legal skills, cases are very often decided in favor

Head Laments State of Media", *op.cit.* note 52; and interview with Svetlana Svistunova and Nadezhda Azhgikhina, *op.cit.* note 40.

174 Simonov, *op cit.* note 67, 71.

175 Becker, *op.cit.* note 30, 152ff.; and Bachinin, *op.cit.* note 45, 133.

176 For further discussion see, *inter alia*, Burkov, *op.cit.* note 10, 69ff.; Kowaljow, *op.cit.* note 158, 47ff.; and Rudinsky, *op.cit.* note 6, 14ff.

of the accused.[177] For many scholars, legal defense is one of the most promising ways to defend freedom of expression in Russia.[178]

To some extent, European organizations are already aware of the fact that media freedom has to be promoted more systematically: often naming the situation of the media and impunity in the same breath. It is high on the agenda of the CoE to promote reforms of the legal system in Russia through conferences, consultations and training of lawyers by the European Commission for Democracy through Law, the so-called Venice Commission.[179] After a visit of a Court delegation to Moscow, the President of the Court, Jean Paul Costa, said in a press release in May 2007 "that the meetings with senior Russian judges had shown that there was a high degree of support within the judiciary for the international human-rights protection system set up by the European Convention on Human Rights".[180] In the long run, a well-functioning domestic legal system would protect journalists against undue interference by state authorities.

Public Unawareness

Most Russian citizens are unaware of the media's current situation, as activists working in the field of media rights and journalists acknowledge.[181] In a way, this is not surprising: propaganda always intends to create a society that is oblivious of the forces leading it and of the dangers lurking in the current political regime. Excessive use of entertainment programs works such as narcotics—making people forget about social problems and political challenges. Possibly, many Russian citizens who get their main information from television would even say that the media are free, as seemingly there is such a wide array of topics. Unlike Soviet times, where one could not escape the communist propaganda and where people felt controlled, today, propaganda is less apparent; this is why the current regime is much more successful. From a philosophical point of view, it is not a counter-argument against control of the media that people are not aware of it; quite the reverse: it is evidence of how successfully society has already been manipulated. But even if one can explain the ignorance of the people, the situation is rather

177 See, for instance, case of *Filatenko v. Russia*, *op.cit.* note 134, para. 34.

178 Burkov, *op.cit.* note 10, 53ff., 65.

179 Jordan, *op.cit.* note 109, 685ff.; and Egbert Myer, "Cooperation between National Authorities and the Council of Europe: Experiences in Capacity Building of the Judiciary", Report of the Seminar "Implementation of Human Rights: The Efficiency of Justice in the Council of Europe and its Member States", Netherlands Ministry of Foreign Affairs, NCJM, Dutch section of the International Commission of Jurists (19-20 April 2004), The Hague, Leiden, 59.

180 CoE, ECtHR, "Russian visit encouraging says Court President" (15 May 2007) Press release 312.

181 Zherdeva, interview, *op.cit.* note 47; Grishina, interview, *op.cit.* note 28; and Rostova, interview, *op.cit.* note 32.

tricky. How can European organizations possibly interfere in Russia, if Russian society itself does not want to change the situation? And how can it be justified to the Russian government?

In the first place, European organizations could ignore Russian society. Most of them, most notably the EU, have indeed adopted this way of thinking when solely consulting with government officials. When confronted with the objection that Russian citizens themselves do not want to change the situation, they could simply point at their own experience with totalitarianism and people's unquestioning obedience to have 'moral' legitimacy to interfere. From that perspective, any such interference would not cause harm to the Russian people but change the situation in Russia for their own good. However, even if the basic assumptions might be right, it is a very dangerous attitude. With some talent, leaders in Russia could turn the Russian people against Europe—arguing in the same categories as discussed in "The Never-Ceasing Debate..." above. Interference by European organizations could be interpreted as an arrogant attitude towards Russia. As an answer, concepts of collectivism, sovereign democracy and the responsibilities of journalists for the country's unity and security would come up again. It is obvious that the method of ignorance is not the best means of promoting freedom of expression, as it plays into the hands of nationalists.

The only possibility to avoid such negative effects is to take the country's society into account. Human-rights protection can only be lasting if both governmental officials and normal citizens internalize the values promoted. Without the individual desire to freely express one's opinion, freedom of expression will never have social effect. Below, I will present some of the main reasons why Russian society is not (yet) willing to promote freedom of expression and prospects to overcome them.

Public Unawareness: Trust in the Authorities

A common stereotype about the Russian people is their trust in authorities. As 'proved' by Russian history, the Russian nation seems to need a strong leader. Many Russian scholars claim that the 'Russian national tradition' still determines the relationship between the citizen and state power. People would submit uncritically to the leader's will.[182] Sometimes, state authorities confirm that they still see themselves as sovereigns in the literal sense:

> "Only a strong state can ensure human rights, equality and freedom for all and not only those who had good luck in the course of privatization. We are still in the stage of creating it—we're in the process of a search for optimal forms of a state model for Russia."[183]

In such a model, individuals are mere servants of greater powers. Frustrated, Babchenko remarks: "The Russian people never aspired to freedom; they always

182 Kowaljow, *op.cit.* note 158, 43f; Rostova, *op.cit.* note 35, 159; Trudolyubov, *op.cit.* note 46, 98, 101; and Lucas, *op.cit.* note 33, 34.

183 Lavrov, interview, *op.cit.* note 151.

aspired to having a kind tsar. In fact, we're closer to Ancient Egypt—where a pharaoh was seen as the embodiment of God—than to modern civilisation."[184] Is it really true that the model of civil society that has proved successful in Europe does not work in Russia and that Russians simply need a strong leader?

These ideas are not uncontested within Russia. Indeed, there are very good arguments against a specific Russian mentality and historical necessity. *First of all*, history is certainly not as simple as depicted in the narrative of the strong leader. In opposition to this one-sided interpretation, democratic thinkers point at the democratic administration of Velikii Novgorod to prove that democracy is not (only) a Western European invention. Or they show that the constitutional movement in Russia is as old as authoritarianism. In the worst times of the USSR, dissidents were protesting against the regime, often risking their lives in seemingly hopeless situations. They maintain that even if the course of history has often favored other positions, the battle for individual rights, public participation and a just society also is deep in the heart of Russians.[185] *Second*, there are examples of other (now democratic) countries, which have been confronted with similar arguments, most notably Germany, which had been struggling with the argument of the German '*Sonderweg*' until 1945. Recent history, however, shows that German society is not fixed to a trust in authorities. Certainly it had to undergo bitter historical experience, but eventually public awareness changed. As the future course of (Russian) history is unknown, no one can eliminate the possibility that one day Russia could also overcome authoritarian tendencies. And *third*, it is very difficult to assess how many Russians indeed support the regime of Putin/Medvedev. The often quoted number of 80-90%[186] has to be read carefully: as the only means of measuring popular opinions are "public opinion polls, most of which are conducted by Putin loyalists such as *VTsIOM* (All-Russia Center for the Study of Public Opinion)",[187] they are not reliable. Neutrally measured, the outcome of surveys would be different. Probably the number of supporters would still be very high, but it is unlikely that nearly everybody would sacrifice their human rights for the benefit of a strong hand in the Kremlin. Hence, foreign observers and scholars themselves have to be careful not to be misled by the data that opinion polls produce and by the pro-Kremlin atmosphere of the mass media. This all shows that the idea of a flourishing civil society is not a utopia but a realistic aim for the years to come; at least it is not incompatible with Russian society. How long it will take to make democrats out of people with

184 Babchenko, *op.cit.* note 51, 119.

185 Alexander Daniel, "Im Geist der Freiheit: Zur Geschichte der Menschen- und Bürgerrechtsbewegung in Russland", in *Russland auf dem Weg zum Rechtstaat? Antworten aus der Zivilgesellschaft*, *op.cit.* note 30, 18-41, at 18ff.; and Kowaljow, *op.cit.* note 158, 47ff.

186 Leonard and Popescu, *op.cit.* note 93, 7; and Lucas, *op.cit.* note 33, 33.

187 Medvedev, *op.cit.* note 93, 21.

a tendency to look up to a 'tsar' is unclear, but it is certainly not as improbable as some writers might suggest.

This is especially important for freedom of expression, the exercise of which presupposes that the individual and the state authorities are not in a mere relationship of obedience. If people were not allowed to criticize the state authorities and to adopt a position different from the official point of view, the right to freedom of expression would lose its true meaning. European organizations are right that one can only exercise this right in a democratic society, where different opinions are not only permitted but even asked for. In the end, it is the same choice between authoritarianism and democracy again, but this time by the Russian people and especially by journalists. Either Russian society maintains its passivity, submissiveness and 'support' as the narrative of the 'Russian way' tells it—but then democracy and a state under the rule of law cannot be realized—or it chooses democracy more decisively to gain all the human rights that democracy promises. But this implies that Russian society itself has to become more active, challenging and critical. Obviously, it is not an easy task to overcome the legacy of the 'all-enveloping state',[188] but it is not impossible.

Public Unawareness: Democratization: A Swearword?

But exactly this choice for democracy is another deep problem for many in Russia. Unlike in the West, in Russia the word democracy, and with it the implied rights of freedom of assembly and freedom of expression, evokes very bad associations: as the 1990s are commonly referred to as 'democratic', many people think that democratic societies have similar problems as experienced under El'tsin, *i.e.*, ideological and economic insecurity.[189] Only when the more authoritarian ruler Putin came to power did the overall situation of the country improve, which is seen as proof that democracy does not work.

In theory, it is very easy to rebut this idea. *First and foremost*, one would have to show that the situation in the 1990s was not as democratic as many politicians claimed and as the West wanted to believe. Against the initial hope of people to decide the destiny of their country on their own, they were again dominated by the old political elites, who simply turned to other parties, or by new economic elites—partly because they had no experience of resisting the authorities or of actively participating in political decision-making processes.[190] *Second*, one would have to establish that the amelioration of the economic situation at the end of the 1990s had nothing to do with abandoning democracy. After the severe depression in the 1990s, an economic conjuncture was more than probable.

188 Crowfoot, *op.cit.* note 76, 78; and Simons and Strovsky, *op.cit.* note 19, 201.

189 Lucas, *op.cit.* note 33, 34; Trudolyubov, *op.cit.* note 46, 98; Medvedev, *op.cit.* note 93, 17; and interview with Nataliia Rostova, *op.cit.* note 32.

190 Lucas, *op.cit.* note 33, 26.

In practice, however, it is much more difficult to disentangle the transitional problems of the 1990s and the idea of democracy. How to argue against the life experience of so many people? Certainly the process of 'enlightenment' will take time. One option would be to educate people to account for the past. Only if people understand their own process of transition from a totalitarian regime to an unconsolidated democracy and market economy could they see problems and shortcomings. Thus, they would understand that it is not the notion of democracy itself that is the reason for the disastrous circumstances in the 1990s. Another option would be to point at other countries in the world that have had similar problems and that were successfully transformed into democracies. This takes considerable reflection and, first and foremost, willingness. Russians would have to make a well-founded choice between old imperialistic ideas and social patterns on the one hand, and a democratic society on the other. The very last option is personal experience. If people experience that democracy—but perhaps one would have to invent another word for Russians—also brings benefits, there is a fair chance that people will change their minds.

Public Unawareness: Business Orientation

The latter problem is closely connected with another obstacle to a comprehensive democratization process, which is business orientation. For many people, it is sufficient to have a good life in an economic sense to feel satisfied with the current political situation.[191] According to an opinion poll by the BBC in December 2007, only 40% of Russians would agree that freedom of the press is very important,[192] and according to a Public Opinion Fund survey, most Russian citizens would rank it behind "welfare benefits, the right to work and a decent income".[193] In the regions, where poverty is still a considerable problem, people have other pressing needs than political participation and the exercise of freedom of expression. Often, they cannot or do not want to spend money on high-quality newspapers that are often more expensive than government-funded tabloids.[194] In the big cities, where the overall level of living is higher, many people do not care about civil and political rights either, contenting themselves with the benefits of a rich life. Especially in Moscow, one of the richest cities in Europe, a new business elite is forming that cooperates closely with the government. 'Having learned their lesson' from the experience of oligarchs such as Gusinskii and Berezovskii, today they do not oppose the government, and they are more successful. Indeed, they often receive grants and other forms of assistance from the state.[195]

191 Svistunova and Azhgikhina, interview, *op.cit.* note 40.

192 Lucas, *op.cit.* note 33, 34.

193 Trudolyubov, *op.cit.* note 46, 97.

194 Bachinin, *op.cit.* note 45, 134.

195 Becker, *op.cit.* note 30, 152.

For many critical journalists, it is very frustrating that this way of thinking is also present in the media sector—a sector that, by its nature, should follow other principles than economic interests and that has a serious responsibility toward readers. Many editors-in-chief of the big television channels and of tabloids have aligned themselves with the political leadership, and regional editors have also successfully adopted a business-oriented approach. Seemingly, many media theories that are "based on the prediction that financial sustainability of media companies would eventually lead to editorial independence" do not work—at least, not in the short run.[196] Adequate funding is a necessary condition for independence, but it is not sufficient.

Skillfully, the government takes advantage of the dominant interest in economic and social matters. In contrast to political reforms, social problems are dealt with much faster and are also discussed critically in public. The business orientation of society gives local and governmental elites the possibility to present themselves in the best way and thus to make the people satisfied with the regime. At the same time, it is a convenient means of distracting society from other problems.

Again, there is no easy solution for overcoming this utility thinking. One could argue in the same framework that true economic stability cannot be achieved without a certain level of political participation and the possibility to express one's opinion and problems. Otherwise, state authorities would always be in a position to arbitrarily exploit people or to illegitimately interfere in economic matters. However, as long as people do not feel this danger, the argument is rather soft. Apart from purely economic considerations, there are also strong moral and philosophical arguments. At first, one is reminded of the prominent discussion about the relation of civil and political rights, on the one hand, and economic, social and cultural rights, on the other. At the 1993 Vienna World Conference on Human Rights, it was concluded that none of these rights can be realized without the others due to their interdependence, so that it is not possible to maintain a hierarchy of these rights.[197] Another argument is perhaps more abstract, but strong all the same. Since antiquity, philosophers have been claiming human life to be more than the fulfillment of basic needs. Accordingly, society is more than a guarantor of welfare. There is perhaps another point in history when people would 'wake up' in the sense of the Greek enlightenment or the enlightenment in the eighteenth century and think of other benefits than economic ones. One cannot exclude the possibility that such a 'revolution' will happen in Russia again.

196 Eismont, *op.cit.* note 45, 125; see, also, Trudolyubov, *op.cit.* note 46, 101ff.

197 See the 1993 Vienna Declaration and Programme of Action: Sec.I para.5: "All human rights are universal, indivisible and interdependent and interrelated", available at <http://www.ohchr.org/en/professionalinterest/pages/vienna.aspx>.

Public Unawareness: Marginal Groups or the Beginning of a Civil Movement?

Due to these obstacles, formation of civil society is not an easy task, but many people working in existing civil-society organizations have a vision that one day the overall situation in the country could change toward broader public participation. Against the official emphasis of the government, NGOs, opposition parties and other civil-society organizations were only marginal groups, civil society, with over 30,000 different organizations, is booming in Russia and is probably stronger than leading figures want to believe.[198] As it is not possible to analyze the history, development and aims of the civil movement in Russia and the composition of the entire NGO sector with its manifold fields of interest,[199] only some organizations with a focus on media freedom will be mentioned in the following paragraphs. In a certain manner, these NGOs are pioneers paving the way for free exercise of freedom of expression and a flourishing civil society.

The mere existence of the RUJ, the largest organization of journalists in Russia, and of several Russian NGOs working in the field of media rights such as the GDF or the CJES shows that resistance is growing slowly but surely. To raise public awareness, they are constantly monitoring the situation on the ground and producing statistics and reports. Without their contribution, European observers would not know how serious the situation is. For these organizations themselves, it is very important that European organizations learn the truth. As an acknowledgement for their work, in 2007 the International Federation of Journalists (IFJ) held its world congress in Moscow, giving journalists and journalistic organizations the chance to speak up in public and to present their surveys. Much to the regret of the organizers, fewer officials appeared at the meeting than expected, and the mass media were nearly silent on the event.[200] But these organizations are not only passive; very often, they call for public action. To this effect, they have protested against further tightening of laws on several occasions—and sometimes successfully[201]—or organized marches in favor of freedom of expression. The RUJ and the Center for Public Information called for a public gathering in memory of Anna Politkovskaia, for example.[202] Furthermore,

198 Daniel, *op.cit.* note 185, 36; Simonow, *op.cit.* note 30, 84; and Tscherkassow, *op.cit.* note 30, 100.

199 See, *inter alia*, Daniel, *op.cit.* note 185, 18ff.

200 "'Our Journalists Have No Protection': An International Congress of Journalists is Convening in Moscow This Week as Concerns about Media Freedom in Russia Continue to Grow", *Radio Free Europe/Radio Liberty*, (29 May 2007), available at <http://www.rferl.org/content/article/1076780.html>; and Azhgikhina, *op.cit.* note 29, 1261.

201 Gessen, *op.cit.* note 34, 106; and "Russlands Präsident strukturiert um: Medwedjew kippt schärferes Mediengesetz", *Tagesschau* (4 June 2008), available at <http://archive.today/1SR2r>.

202 Grishina, interview, *op.cit.* note 28.

they have already initiated several projects—occasionally cooperating with European organizations. These are financial projects such as cooperation with Microsoft, as already mentioned, to prevent lawsuits for crimes in the IT sphere but, also, educational projects such as establishment of a center for independent media studies and journalism in the post-Soviet space. Organized by the RUJ, it is planned to function as a scientific institution, thus producing analytical surveys and reports, and also as a training center for journalists and other civil-society activists.[203] Moreover, the Moscow Helsinki Group, the oldest Russian NGO, has established educational projects (Youth Human-Rights Movement) promoting human rights and democratization in schools and universities in a systematic manner.[204] Apart from that, organizations such as the Center for Public Information, which connects the NGO sphere with the media, try to spread as much critical information as possible in newspapers—undermining strong governmental control: "NGOs should and must continue to work with the media, but they should do it in the right way not to make journalists nervous, not to be incorrect, not to unduly interfere with their work."[205] These are only some examples of a wide array of initiatives coming from committed Russian activists. Today, these organizations are not as powerful as they would like to be; but, with some governmental or social changes, they could develop their huge potential in the future.

European organizations should support these organizations and existing initiatives in a more comprehensive manner, instead of addressing only government authorities or randomly talking to 'the' media in Russia. This will lend credence to the struggle for media freedom—showing that freedom of expression is not only a European idea, but an idea for which the Russians also are fighting.

Conclusions

Finally, it is possible to identify the root cause of the malfunction of the European human-rights system. Surprisingly, it is not primarily an ideological clash between different cultures but, rather, a problem of implementation: in their function as intergovernmental organizations, most European organizations address their proposals first and foremost to governmental authorities instead of taking into account the institutional framework and the broader society of a country. Apparently, this model of government-centered human-rights and democracy promotion does not work satisfactorily in practice. On several occasions, the reluctance of the Russian authorities—consolidating their power by all possible means—has been insurmountable, which has then lead to nothing more than paperwork and a lot of rhetoric on both sides. To avoid similar results, European

203 Iakovenko, interview, *op.cit.* note 38.

204 Zherdeva, interview, *op.cit.* note 47.

205 Grishina, interview, *op.cit.* note 28.

organizations have to revise their enforcement mechanisms. I suggest that a true change in the Russian situation can only be achieved if the direction of their intervention changes.[206]

In a radical bottom-up approach, their missions should start with consultations with civil society in Russia. Effective protection of freedom of expression at the domestic level starts with the work of journalistic organizations and Russian NGOs that are also ready to fight for this right against an unwilling Russian government. Initially, they provide European organizations with the necessary information about the daily working conditions of journalists in Russia, follow up to lawsuits before domestic courts and measure the resonance of the independent media in broader society. Without their monitoring, intergovernmental human-rights organizations would not be able to fulfill their mandate in an appropriate manner. Today, some bodies—such as the RFOM or the Committee of Ministers of the CoE—are actually consulting with Russian organizations when assessing the situation on the ground. But Russian NGOs should not be reduced to mere monitoring organizations. More importantly, they create projects and programs to promote freedom of expression in Russia in a systematic way. Obviously, domestic civil-society organizations have the best insight to decide what action is truly effective. It would strengthen the power of both domestic organizations and intergovernmental organizations if they cooperated more closely.

As a second step, they could jointly implement freedom of expression at different levels. One has to be fair that there are already several attempts to integrate other sectors of society, most notably legal projects issued by the CoE and the individual complaint procedure of the ECtHR; but, so far, only a few truly comprehensive projects have been created. As media freedom is closely linked with educational matters and judicial review in particular and the overall process of democratization in general, all measures by European organizations have to be very broad as well. Only systematic implementation of freedom of expression in schools and universities, in the courts and in editorial offices themselves, will ensure that freedom of expression is protected in the long run. Taken separately, all measures are rather weak and limited. Promotion of freedom of expression and other human rights would be more effective with more actors actively participating in the very process of democratization.

Only as a last step should European organizations address the governmental authorities, or at least in parallel to other measures. It would lend credence to their struggle for media freedom, if they were supported by Russian civil society and by the relevant institutions in a state under the rule of law. Concertedly, they could

206 This is possible without changing the respective statutes/charters of European organizations, as the aims of these organizations are still the same. Mostly, the particular way of implementation is a political choice by the majority of member states, not prescribed in detail by the respective treaties.

question the legitimacy of the current regime with sufficient authority by making the government appear to be a power-crazed elite. A premature and unbolstered appeal to the government, by contrast, would indirectly play into the hands of those elites arguing in old patterns: again, Europe would be blamed for imposing its own ideas on the Russian people and its government. Deliberately, they would maintain the distinction between a united Russian people and government, on the one hand, and illegitimate external intruders on the other. There is certainly no better way to circumvent these historical arguments than a joint campaign from the most influential groups in Russia and European organizations. This new strategy obviously requires more money and commitment from the European side, but I argue that it is certainly the only way to improve the situation.

Understandably enough, opinions are divided whether it is possible to change the situation of the media in Russia or whether the proposed reform of European measures can be successful. Depending on their experiences and certainly also on their personalities, the reactions of journalists and civil-society activists range from outright pessimism, resignation and tiredness[207] to irrepressible optimism and activism.[208] The majority of human-rights defenders, though—including those I was able to speak with in the course of this research—still cling to the hope for a better future. Although most of them are quite realistic that change will not take place in the next few years, they do not believe that Russian society will remain passive and powerless forever. As Azhgikhina writes:

> "Society's need for such [independent] journalism is too strong, and the desire of very young journalists to practice precisely this kind of journalism is obvious—I see it in the students at the journalism department in Moscow University, in my young colleagues who work in the regions and who will not leave corrupt officials or the powers that be in peace. These are colleagues who prefer the more traditional values of the Russian intelligentsia—civic service and loyalty to truth—to those of mass culture. I would like to believe that these young people will look at the world without the rose-colored glasses and surrealistic specters of perestroika, and will break through the bastions of the predatory market and administrative interdictions just as grass pushes up through the asphalt."[209]

Mostly those activists cherishing hope are more active and effective in creating new projects and constantly addressing the government and international society. Seemingly, human-rights activists need the prospect of change for their daily work. European organizations do well to support these optimistic tendencies. When different action both at the domestic level and the international level comes together, the idea of a free society in which everyone can express their

207 "Ex-Kremlin Journalist Talks from UK Asylum", *Radio Free Europe/Radio Liberty* (8 April 2008), available at <http://www.rferl.org/featuresarticle/2008/04/22035904-7986-4176-b919-23f062624f9d.html>; Babchenko, *op.cit.* note 51, 119; and interview with Nataliia Rostova, *op.cit.* note 32.

208 Daniel, *op.cit.* note 185, 40; Zherdeva, interview, *op.cit.* note 47; and Grishina, interview, *op.cit.* note 28.

209 Azhgikhina, *op.cit.* note 29, 1254.

own views and share information without interference will not remain an empty philosophical promise, a legal standard with no impact in reality or a rhetorical tool in international relations. With Russia re-evaluating media freedom, freedom of expression would take a step forward to become a true European value—a Europe that cannot exist without Russia. Time will tell.

Orthodox Pluralism: Contours of Freedom of Religion in the Russian Federation and Strasbourg Jurisprudence

Dara Hallinan

Introduction

This chapter is devoted to the question of whether the system for protection of freedom of religion in the Russian Federation is compatible with the concept of freedom of religion perceived in the European Convention on Human Rights (ECHR) and developed by Strasbourg jurisprudence.

As one of the foundation stones of a democratic society, the right to freedom of religion and belief is vital to consideration of the Council of Europe's achievements and aims. It is perhaps one of the most elusive and difficult rights to define, and yet it protects the very heart of liberal society, the inner world of the individual, and is vital for the social structure of liberal democracy. Accordingly, analysis of the development of the right in a specific context provides great insight into the nature of all the relationships and structures it touches. It is especially interesting due to the unique role and manifestation of religion in each individual European society.

Developments in Russia regarding the continuation of the process of democratization and its relationship with the Council of Europe, and question marks over the synergy between the two have become increasingly fascinating over the last few years and are now at a critical point. Considering the worrying amount of religious persecution and restriction, and a seeming trend towards preference and influence for the Russian Orthodox Church by the state, now is a fascinating time to consider the compatibility of the two systems in the context of freedom of religion.

Given the significance of the right, an analysis of the dynamics of its development in Russia in comparison with the ideal model set out by Strasbourg also provides a starting point from which to begin to consider much broader issues. Within Russia, it provides a contextual snapshot of the Russian legal system, its changing approach to fundamental rights, and the efficacy and solidity of its role in society, while a consideration of the practical mechanics of development allow an insight into the complex alteration of a series of relationships outside the field of religion—for example, the balance between citizen and state. In an international context, the observation of the interaction between Russian and Strasbourgian systems highlights the dynamics of Russia's developing relation with European systems and Europe in general.

There have been considerations of the similarities and differences between Western Europe and Russia in terms of religion before. However, they have

Lauri Mälksoo, ed.
Russia and European Human-Rights Law: The Rise of the Civilizational Argument 151-205

tended to analyze events or to consider religion in broader terms. This analysis will consider religion in the context of Russia as a member of the Council of Europe and, thus, its obligations to a certain model of society.

The chapter will briefly look at the right developed by Strasbourg, elaborating the system of protection, its development, its key features and what trends in jurisprudence can be isolated. It will then look at the Russian system in the same way, considering the Russian legal system and how it functions, its development and core themes and trends, as well as the place and function of the ECHR and Strasbourg jurisprudence in it. Thereafter, it will consider how this protection functions in a wider context in Russia, considering the practical issues that have an effect on the system and how the principles of the system fit into a broader context. Finally, it will compare the two systems, considering their similarities and differences but concluding that the reality of protection and fluidity of the efficacy of law within Russia makes true compatibility impossible.

Article 9 in the Strasbourg System

The basic mandate for the Strasbourg system is to provide a base level of protection using the ECHR as a template.[1] In the ECHR, Article 9 is the main article that secures freedom of religion and belief, and forms the basis of the Strasbourg system. The right is considered one of the fundamental rights contained in the ECHR, with the freedoms given in Article 9(1) being absolute, subject only to the restrictions laid out in Article 9(2).[2]

Key Principles in the Strasbourg Model of Protection

The ECHR provides a minimum level of protection for individuals from interference on the part of the state.[3] For each right, the Court essentially tries to map out the boundaries and obligations involved in the relationship between the individual and the state. The way the right to freedom of religion has developed,

1 Council of Europe, European Convention on Human Rights, Accession of the European Union, available at <http://hub.coe.int/what-we-do/human-rights/eu-accession-to-the-convention>.

2 Convention for the Protection of Human Rights and Fundamental Freedoms, ETS 5, Art.9, paras. 1 and 2, available at <http://conventions.coe.int/treaty/en/treaties/html/005.htm>.

Art.9: "1. Everyone has the right to freedom of thought, conscience and religion; this right includes freedom to change his religion or belief and freedom, either alone or in community with others and in public or private, to manifest his religion or belief, in worship, teaching, practice and observance.

2. Freedom to manifest one's religion or beliefs shall be subject only to such limitation as are prescribed by law and are necessary in a democratic society in the interests of public safety, for the protection of public order, health or morals, or for the protection of the rights and freedoms of others."

3 See case of *Refah Partisi* [Prosperity Party] *and Ors v. Turkey* (13 February 2003) No.41340/98, No.41342/98, No.41343/98 and No.41344/98, para. 86.

historically differently in each state, and the difficulty of its subject matter, make the right slightly different from other Convention rights. The Court must analyze and map out standards for a plurality of relationships: namely, the relationships that exist between the individual and the state, the state and religious groupings and between different religions (and other groups). It must also apply these standards coherently across a variety of different models, arguably with little common consensus.[4] Certain key principles are laid out helpfully in various cases, for example in *Leyla Şahin v. Turkey* (paras. 104-111).[5]

4 Jean-Paul Willaime, "European Integration, Laïcité and Religion", 37 *Religion, State & Society* (2009), 23-35, at 24-26. This article provides an idea of the difference between the models and religions existing within EU states and can be used as an example of the differences that exist among Council of Europe states.

5 Case of *Leyla Şahin v. Turkey* (10 November 2005) No.44774/98. The same principles can be found in a variety of cases concerning freedom of religion. *Leyla Şahin* has been chosen for its comparatively full list, its relevance, and the range of important issues. The Court *begins* by stating that freedom of religion and belief is one of the foundations of a democratic society and is a vital element for the identity of believers and vitally important for non-believers and the unconcerned. It states that it is fundamental for the existence of pluralism, which is in turn "indissociable from a democratic society". It *follows* by reiterating that freedom of religion is primarily an individual right, but that this implies freedom to manifest one's religion alone or in "community with others whose faith one shares" and then briefly lays out the forms manifestation may take, while pointing out that Art.9 does not cover all acts motivated by religion. *Thirdly*, the Court considers the role of the state, saying that "in a democratic society in which several religions coexist within one and the same population it may be necessary to place restrictions on freedom to manifest one's religion or belief in order to reconcile the interests of various groups and make sure everyone's interests are respected". This can also be said to create a positive obligation under Art.1 of the Convention. After this, the Court briefly clarifies its opinion on the role of the state as a "neutral and impartial organiser of various religions, faiths and beliefs", with the reasoning that this is "conducive to public order, religious harmony and tolerance in a democratic society". This impartiality goes hand in hand with lack of power on the state's part to assess the legitimacy of religious beliefs. The obligation of the state to ensure mutual tolerance between groups is emphasized, and in situations of dispute, it is improper to simply remove the cause of the tension at the expense of plurality. Next, the Court lays out again that "pluralism, tolerance and broadmindedness are hallmarks of a democratic society" and states that sometimes individual interests must cede to the interests of the group. However, it emphasizes the need to strike a balance that achieves the fair and proper treatment of minorities and avoids abuse of a majority position and that "pluralism and democracy must also be based on a dialogue and a spirit of compromise which may entail concessions on the part of individuals or groups which are justified in order to maintain and promote the ideas and values of a democratic society". It also puts this need to strike a balance in terms of the need to balance rights in the Convention, and that the priority of freedom of religion may necessarily require a restriction on certain other rights. The Court then considers the difference in European models, and where there are broad differences of opinion on matters, it will assign 'special importance' to the opinion of the national decision-making body. In this respect, it accepts that:

> "It is not possible to discern a uniform conception of the significance of religion in society throughout Europe and the meaning and impact of the public expression will differ according to time and context [...] Rules in this sphere will consequently vary

Pluralism

The principle of pluralism is stressed by the Court to be "indissociable from" a democratic society and is the foundation stone of the current model of protection.[6] Briefly, the concept of pluralism points to the existence of all kinds of associations and groupings that aim for political influence, without one group being politically dominant.[7] Ambiguously, the existence of these group rights is seen by the Court as a collective manifestation of individual rights on the one hand, but on the other, as a condition for the exercise of individual rights—the aspect of freedom to exercise one's right of freedom of religion stemming from the existence of a choice.[8] The concept was applied specifically to freedom of religion in the 1993 *Kokkinakis v. Greece* case, where the Court clarified the relationship of the concept to the right:

> "Freedom of thought, conscience and religion is one of the foundations of a democratic society [...] It is in its religious dimension, one of the most vital elements that go to make up the identity of believers and their conception of life, but is also a precious asset for atheists, agnostics and the unconcerned. The pluralism indissociable from a democratic society, which has been clearly won over the centuries, depends on it."[9]

The need to protect pluralism as a prerequisite for a 'democratic society' leads it to be used in connection with legitimization of interference, as well as prevention of undue interference.[10] Particularly in cases of religion in the public sphere and in connection with a threat to pluralism, there is a wide margin of appreciation (see below) given to local authorities (although, should the authorities act contrary to the principles of pluralism, the margin will be narrow). Even further, one can

> from one country to another according to national traditions and requirements imposed by the need to protect the rights and freedoms of others and to maintain public order. Accordingly, the choice of the extent and form such regulations should take must inevitably be left up to the state, as it will depend on the specific domestic context."

This margin of appreciation will be overseen by the Court, which will decide whether measures taken and the laws under which they were taken were 'justified in principle and proportionate'.

6 Craig Calhoun (ed.), *Dictionary of the Social Sciences* (Oxford University Press, New York, NY, 2002), 363-364. For a full description of pluralism in jurisprudence, see Arend Soeteman (ed.), *Pluralism and Law* (Kluwer, Amsterdam, 2001), particularly the chapters by Leslie Green, "Pluralism, Social Conflict and Tolerance", 87-107; and Alon Harel, "The Boundaries of Democratic Pluralism", 133-155, respectively.

7 For a full explanation, see Avigail I. Eisenberg, *Reconstructing Political Pluralism* (State University of New York Press, New York, NY, 1995); and Aernout Nieuwenhuis, "The Concept of Pluralism in the Case Law of the European Court of Human Rights", 3 *European Constitutional Law Review* (2007), 367-384, at 373.

8 *Ibid.*, 367-374.

9 Case of *Kokkinakis v. Greece* (25 May 1993) No.14307/88), para. 31.

10 Cases of *Refah Partisi, op.cit.* note 3, para. 125 (and body of judgment) and *Leyla Şahin, op.cit.* note 5, para. 115

suggest that the Court sees this value as so important that the normally required standard of proof is also given a certain 'margin of appreciation'. In the 2005 *Leyla Şahin v. Turkey* case, there was little solid proof of a link between wearing a headscarf and any danger to the freedom of others, yet the specter of a threat to pluralism was enough to find legitimacy in state interference.[11]

The concept certainly has importance in defining religion's place in society and relating to the right of freedom of religion. However, as can be seen from the above examples and a consideration of interference between groups, this concept also serves to group religions to some extent with other groups in society.[12] This takes away elements of the special position to which a religion may lay claim and which, in terms of social order, puts it on a playing field with other groups.[13] Essentially, religious freedom is defined along political lines, in a political model, rather than existing as a special entity.

Between groups, the doctrine has been used to regulate interaction on the basis that "pluralism, tolerance and broadmindedness must go together".[14] This is mostly relevant in the balancing of different groups' rights on the basis of equality within a society. An example of this is the reasoning given in the 1994 *Otto Preminger-Institut v. Austria* case in which it was made clear, on the one hand, that "those who choose to exercise the freedom to manifest their religion [...] cannot reasonably expect to be exempt from all criticism". [15] However, in the same case, the need for religious groupings to express their convictions means that the Court is willing to use the ideas of pluralism as a reason that groups must be protected from overly vehement attacks.[16]

Between the individual and the state, the concept acts as a double-edged sword. Throughout the jurisprudence, it is maintained that, at its core, freedom

11 Jill Marshall, "Conditions for Freedom: European Human Rights Law and the Islamic Headscarf Debate", 30 *Human Rights Quarterly* (2008), 631-654, at 646-648; see, also, Christian Moe, "Refah Partisi (Welfare Party) v Turkey", 6(1) *International Journal for Not-For-Profit Law* (2003), available at <http://www.icnl.org/research/journal/vol6iss1/special_5.htm>, for a demonstration of lack of thorough proof of the dangers inherent in Sharia to a democratic society; *Refah Partisi, op.cit.* note 3; and case of *Manoussakis and Others v. Greece* (26 September 1996), Reports 1996-IV, 1365, para. 40.

12 Martin Steven, "Religious Lobbies in the EU: From Dominant Faith to Faith Based Organisations", 37 *Religion, State & Society* (2009), 181-191. This elaborates an interaction between religions and supra-territorial organizations as regulated according to their place in a democratic society.

13 *Ibid.*

14 *Leyla Şahin, op.cit.* note 5, para. 108.

15 Case of *Otto-Preminger-Institut v. Austria* (20 September 1994) No.11/1993/406/485), para. 47. The Court went on to state: "[...] They [religious groups] must tolerate and accept the denial by others of their religious beliefs and even the propagations of others of doctrines hostile to their faith."

16 *Ibid.*

of religion is an individual right. This in itself is compatible with the doctrine of pluralism.[17] However, due to the prominence of the group in the nature of the relevant cases, the focus of protection has shifted away from the individual. The key relationship is thus that of religious groups and the state.[18] In light of cases concerning religious groups such as the 1996 *Manoussakis v. Greece* or the 2002 *Metropolitan Church of Bessarabia v. Moldova*—where the considerations were the structural impact on the nature of pluralism of religious groupings and pluralism in society rather than on the effect on the individual—it seems that the level of protection granted to individuals, in comparison, is lower as a result. The language of pluralism may be formed on the basis of individual rights, but in jurisprudence it creates a system based on the group.[19]

Between religious groups and the state, the concept is used to keep the state out of undue interference in the religious sphere as much as possible and *vice versa*. A certain amount of overlap is acceptable, as it is inevitable, but must not endanger key principles. This principle is also supported by Council of Europe recommendations and statements, such as Recommendation 1804 on State, Religion, Secularity and Human Rights, where it is clearly stated in paragraph 10 that "religion and governance should not mix".[20] As has been seen above, the margin of appreciation for authorities grows with any threat to democratic principles, pluralism, or protection of minorities and the situation of manifestation and entry of religion into the government sphere.[21]

Finally, pluralism is one of the ideas through which the Court secures non-interference in religious society by the government. The idea of pluralism is based on the idea that there must be organization so that religion can thrive, and this is the duty of the state. As mentioned above, this means the state has the obligation to ensure tolerance and broadmindedness between groups, and also where necessary, respect.[22] In a situation where there is an issue between various groups, the nature of the state as organizer must not go against the principles of

17 Nieuwenhuis, *op.cit.* note 7, 368.

18 Due to the scarcity of case law relating to freedom of religion, this is a hard point to prove. The given examples seem to show this trend. For further argumentation regarding these cases, see Aernout Nieuwenhuis, "European Court of Human Rights: State and Religion, Schools and Scarves. An Analysis of the Margin of Appreciation as Used in the Case of Leyla Sahin v Turkey", 1 *European Constitutional Law Review* (2005), 459-510.

19 Case of *Kalaç v. Turkey* (23 June 1997) No.61/1996/680/870, para. 28. This was clarified in *Kalaç v. Turkey*, where the Court said that when manifesting one's religion one must "take his specific situation into account" as part of a general principle of proportionality.

20 PACE, "State, Religion, Secularity and Human Rights" (2007) Recommendation 1804, available at <http://assembly.coe.int/Main.asp?link=/Documents/AdoptedText/ta07/EREC1804.htm>.

21 *Ibid.*, para. 10.

22 Principles in *Leyla Şahin, op.cit.* note 5, paras. 104-111; see, also, Eisenberg, *op.cit.* note 7.

pluralism. This is manifested in the principles laid out in the cases of *Serif v. Greece* and, also, *Metropolitan Church of Bessarabia and Others v. Moldova* (1999 and 2002 respectively).[23] This role of the state as organizer is tied to other principles relied on by the Court; namely, that the state does not validate the legitimacy of a belief and that the state ought to be neutral.

Neutrality

From the statements of the Court in the above cases, it seems clear that state impartiality is a necessary pillar of the model which the Court promotes. However, it is necessary to consider how this principle reconciles itself with the diverse reality of models of state-religion interaction, and in particular, with the existence of state churches. Almost all states have some manifestation of state church, for example, the state church in Denmark, which enjoys preferences in all aspects of public life.[24] Exceptions include the secular states of France and Turkey (although their *de facto* secularity can be debated).

The Court has said that it found no breach of the ECHR with the existence of state churches in cases such as the 1990 *Darby v. Sweden*, and has elaborated certain points around which the existence of a state church may alter the boundaries of neutrality. *First*, the nature of a state church means that the state may be allowed much more say in the organization, leadership and direction of its affiliate church.[25] The Court has elaborated the boundaries of interaction with the principle that the state church system—in order to satisfy the requirements of Article 9—must include specific safeguards for the individual's freedom of religion. The protection of all forms of religion must be ensured, meaning all measures that would threaten this would be closely scrutinized. A theocratic state would, for example, be inadmissible, as would putting the state religion in charge of a registry for other religions.[26]

The Court has clarified to some extent the scope of support a state church might enjoy. The state can fund a state church, but the ways this can be done have been regulated. A state church can, for example, be put in charge of certain secular functions such as maintenance of birth and death registers and be paid by the state for the service.[27] General tax can be used to pay for these services,

23 Cases of *Metropolitan Church of Bessarabia v. Moldova* (27 March 2002) No.45701/99, para. 116; and *Serif v. Greece* (14 December 1999) No.38178/97, para. 53.

24 Carin Laudrup, "A European Battlefield: Does the EU Have a Soul?", 37 *Religion, State & Society* (2009), 51-61, at 53-61.

25 Cases of *Darby v. Sweden* (1990) No.11581/85; *Karlsson v. Sweden* (1988), 57 *Eur. Comm. H.R. Dec. & Rep.* 172, 172-73; and *Knudsen v. Norway* (1985), 42 *Eur. Comm'n H.R. Dec. & Rep.* 247.

26 *Manoussakis, op.cit.* note 11, paras. 23-48; and *Kokkinakis, op.cit.* note 9, paras. 31-35.

27 Carolyn Evans and Christopher A. Thomas, "Church State Relations in the European Court

even though a non-believer cannot be taxed directly to pay for the state church as confirmed in the 2001 case of *Lundberg v. Sweden.*[28] On the one hand, the course of the Court is understandable. There are requirements that must be fulfilled under the ECHR for freedom of religion in the model, and in practice, to be realized. Among these are a certain protection for minorities and a respect for pluralism. A requirement for this is a degree of state neutrality; thus, the Court acts to protect this and to establish a framework under which this can thrive. However, the societies in which this framework is to be implemented are not models but living societies with histories that must be respected and incorporated in adaptation of the law to each situation.

Indeed, at the time the ECHR was drafted, should it have been construed that state churches were anti-Convention, there is a good chance that many of the signatories would not have signed. Further, any attempt to go against the idea of a state church would likely meet firm opposition from countries in which the state church is a very strong social institution.[29] Finally, in many instances, the majority of people who associate with state churches on cultural and nationalistic levels would perceive that to refuse their eminence in a particular society where they enjoy privilege would be, in a different way, undemocratic, with the will of the many not being represented. Further, it would exclude religion from public life in a way that would be contrary to the democratic principles of many states. "It is just as bad to treat unequal legal relationships as equal, as it is to treat equal legal relationships as unequal."[30] Thus, what the Court will do is judge the acceptability of the link in each situation rather than tackle the social and structural issue of a state church head on.

The state church is thus regulated so that the fewest breaches of the principles of neutrality and plurality are allowed to occur. However, in the nature of the idea of a state church, there are breaches of the principle of neutrality, and it is not feasible to consider, for example, that the state church in Denmark—which enjoys incomparable access to public opportunities—does not benefit in comparison to other religions.[31] For this reason, the Court takes a form of

of Human Rights", 3 *Brigham Young University Law Review* (2006), 699-725, at 703-709. This is the case in Spain.

28 Case of *Lundberg v. Sweden* (2001) No.36846/97.

29 See Steven Livingstone, "Article 14 and the Prevention of Discrimination in the European Convention on Human Rights", 25 *European Human Rights Law Review* (1997), 25-34.

30 Francesco Ruffini, *Diritti di liberta* (La Nuova Italia, Firenze, 1945, originally published in 1926), 84.

31 The 1975 Constitution of Greece (as amended); English translation available at <http://www.hellenicparliament.gr/UserFiles/f3c70a23-7696-49db-9148-f24dce6a27c8/001-156%20aggliko.pdf>. Reference to the specificity of the place of the Orthodox Church appears in Art.3. Reference to religion's importance to the state appears various times; See Malcolm Evans and Peter Petkoff, "A Separation of Convenience? The Concept of Neutrality in the

dynamic stance on the issue. *First*, the Court is very protective against moves that potentially affect pluralism or neutrality in any given state.[32] This is a way of saying the state church is tolerated as it exists, as long as it follows certain principles, but ensuring that it will encroach no further onto those principles.[33]

Second, the Court erodes the influence of state churches in situations that are in violation of the principles of plurality or neutrality. This was particularly obvious in Greece, where the cases of *Kokkinakis* and *Manoussakis* (1993 and 1996) affirmed the freedom of Jehovah's Witnesses at the expense of the Greek Orthodox Church.[34]

In this context, we must consider the difference in treatment between older and newer members of the Council of Europe. There are two strands of case law followed by the Court. The first follows that state churches are acceptable and that the concept of neutrality as applied by each state is to be given a wide margin of appreciation. This can be seen as the existing paradigm model. However, in the context of newer member states (largely the ex-communist states), this concept has been reversed. Attempts at creating a state-church paradigm are strongly considered in light of a need to develop according to ECHR-approved concepts of democracy, pluralism, and neutrality.[35]

Margin of Appreciation

The margin of appreciation is a legal tool that originated in the 1961 Commission case of *Lawless v. Ireland*, and was developed by the Court in the 1976 case of *Handyside* as a way of dealing with the issue of state sovereignty.[36] The Court claimed that, as the Convention was an international legal document, the primary responsibility for securing rights for individuals lay with the state. The obligation was not for the Court to put itself in the position of the state in situations of adversarial proceedings but, rather, to examine the decision of the government for compatibility with the ECHR and then intervene when necessary. In this regard, the Court viewed certain issues as less applicable to be

Jurisprudence of the of the European Court of Human Rights", 36 *Religion, State & Society* (2008), 205-223, at 210. Reference to the judgment in the case of *Metropolitan Church of Bessarabia, op.cit.* note 23.

32 Evans and Petkoff, *op.cit.* note 31, 210.

33 Case of *Metropolitan Church of Bessarabia, op.cit.* note 23; and *Refah Partisi, op.cit.* note 3.

34 Case of *Kokkinakis, op.cit.* note 9; and *Manoussakis, op.cit.* note 11.

35 In the case of *Metropolitan Church of Bessarabia and Others, op.cit.* note 23, while the Orthodox religion was given as a central pillar of the state, a threat to which also gave rise to issues of national security, the Court found that the importance of not interfering in freedom of religion was important enough to rule against Moldova: Cases of *Jehovah's Witnesses v. Romania* (11 July 2006) No.63108/00 (and 14 other applications).

36 Cases of *Lawless v. Ireland* (1 July 1961) No.332/57; and *Handyside v. UK* (7 December 1976) No.5493/72.

judged by an international body, for example, morals.[37] However, when the state exceeds its authority in relation to the fundamental principles of the ECHR, the Court will act.

When there is little European consensus on a certain matter, the margin will generally be higher, and the state will have more room for maneuver; if there is a higher degree of consensus, the margin will fall.[38]

Relating to freedom of religion, the Court repeats in its general principles, what it had said in *Handyside.*[39] The great difference across Europe in development and interaction of religions among one another and with the state means that common European consensus regarding religious issues is difficult to pinpoint. The nature of the right, however, as centrally important to a democratic society, is possible to assess on a case-by-case basis. Thus, the use of a margin is an understanding that there are areas in which there is little consensus and, therefore, the Court has less jurisdiction to rule, that the models employed can differ greatly and that in the area of freedom of religion, the national manifestation can be tightly tied to issues of culture meaning, that to define universally, would be dangerous. A wide margin is also given in areas of traditionally defined religion-society relationships. However, when the central principles of religion-society interaction are touched upon, *i.e.*, those that concern the functioning of a democratic society, the Court will narrow the margin (depending also on other relevant factors, such as the reason for interference).

This can lead to very confusing case law. It can appear that the Court will rule on similar cases differently due to their country of origin, citing different margins of appreciation. However, it really represents an understanding that the ECHR is not a complete legal order and its development must be tempered with a respect for the difference between states and the boundaries of function it has as a legal order.

37 In *Handyside,* the Court stated: "[...] by reason of their direct and continuous contact with the vital forces of their countries, state authorities are in principle in a better position than the international judge to give an opinion on the exact content of the limitations required to protect morals as well as on the necessity of a restriction or penalty intended to meet them". However, it goes on to say that this discretion "will go hand in hand with European supervision".

38 For further information, see Michael R. Hutchinson, "The Margin of Appreciation Doctrine in the European Court of Human Rights", 48 *International and Comparative Law Quarterly* (1999), 638-650; Pieter Van Dijk and Godefridus J.H. Van Hoof, *Theory and Practice of the European Convention on Human Rights* (Kluwer, Amsterdam, 2006), 88; and the case of *Leander v. Sweden* (26 March 1987) No.9248/8, para. 59.

39 Case of *Leander v. Sweden, op.cit.* note 38; see, also, note 37.

Russian Legal Protection

The Russian Constitution

The 1993 Russian Constitution is the foundation stone of the Russian state and lays down the principles under which freedom of religion in Russia should be regulated.

The key relevant principles concerning freedom of religion in the Russian Constitution are laid out in Articles 13 and 14 which, together, form the foundations for pluralism and the secular nature of the Russian state. These articles specifically rule out the existence of a state-sponsored ideology. This constitutional solution rules out the adoption of a state church. Equality of religions is assured, as is their separation from the state, which also confirms the principle of the neutrality of the state. The language constructs a model very close to that of the ECHR, the Court's jurisprudence, and Council of Europe documentation on church-state relations. There is the caveat that associations—the aims of which contravene the security of the state or which incite social, national or religious strife—may be prohibited.[40]

Article 28 lays the foundations for individual and collective manifestation of religion.[41] It also lays out the right to manifest one's religion, including the right to disseminate beliefs. This includes teaching one's religion (no restriction is mentioned concerning to whom). This article mimics Article 9(1) of the ECHR,

40 The 1993 RF Constitution: "Konstitutsiia Rossiiskoi Federatsii, *Rossiiskaia gazeta* (25 December 1993), available (as amended) at <http://www.rg.ru/2009/01/21/konstitucia-dok.html>; English translation of the 1993 RF Constitution available at <http://www.legislationline.org/documents/section/constitutions/country/7>.
Art.13 states:
"1. In the Russian Federation ideological diversity shall be recognized.
2. No ideology may be established as state or obligatory one.
3. In the Russian Federation political diversity and multi-party system shall be recognized.
4. Public associations shall be equal before the law.
5. The creation and activities of public associations whose aims and actions are aimed at a forced change of the fundamental principles of the constitutional system and at violating the integrity of the Russian Federation, at undermining its security, at setting up armed units, and at instigating social, racial, national and religious strife shall be prohibited."
Art.14 states:
"1. The Russian Federation is a secular state. No religion may be established as a state or obligatory one.
2. Religious associations shall be separated from the State and shall be equal before the law."

41 *Ibid.*, Art.28: "Everyone shall be guaranteed the right to freedom of conscience, to freedom of religious worship, including the right to profess, individually or jointly with others, any religion, or to profess no religion, to freely choose, possess and disseminate religious or other beliefs, and to act in conformity with them."

apparently guaranteeing all the same rights. We can presume from this article and the principles of the Constitution that the right is based in individual terms but retains the collective element demanded by the principle of pluralism.[42]

Article 29 puts certain restrictions on the dissemination of one's religious views, but in no unusual terms.[43] Strong parallels can be found with the idea of the state as a neutral organizer of the plural public sphere, arranging for freedom to assert one's opinion on the one hand but tolerance between groups on the other.[44]

Other articles have a bearing on the freedom for religions to operate. For example, Article 35 asserts that no one may be arbitrarily deprived of their property, which has specific relevance for many Muslim and Protestant denominations.[45]

In general, the Russian Constitution is seen to be very forward-looking and adheres to the principles of protection of human rights, the rule of law, and democratic ideology, *i.e.*, the essence of the Strasbourg system. However, when considering the Constitution, it is important to understand that, at the time, the drafters had embraced a liberal system and had just entered a new age in which manifestos of international human rights were seen as a keystone for gaining trust in the international community and, therefore, as a keystone to Russia's future. This manifests in the Constitution, which can almost be read as imported rather than a legal framework that grew from the specifics of Russian society.[46] This must be considered in light of the present day, when liberal, Western-looking ideology is perhaps not seen so favorably. Moreover, it is one thing to proclaim things on the constitutional level; their implementation in significant 'detail' is another. Connected with other developments, this consistently brings up the question of the exact status of the Constitution. Is it a malleable instrument and general basis to be adapted, or is it solid law?

42 Nieuwenhuis, *op.cit.* note 7, 367-369.

43 1993 RF Constitution, *op.cit.* note 40, Art.29:

"1. Everyone shall have the right to freedom of thought and speech.

2. Propaganda or campaigning inciting social, racial, national or religious hatred and strife is impermissible. The propaganda of social, racial, national, religious or language superiority is forbidden.

3. Nobody may be coerced into expressing their views and convictions or into renouncing them.

5. The freedom of the mass media shall be guaranteed. Censorship shall be prohibited."

44 For an explanation of the logic see *Otto-Preminger-Institut v. Austria, op.cit.* note 15.

45 For examples of property issues concerning various religious groups see Alexander Verkhovsky and Olga Sibireva, "Restrictions and Challenges in 2008 on Freedom of Conscience in Russia", available at <http://www.sova-center.ru/en/religion/publications/2009/04/d15726/>.

46 I.U. Kozlychin, "Pravo, zakon i vlast' v sovremennoi Rossii", in V.G. Grafskii (ed.), *Nash trudnyi put' k pravu. Materialy filosofsko-pravovykh chtenii pamiati akademika V.S. Nersesiantsa* (Norma, Moscow, 2006), 62-75, at 74.

Reception of Council of Europe Law in Russia

Russia signed the Statute of the Council of Europe in 1996, along with the ECHR, and agreed to fulfill obligations set out in PACE Opinion 193.[47] Two years after this, Russia ratified the ECHR which, in Article 1, requires states to "secure to everyone within their jurisdiction the rights and freedoms defined in Section I of the Convention", as well as (since *Ireland v. UK* in 1978) requiring states to protect against and remedy breaches of these rights at subordinate levels.[48] Even at this point there were doubts surrounding the compatibility of the systems as evidenced by such reports as the *ad hoc* Eminent Lawyers' Report prepared at the request of the Bureau of the Parliamentary Assembly, which claimed that "the legal order of the Russian Federation does not, at the present moment, meet the Council of Europe standards as enshrined in the Statute of the Council and developed by the organs of the ECHR" and by the evaluation of Aleksander G. Khodakov (then-Director of the Legal Department of the Russian Ministry of Foreign Affairs and, later, RF Ambassador in The Netherlands) in the Explanatory Note on the Issue of Signing the European Convention of Human Rights and Fundamental Freedoms signed in 1996, stating "at the present moment Russian legislation, with the exception of the Constitution, and law enforcement practice do not fully comply with the Council of Europe's standards".[49]

Considering the Constitution as the base of the Russian legal order, we can isolate certain key articles that suggest the correct theoretical place the ECHR occupies in the Russian system.

Article 15 assures the supremacy of the Constitution.[50] It also states the monistic nature of the Russian Federation, with international treaties entered

47 PACE, "On Russia's Request for Membership of the Council of Europe" (1996) Opinion 193, available at <http://assembly.coe.int/Main.asp?link=/Documents/AdoptedText/ta96/EOPI193.htm>.

48 Convention for the Protection of Human Rights and Fundamental Freedoms , *op.cit.* note 2, Art.1; and *Ireland v. UK* (1978) Series A No.25.

49 PACE, "Report on the Conformity of the Legal Order of the Russian Federation with Council of Europe Standards" (2 January 1996) Document 7443, available at <http://www.assembly.coe.int/nw/xml/XRef/Xref-DocDetails-EN.asp?FileID=10250&lang=EN>; Rudolf Bernhardt *et al.*, "Report on the Conformity of the Legal Order of the Russian Federation with Council of Europe Standards", 15(7) *Human Rights Law Journal* (1994), 287; and Aleksandr Khodakov, "Poiasnitel'naia zapiska po voprosu o podpisanii Rossiiskoi Federatsiei Evropeiskoi Konventsii o zashchite prav cheloveka i osnovnykh svobod ot 4 noiabria 1950 g. i protokolov k nei" (10 January1996), reproduced in A. Burkov, *Konventsiia o zashchite prav cheloveka v sudakh Rossii* (Wolters Kluwer, Moscow, 2010), 338ff.

50 1993 RF Constitution, *op.cit.* note 40, Art.15:

"1. The Constitution of the Russian Federation shall have supreme legal force and direct effect, and shall be applicable throughout the entire territory of the Russian Federation. Laws and other legal acts adopted by the Russian Federation may not contravene the Constitution of the Russian Federation.

into by the Russian Federation having, in principle, direct effect in national law and supremacy over contradictory national legislation.[51]

This was confirmed by the 2003 Resolution of the Plenum of the RF Supreme Court that gave instructions on international treaties to the lower courts as to how to interpret and apply Article 15(4) and the RF Federal Law on International Treaties.[52]

Articles 17 and 18 of the Constitution may be interpreted to indicate that international treaties and obligations may actually have supremacy over the Constitution.[53] However, this has never been realized in practice. Article 22 of

> 3. The laws shall be officially published. Unpublished laws shall not be applicable. No regulatory legal act affecting the rights, liberties or duties of the human being and citizen may apply unless it has been published officially for general knowledge.
> 4. The commonly recognized principles and norms of international law and the international treaties of the Russian Federation shall be a component part of its legal system. If an international treaty of the Russian Federation stipulates other rules than those stipulated by the law, the rules of the international treaty shall apply."

51 1993 RF Constitution, *op.cit.* note 40, Art.(3). There is some debate over when this exactly happens and which treaties this includes. For example, there is the question whether this includes treaties that have been signed and not ratified, although the logic of Art.15(3) and opinion surrounding it suggests that it applies only to treaties that have been signed, ratified and published. These concerns are not relevant as regards the ECHR (which already has been signed, ratified and published).

52 Postanovlenie Plenuma Verkhovnogo Suda "O primenenii sudami obshchei iurisdiktsii obshchepriznannykh printsipov i norm mezhdunarodnogo prava i mezhdunarodnykh dogovorov Rossiiskoi Federatsii" (10 October 2003) No.5, *Rossiiskaia gazeta* (2 December 2003), (hereinafter the "Resolution on Application by Courts of General Jurisdiction of the Generally Recognized Principles and Norms of International Law and International Treaties of the Russian Federation"), available at <http://www.rg.ru/2003/12/02/pravo-doc.html>. It states:

> "The rights and liberties of man in conformity with the commonly recognized principles and the norms of international law, as well as the international treaties of the Russian Federation shall have direct effect within the jurisdiction of the Russian Federation. They shall determine the meaning, content and application of the laws, and the activities of the legislative and executive branches and local governments, and shall be secured by the judiciary."

Translation from <http://www.supcourt.ru/catalog.php?c1=English&c2=Documents&c3=&id=6801>.

53 1993 RF Constitution, *op.cit.* note 40:
Art.17:

> "1. The basic rights and liberties in conformity with the commonly recognized principles and norms of the international law shall be recognized and guaranteed in the Russian Federation and under this Constitution.
> 2. The exercise of rights and liberties of a human being and citizen may not violate the rights and liberties of other persons."

Art.18:

> "1. The rights and liberties of man and citizen shall have direct effect. They shall determine the meaning, content and application of the laws, and the activities of the legislative and executive branches and local self-government, and shall be secured by the judiciary."

the 1995 RF Law on International Treaties of the Russian Federation indicates that a treaty that would require changes to the Constitution can only be ratified after amendments to the Constitution have already been made.[54] In theory, international treaties—and, therefore, the ECHR—slot in between the Constitution and legislation subordinate to it. In this instance, the protection provided by the language in the Constitution theoretically provides no less protection than that provided by the ECHR.

Article 46 recognizes the right of appeal to interstate human-rights organs should this have been agreed to in treaties signed (and ratified) by the Russian Federation.[55] Thus, the right of appeal to Strasbourg is recognized. Logically, this would be an illusory right and the article a moot point should the authority of the Court—and, therefore, also its decisions—not be recognized.

The Court is the living interpretation of the Convention, adapting and developing the sixty-two-year old Convention. That the Court regards the Convention as a living instrument is clearly evident from the principle of case law and the case law itself: take, for example, the Court's statements in the 1996 *Loizidou v. Turkey* case.[56] Thus, the jurisprudence and principles of the Court are key elements of the contemporary existence of the Convention.

However, in what way these interpretations are binding on Russia is still in doubt, as guidelines are not laid out in any binding instrument. Various interpretations have been offered. The 1998 RF Federal Law on ratification of the Convention suggests that interpretations are binding in cases of violations by Russia, which may suggest that heed need not be taken of interpretations concerning cases that do not involve Russia, while decisions of the Constitutional Court suggest that case law may be transformed into domestic law.[57] Further

54 RF Federal'nyi Zakon RF "O mezhdunarodnykh dogovorakh Rossiiskoi Federatsii" (15 July 1995) No.101-FZ (with subsequent amendments), *Rossiiskaia gazeta* (21 July 1995). See the debate in Margareta Alexandrovna Zanina, "Kollizii norm natsional'nogo prava i Evropeiskoi konventsii prav cheloveka i osnovnykh svobod", 11 *Rossiiskaia iustitsiia* (2005), 58-61; and Gennady M. Danilenko, "Implementation of International Law in CIS States: Theory and Practice", 10 *European Journal of International Law* (1999), 51-69.

55 1993 RF Constitution, *op.cit.* note 40, Art.46:

"3. The conformity with the international treaties of the Russian Federation, everyone shall have the right to turn to interstate organs concerned with the protection of human rights and liberties when all the means of legal protection available within the state have been exhausted."

56 Case of *Loizidou v. Turkey* (18 December 1996) No.15318/89.

57 RF Federal'nyi Zakon, "O Ratifikatsii Konventsii o zashchite prav cheloveka i osnovnykh svobod i protokolov k nei" (30 March 1998) No.54-FZ, (hereinafter the "Law on the Ratification of the Convention on the Protection of Human Rights and Fundamental Freedoms"), *Rossiiskaia gazeta* (7 April 1998), also available at <http://www.echr.ru/documents/doc/12011157/12011157.htm>; and Postanovlenie Konstitutsionnogo Suda Rossiiskoi Federatsii, "Po delu o proverke konstitutsonnosti punkta 5 chasti vtoroi stat'i 371, chast tret'ei stat'i 374 i punkta 4 chasti vtoroi stat'i 384 ugolovno-protsessual'nogo kodeksa

issues exist over the meaning of case law; these are seldom addressed and remain largely unresolved.

Referring to the area of protection for freedom of religion, the legal solution that presents itself most readily is the following. Considering that there is no bar domestically to use of interpretations of the Court, and that the Court is a body to which Russian citizens can appeal and whose decisions are the contemporary manifestation of the ECHR, which was ratified by the Russian government, which occupies a highly authoritative position in the Russian legal system, and whose judgments also come with an obligation to act to remedy a breach of the ECHR, it is evident that case law must have an effect so far as it involves Russia itself. However, considering the example of the doctrine of plurality as developed in relation to freedom of religion, we can see that the protection the ECHR offers is more than a simple set of rules for one situation; it attempts to provide certain benchmarks for a democratic society, the specifics of which are fleshed out by case law and jurisprudence.[58] Therefore, principles developed by case law are founded and interlinked across decisions concerning different countries and articles. In the principles laid out in 2005 in *Leyla Şahin*, for example, we can observe that the 2004 case of *Gorzelik and Others* has been used as authority.[59] This is not a case that concerned freedom of religion directly or that involved Turkey.[60] Thus, the Court's case law must be taken as a whole (obviously within sensible limits, references to the specificity of a society may preclude certain specifics from being widely relevant in jurisprudence, but this will not apply to a developing strand of interpretation of a legal instrument). A consideration of the Court's jurisprudence that considers only cases relating to the state in question would make the idea of a supra-state legal system impossible to develop in any coherent way.

Therefore, considering the Constitution and interpretations of the ECHR and the Russian system, it seems only logical to assume that the interpretations of the Court—so long as they are obviously not directed deliberately at one state in particular, are applicable as concerns Russia, whether or not Russia was a party to the case.

RSFSR v sviazi s zhalobami grazhdan K.M. Kul'neva, V.S. Lalueva, Iu.V. Lukashova i I.P. Serebrennikova" (2 February 1996) No.4-P, *Rossiiskaia gazeta* (15 February 1996).

58 Case of *Refah Partisi, op.cit.* note 3, paras. 86-95, for example.

59 Cases of *Leyla Şahin, op.cit.* note 5, para. 109; and *Gorzelik and Others v. Poland* (17 February) No.44158/98 (a case concerning minority identity in Poland).

60 See, also, case of *Otto-Preminger-Institut, op.cit.* note 15, which concerned a balancing of rights between freedom of expression and freedom of religion.

A Federal Law on Freedom of Conscience and on Religious Associations

In 1997, the Law on Freedom of Conscience and on Religious Associations was adopted at the federal level. That law—rather than placing religion in its societal context—seeks to regulate "legal relationships in the area of human and civil rights to freedom of conscience and to freedom of religious profession creed, as well as the legal status of religious associations".[61] This replaced an earlier federal law from 1990 on religion, which was considered very liberal.[62] Its inception was the result of sustained lobbying activity (not least on the part of the Russian Orthodox Church) at both the federal and regional levels.[63] However, already between 1993 and 1997, more than one-third of all Russia's regions had introduced laws that went against the permissive 1990 legislation.[64]

Since then, the law has been the subject of much criticism on the grounds of its restrictive language and has been a specific subject of concern for the Council of Europe. Questions have been raised as to its compatibility with the ECHR, as well as with the 1993 RF Constitution.[65] It is necessary to consider the aims of this law, as well as some of its key features and the issues they raise in greater detail.

The law suggests that it adheres to the principles outlined in the Constitution and encourages and protects a liberal conception of freedom of religion. We can see this from the very beginning of the document in the preamble and in the first section (Chapter I. General Provisions). The first few sentences of the preamble are "affirming the right of each person to freedom of conscience and freedom of religious profession, as well as to equality before the law irrespective of religious affiliation and convictions" and "assuming that the Russian Federa-

61 RF Federal'nyi Zakon "O svobode sovesti i o religioznykh ob"edineniiakh" (1 October 1997) No.FZ-125, (hereinafter the "Law on Freedom of Conscience and on Religious Associations"), *Rossiiskaia gazeta* (1 October 1997), Art.1. Translation from Paul D. Steeves, available at <http://www2.stetson.edu/~psteeves/relnews/freedomofconscienceeng.html>.

62 James T. Richardson and Marat S. Shterin, "Constitutional Courts in Post Communist Russia and Hungary: How Do They Treat Religion?", 36 *Religion, State & Society* (2008), 251-267, at 258.

63 Joachim Willems, "The Religio-Political Strategies of the ROC as a Politics of Discourse", 34 *Religion State & Society* (2006), 287-298 at 287.

64 Lauren B. Homer and Lawrence A. Uzzell, "Federal and Provincial Religious Freedom Laws in Russia: a Struggle for and against Federalism and the Rule of Law", in John Witte and Michael Bourdeaux (eds.), *Proselytism and Orthodoxy in Russia: The New War for Souls* (Orbis Books, New York, NY, 1999), 284-320.

65 See, *inter alia*, PACE, "Motion for a Recommendation, 'New Russian Law on Religion'" (1997) Document 7957, available at <http://assembly.coe.int/ASP/Doc/DocListingSession_E.asp?IDSession=151&offset=30>; PACE, "Russia's Law on Religion" (2002) Document 9404, available at <http://assembly.coe.int/ASP/Doc/DocListingSession_E.asp?IDSession=179>; and PACE, "Russia's Law on Religion" (2002) Resolution 1278, available at <http://assembly.coe.int/Main.asp?link=/Documents/AdoptedText/ta02/ERES1278.htm>.

tion is a secular state".[66] This seems to be a commitment in the foundation of the law to the principles mentioned in the Constitution and the ECHR. Further examples of this are found in various articles of the law.

> "Article 2(3)
>
> Nothing in the legislation on freedom of conscience, freedom of religious profession, and of religious associations should be interpreted in a sense that lessens or infringes the human and civil rights to freedom of conscience and freedom of religious profession that are guaranteed in the constitution of the Russian Federation or derive from international treaties of the Russian Federation."[67]

Article 3(1) of the 1997 Law repeats Article 28 of the Constitution.[68]

> "Article 4(1)
>
> The Russian Federation is a secular state. No religion may be established as a state or obligatory religion; religious associations are separated from the state and are equal before the law."[69]

This confirms the law's commitment to the secularity of the state and, when read in connection with the rest of Article 4, echoes the Constitution in terms of the principle of state neutrality.

Following this, the law becomes more ambiguous in its intentions. Its interpretation and other trends have led to various articles and their use being heavily criticized as incompatible with the Constitution and the ECHR model.

The preamble includes weighted language such as:

> "recognizing the special role of Orthodoxy in the history of Russia and in the establishment and development of its spirituality and culture,"

and

> "respecting Christianity, Islam, Buddhism, Judaism, and other religions, constituting an integral part of the historical heritage of the peoples of Russia."[70]

Recognition of the reference to certain religions as forming an inseparable part of Russia's historic heritage lays the foundations for introduction of the idea of traditional religions, adoption of which has been seen to violate the idea of equality of religions before the law.[71] It is suggested that this reference begins to construct the framework for giving the Russian Orthodox Church a preeminent position above other religions. Further issues are raised by this concept due to its imprecise nature. For example, although the Catholic and Protestant denomina-

66 Law on Freedom of Conscience and on Religious Associations, *op.cit.* note 61, preamble. Translation from Paul D. Steeves, available at <http://www2.stetson.edu/~psteeves/relnews/freedomofconscienceeng.html>.

67 *Ibid.*, Art.2(3).

68 *Ibid.*, Art.3(1).

69 *Ibid.*, Art.4(1).

70 *Ibid.*, preamble.

71 Giovanni Codevilla, "Relations between Church and State in Russia Today", 36 *Religion, State & Society* (2008), 113-138, at 115.

tions are widely regarded as segments of the Christian faith, why they receive second-class treatment in comparison with Orthodoxy is unclear; it is also unclear why Orthodox Old Believer faiths do not fall into the same category as the Russian Orthodox Church.[72] The imprecise nature of this concept is confirmed by the contradictory and often arbitrary nature of its definition by various authorities, legislators and administrative organs. For example, one can compare the definition given by V.I. Korolev (then-head of the Department for Registration of Religious Associations at the Ministry of Justice), who said that "traditional religions include Lutherans, Pentecostals, Baptists, Evangelicals [...]", with the definition given by then-Metropolitan Kirill (now Patriarch and a key figure in Russian religion-state interaction), who stated that "the traditional religions of Russia are Orthodoxy, Islam, Judaism and Buddhism, but not Catholicism".[73] Although these references are only in the preamble, it can be argued that they have certain normative force, and at least construct the foundations for the reading of the law and, thus, the restrictions the law places on freedom of religion. Codevilla argues: "The concept 'traditional religion' is simply a tool used by the law to mark the boundary between tolerance and intolerance."[74]

Consequently, in Chapter II, "Religious Associations", the law begins to outline legal differences between religious entities. The key differentiation is the categorization of religious groups and organizations. The law makes it certain that religious bodies that have not functioned legally in an area for a period of fifteen years are deemed to be religious groups (as opposed to religious organizations). This provision goes a certain way toward creating a hierarchy of religions: the traditional religions mentioned in the preamble with Orthodoxy at the top, other traditional religions, religions of fifteen years standing (these first three all counting as religious organizations), and finally new religions (religious groups). Article 7 clarifies that these newer religious groups will not attain legal personality of the same order as religious organizations and that their activities will be limited to private affairs among the participants of the group.[75] Article 7(1) states that "premises and property necessary for the activities of a religious group are to be provided for the use of the group by its participants".[76] This means that the religion cannot actually own property or engage in transactions—such as renting premises for religious services—but relies on the use of its members' property

72 *Ibid.*, 114. See, also, Irina Budkina, "Religious Freedom since 1905: Any Progress in Russia", available at <http://www.forum18.org/Archive.php?article_id=570>.

73 Metropolitan Kirill told the French Newspaper *Diplomatie* in 2005 that "the four traditional religions of our country are: Orthodoxy, Islam, Judaism and Buddhism". See, also, Kirill's speech at the first meeting of the Federation Council's Joint Commission on National Policy and Relations between the State and Religious Organizations (22 June 2006).

74 Codevilla, *op.cit.* note 71, 115.

75 Law on Freedom of Conscience and on Religious Associations, *op.cit.* note 61, Art.7.

76 *Ibid.*

for this function. This raises various issues such as violation of the principle of all religions being equal before the law, as well as issues concerning the practical equality of religious organizations and religious groups.[77] Article 7(3) states that these religious groups can carry out religious services yet may only carry out the "teaching and religious upbringing of their followers". This can clearly be seen as questionable when we consider the protection granted to the right to "freely choose, possess and disseminate religious or other beliefs, and to act in conformity with them" as stated in the Constitution.[78] This also potentially raises issues concerning the idea of the right to freely choose one's religious belief on the part of an ordinary citizen. By restricting the right of a group that has not existed legally for longer than fifteen years to its own private sphere outside the public realm, the right to choose one's religious belief on the part of the ordinary citizen is restricted.[79] Interpreting Article 6(1), it is possible to suggest that a general failure to protect the right to disseminate one's religion exists for religious organizations as well as groups.[80] Evidence clearly shows that this is not enforced equally for all religions—the dominant religion in an area not being subject to these restrictions in the same way as others. For example, the Orthodox Church is rarely, if ever, subject to limitations on proselytism.[81] Many further contradictions with constitutional principles have also been pointed out, such as Article 27(3) being seen to violate the principle of non-retroactivity by placing demands on already registered religions, issues created by a separation between foreign and domestic founders of religions and the possibility of liquidation for unregistered religions (2006 case of the *Moscow Branch of the Salvation Army*).[82]

While considering these objections on the basis of the law's adherence to constitutional and ECHR principles, it is important to remember that this law was considered specifically by the Council of Europe and was found to constitute an acceptable basis for regulating church-state relations (although this has been disputed).[83] Many of the problem issues appear to have good argumentation

77 Speech by Galina A. Krylova, delivered at the International Coalition for Religious Freedom Conference on "Religious Freedom and the New Millennium" (Washington, DC, 1998), available at <http://www.religiousfreedom.com/Conference/DC/krylova.htm>.

78 Law on Freedom of Conscience and on Religious Associations, *op.cit.* note 61, Art.7.

79 *Ibid.*

80 *Ibid.*, Art.6(1).

81 Verkhovsky and Sibireva, *op.cit.* note 45.

82 Case of the *Moscow Branch of the Salvation Army v. Russia* (5 October 2006) No.72881/01. Among the issues raised in this case were the threat of liquidation for unregistered religions and those concerning the difference between foreign and domestic religions.

83 PACE, Monitoring Committee Report, "On the Honouring of Obligations and Commitments by the Russian Federation" (2002) Document 9396, available at <http://assembly.coe.int/ASP/Doc/XrefViewHTML.asp?FileID=9675&Language=en>; PACE, "On the Honouring of Obligations and Commitments by the Russian Federation" (2002) Resolution 1277,

behind them, although the arguments tend to come from a consideration of extralegal relationships that influence the law rather than legal considerations of the law itself or revolve around legal grey areas, such as the power of the preamble or the idea of traditional religions existing as an active function of protection. However, these issues are being created from outside the legal sphere and acting independently on the legislation rather than developing through or because of it. While many smaller issues in the text of the law are clearly difficult to justify when scrutinized and when compared with certain fundamental principles, it appears that it is the interpretation and use of the law outside these principles (rather than the law itself *per se*) that causes most issues. For example, although creation of a religious hierarchy may be seen to have come about through use of the law to restrict the possibility of certain religions to act, this has happened due to exertion of power by extralegal forces and their manipulation of legislation rather than being specifically laid out in the law.

The text of the law, what it sets out to do and its effect are very much connected with other developments both politically and socially. The law is also heavily influenced by its subordinate legislation, which is often itself misaligned with the principles of the Constitution and the ECHR, or which puts the articles into practical use with little attempt to correct them for constitutionality. A relevant example would be the Law on the Order of Registration, Opening and Closing in the Russian Federation of Representation of Foreign Religious Organizations.[84] The imperfection of the law from a legal point of view has also left it open to much arbitrary interpretation, particularly at the local level.[85] All these factors together mean that the 1997 Law has a considerable impact in law and in practice on the foundations of the reality of the secular state, the function of pluralism and the relationships and social model they create.

Other, Including Anti-Extremist, Legislation

Freedom of religion is part of a much wider legal system that must consider issues broader than those covered by human rights and the fields regulated by the ECHR. It is inevitable that other legislation directly or indirectly impacts on protection of freedom of religion, for example the 2006 Law on Public Associations (NGO

available at <http://www.assembly.coe.int/Main.asp?link=/Documents/AdoptedText/ta02/ERES1277.htm>; and PACE (2002) Resolution 1278, *op.cit.* note 65.

84 "Poriadok registratsii, otkrytiia i zakrytiia v Rossiiskoi Federatsii predtsavitel'stv inostrannykh religioznykh organizatsii" ("On the Order of Registration, Opening and Closing in the Russian Federation of Representations of Foreign Religious Organizations"), approved by an Order (*prikaz*) of the RF Ministry of Justice (3 March 2009) No.62, available at <http://www.minjust.ru/node/1586> and, in translation, at <http://www2.stetson.edu/~psteeves/relnews/0903b.html#09> (transl. Paul Steeves).

85 US Bureau of Democracy, Human Rights and Labor, "Russia: International Religious Freedom Report 2007", available at <http://www.state.gov/g/drl/rls/irf/2007/90196.htm>.

law).[86] This law gives the Ministry of Justice the right to obtain documents and to send agents to investigate religious events and conduct an annual review of an organization's adherence to its mission statement, as well as requiring religions to fulfill certain other obligations such as new, varied and extensive reporting requirements. Many NGOs have complained about the time and effort required to comply with these reporting requirements, which include the obligation to report the source of funds from foreign countries.[87] Failure to comply with this law can result in the NGO or religious organization being shut down. Arbitrary use and interpretation have led to this law being used to target certain religions.[88]

Another important document (and piece of semi-legislation or 'soft law') is the 1997 National Security Concept of the Russian Federation, which was last updated with a new version in 2009. This document stated that "ensuring national security includes countering the negative effect of foreign religious organizations and missionaries".[89] This is closely linked to ideas about the emergence of new religious movements, cults and sects. The Concept states that:

> "Safeguarding the national security of the Russian Federation also means defending the cultural, spiritual and moral heritage, historical traditions and the norms of social life [...] and formulating state policies on the spiritual and moral education of the population [...]."[90]

This is vocabulary that has leaked into the lexicon and minds of officials, with law-enforcement officials and legislators speaking of protecting 'spiritual security' and discouraging the growth of 'cults and sects'. The Moscow City Prosecutor had promised in 2007 that decisive measures would be introduced to put a

86 RF Federal'nyi Zakon "O vnesenii izmenenii v nekotorye zakonodatel'nye akty Rossiiskoi Federatsii", (23 December 2005) No.3972, *Rossiiskaia gazeta* (17 January 2006), (hereinafter the "Law on Introducing Amendments to Certain Legislative Acts of the Russian Federation"). The Law amends four existing laws: the Civil Code, the Law on Public Associations, the Law on Non-commercial Organizations, and the Law on Closed Administrative Territorial Formations.

87 US Bureau of Democracy, Human Rights and Labor, *op.cit.* note 85.

88 *Ibid.* For example, federal authorities (including branches of the *FSB*) have used the authority granted by this law to investigate the Jehovah's Witnesses' headquarters.

89 Ukaz Prezidenta Rossiiskoi Federatsiia "O kontseptsii natsional'noi bezopasnosti Rossiiskoi Federatsii" (17 December 1997) No.1300, with subsequent amendments (10 January 2000) No.24 (hereinafter the "National Security Concept of the Russian Federation"), available at <http://www.armscontrol.ru/start/rus/docs/sncon00.htm>, Sec.II (Natsional'nye interesy Rossii). The new version is: Ukaz Prezidenta Rossiiskoi Federatsiia "Strategiia natsional'noi bezopasnosti Rossiiskoi Federatsii do 2020 goda" (12 May 2009) No.537. These documents are available at the RF Security Council's website <http://www.scrf.gov.ru/index.html>. Translation from <http://www.princeton.edu/~ransac/recentdocuments/russiastrat2000.htm> (which source has since been removed from the Internet).

90 *Ibid.*, Sec.III (Ugrozy natsional'noi bezopasnosti Rossiiskoi Federatisii). Unless otherwise noted, all translations in this chapter are by the author.

stop to the extremism and danger posed to Russia by new religious movements entering the country.[91]

The broad strokes and lack of definition given for what a sect is, what constitutes missionary activity, and which religions are classed as 'new religious movements' (NRM) can result in arbitrary enforcement of the provisions of the law.[92] For example, the term 'sect' is widely understood to include certain Protestant movements, although no basis for this is given. The lack of a legal definition also seems to lead the authorities on occasion to consult or even to follow the opinion of the Russian Orthodox Church.[93]

The 2002 Russian extremism law has various clauses that place the concept of extremism in a religious context—such as committing a crime motivated by religious hatred or obstruction of lawful religious activity by violence or the threat of violence.[94] In many ways, the nature of Russia as a multi-confessional country—and the specific extremism dangers that it faces as a result—make these clauses largely defensible in theory. However, application of these laws in practice has raised issues. Decisions have been made on the basis of the law relating to religious organizations that have failed to make the required factual connections between the people and groups involved and their supposed danger.[95] This was shown with the 2003 ban on the Hizb-ut-Tahrir group by the RF Supreme Court in a closed session—although the judgment did not refer to proof of any terrorist activity.[96] While this trend obviously has been directed against Islamic groups, its potential to be used against other groups can be seen in the way in which it has been employed in cases involving manuscripts of the Jehovah's Witnesses

91 US Bureau of Democracy, Human Rights and Labor, *op.cit.* note 85.

92 *Ibid.*

93 For an extensive explanation of how the Russian Orthodox Church influences discourse and shapes terminology, see Willems, *op.cit.* note 63, 287-298.

94 RF Federal'nyi Zakon "O protivodeistvii ekstremistskoi deiatel'nosti" (with subsequent amendments), (27 June 2002) No.114-FZ, *Rossiiskaia gazeta* (30 July 2002), (hereinafter the "Law on Counteracting Extremist Activity").

95 For relatively comprehensive coverage of the application of anti-extremism legislation and its effects on freedom of religion, see Alexander Verkhovsky and Galina Kozhevnikova, "Inappropriate Enforcement of Anti-extremist Legistion in Russia in 2008", available at <http://xeno.sova-center.ru/6BA2468/6BB4208/CD49ACB?print=on>.

96 Geraldine Fagan, "RUSSIA: Religious Freedom Survey 2008", available at <http://www.forum18.org/Archive.php?article_id=1196>; Verkhovsky and Kozhevnikova, *op.cit.* note 95; and US Bureau of Democracy, Human Rights and Labor, *op.cit. note* 85. Following this, many Hizb-ut-Tahrir members were prosecuted notwithstanding the lack of meaningful evidence of terrorism, even in some cases in an absence of proof that the accused was actually a member of the group. Rather, in these cases, the prosecution relied on unproven and logically flawed testimony as to the nature of some of the group's materials. This forms part of a trend that has led to further literature bans, such as those imposed upon the works of the moderate Said Nursi.

as well as threats based upon this law which have been made against this group by prosecutors (an interesting side note here is that treatment of Jehovah's Witnesses, due to the specifics of their religion and its interaction with the state, is often seen as a good indicator of how well the system of religious protection is functioning in a state).[97] The dangerous development of this law has not gone unnoticed, with the Human Rights Ombudsman for the Russian Federation, Vladimir Lukin, making the following ominous statement:

> "To my mind, it is extremely important not to allow interference in matters of the convictions and beliefs of millions of citizens which could provoke wide-scale violations of their right to freedom of belief and social-religious conflicts in our country under the pretext of fighting extremism."[98]

Issues Relating to Application of the Framework

The complex political situation within Russia and, indeed, also within its regions can have a direct and significant bearing on the effect of laws and how they operate. An example of this which will be discussed in depth is the relationship between the Russian Orthodox Church and the previous and current government. In particular, at the regional level, officials have been put under considerable pressure by majority and powerful groups. This is also evident when considering the key issue of sects and foreign religions and how this has influenced interpretations (and even the creation) and enforcement of the 1997 Law on Freedom of Conscience. Indeed, the political context can influence the behavior of the various parties to alter the effect and application of the standard of protection. The interplay between the Russian Constitutional Court and the legislature is a key example of this, as will be discussed further below.[99]

To be sure, there is a larger context: issues of arbitrariness and legal nihilism pervade the Russian system. It is evident, from a glimpse at interpretations of law, that the letter of the law is often unclear and subject to the whims of the person enforcing it. For example, this fact came through particularly clearly in the 2007 *Kuznetsov and Others v. Russia,* a case in which the Cheliabinsk authorities followed the wishes of one particular person, who was acting utterly *ultra vires*.[100] This is also evident from the occasional lack of proof required, as in certain cases involving extremist legislation or the illogical reasons given by

97 Verkhovsky and Kozhevnikova, *op.cit.* note 95.

98 Mark Smirnov, "Ombudsmen upolnomochen zaiavit' [...]", (interview with former Russian Ambassador in the US and RF Human Rights Ombudsman V. Lukin), *Nezavisimaia gazeta* (4 June 2008). Translated by the editor of the present volume.

99 See Alexei Trochev, *Judging Russia, The Role of the Russian Constitutional Court in Russian Politics 1990-2006* (Cambridge University Press, New York, NY, 2008), 54-188 for intricate examples of how the legal system and politics are intertwined in the Russian Federation.

100 Case of *Kuznetsov and Others v. Russia* (11 April 2007) No.184/02.

some authorities for their actions.[101] However, while certain actions may appear arbitrary, they can be symptomatic of extralegal structures and relationships that have an impact on the functioning of the law. *First*, in a permissive way, where the arbitrary action of one isolated body does not meet with any objection or opposition and *second*, in a more directed way, as manifestations of deeper structural issues outside legal regulation.

There is another issue of importance: the division of power between federal and regional levels is unclear. This leads to decisions being made or to legislation being passed at regional levels violating the principles of protection in the federal legal framework. Between 1993 and 1997, one-third of all regions had passed religious legislation that directly clashed with the liberal 1990 law. This trend has also been observed by monitoring groups within the last few years. The US Department of State's *International Religious Freedom Report 2007: Russia* states that "contradictions between federal and local laws, and varying interpretations of the law, were used by some regional officials to restrict the activities of religious organizations".[102]

There also is confusion about the nature of the law and how to enforce it—an example being the haphazard use of the ECHR and its jurisprudence at regional levels and confusion about their proper place in the Russian legal system. Imperfections in the language of the instruments and the fact that they contradict each other—or were written without thought for the realities of the situation—also contribute to this confusion. In this context, it has been suggested that the Constitution has become less meaningful because it did not arise from the Russian situation but, rather, was an imported set of values incompatible with existing structures.[103] Confusion also comes from lack of proper education and the lack of access for those in relevant positions to necessary information, many of whom have worked for, or have been educated by, institutions with foundations in the Soviet era. The legal interpretation of international law remaining from Soviet times (where direct application of international law was unimaginable)—when many of the current judges were trained—has a negative

101 Case of the *Moscow Branch of the Salvation Army, op.cit.* note 82. It was claimed that the Salvation Army was a paramilitary organization (as mentioned above, this interpretation was seen as totally irrational by Strasbourg.). In the case of the *Church of Scientology Moscow v. Russia* (5 April 2007) No.18147/02, requests were made for original documentation that was already in the hands of the government, making the opportunity to register illusory. In addition, the government was acting arbitrarily and outside the text of the 1997 law by making these demands initially (there have been other similar instances involving registration requirements).

102 US Bureau of Democracy, Human Rights and Labor, *op.cit.* note 85.

103 Elena A. Lukasheva (ed.), *Prava cheloveka i protsessy globalizatsii sovremennogo mira* (Norma, Moscow, 2007), 35; and Anders Fogelklou, "Constitutionalism and the Presidency in the Russian Federation", 18 *International Sociology* (2003), 181-198, at 186. For an example of laws contradicting each other, one can look at the inconsistencies between the 1993 RF Constitution and the 1997 Law on Religion considered above.

impact on the practical functioning of the principles of the Russian state in its present monist approach to the application of international law.[104]

These deeper issues make it hard to trace cause and effect and to differentiate systemic problems from situational problems. Actions can appear to be at the behest of an official or body rather than as the result of that body following a system and procedure. However, through consideration of so many events and actions on the part of authorities all over Russia following the same pattern and theory, acting against the same actors in the same way—and the fact that these acts follow a trend at the federal as well as at the regional level—a body of evidence is created that points toward the existence of an unwritten code of conduct. The almost universal hatred of Scientology by all levels of authorities illustrates this well. From the Constitutional Court to the *FSB* to local registration discrimination, all act against Scientology. Indeed, there is even a phrase in Russian to describe how a course of action not specifically legislated for is arrived at on a systemic level: 'by means of understanding' (*po poniatiiam*).[105]

The Courts

Analyzing the protection offered by Russian courts for the freedom of religion can be extremely difficult considering the above-mentioned factors and, also, the range of situations in different regions. The RF Constitutional Court offers us an interpretation that is most universally valid—even if apparently not universally followed. Although the Court follows the European model of concentrating power in a special body, there are issues as to how it fits into the complete legal system that must be borne in mind as possibly mitigating its power and effect.[106] *First*, it is not the highest court in the system, this position being reserved for the Supreme Court (and, indeed, the two occasionally come into conflict over constitutional issues).[107] *Second*, its relationship with the political elite can dampen its ability to protect constitutional principles. Since the suspension of

104 For information on the practice of judges, see Sergei Y. Marochkin, "International Law in the Courts of the Russian Federation: Practice of Application", 6 *Chinese Journal of International Law* (2007), 329-344. For information on the inadequacies of the Russian judiciary, see Anton L. Burkov, "Implementation of the Convention for the Protection of Human Rights and Fundamental Freedoms in Russian Courts", 1 *Russian Law: Theory and Practice* (2006), 68-75.

105 It is not within the scope of this chapter to consider how this works in detail; therefore, there will be no tracing of paths of causation, *e.g.*, precisely how the relationship between the Orthodox Church and the state trickles down to cause a specific act of discrimination. It is also clear that certain issues are motivated by the arbitrary (prejudiced) and *ultra vires* acts of certain individuals; therefore, arbitrariness cannot always be discounted and ignored. In general, these conditions fall into a wider pattern and cannot be dismissed as a collection of random acts motivated by individuals without systemic cause.

106 Burkov, *op.cit.* note 104, 68-75

107 For examples and an explanation, see Richardson and Shterin, *op.cit.* note 62, 257.

the Constitutional Court by presidential edict, the Court has been described as having a tendency toward 'political restraint'.[108] As far as the freedom of religion is concerned, this trend has continued under the presidencies of Putin and Medvedev.[109] This is not to say the Court has no power whatsoever; furthermore, it has shown certain interpretative initiative and clever legal logic to walk the line demanded of it. It must fulfill a role in an environment that requires a balance to be found between the need to respect constitutional principles and those of the international community, and to honor, on the one hand, the desires of various parts of Russian society demanding respect for freedom of religion and, on the other, not to lose sight of the more restrictive desires of powerful elements in the legislature and executive.[110]

In this respect, certain trends can be found in the case law of the RF Constitutional Court. *First*, it consistently refers to the importance of constitutional principles as the cornerstone of the legal system. In the 1999 case *Jehovah's Witnesses in Iaroslavl' and the Christian Church of Glorification (in Abakan)*, the Court stated:

> "The introduction of principles related to the establishment and registration of religious organisations should not distort the very essence of freedom of religion [...] and the introduction of restrictions on these rights should be justified and proportionate to constitutional principles."[111]

This principle is repeated throughout the jurisprudence in cases such as the *Independent Russian Region of the Society of Jesus* and the *Moscow Branch of the Salvation Army* (2000 and 2006 respectively).[112]

However, in the same cases, the Court recognizes the right of the state to:

> "[...] introduce certain legal barriers in order to avoid automatic conferment of the status of religious organisation; to disallow legalisation of sects that violate human rights and perpetuate unlawful and criminal acts; to prohibit missionary activities (including in connection

108 Anders Fogelklou, "Constitutionalism and the Presidency in the Russian Federation", 18 *International Sociology* (2003), 181-198, at 191.

109 Whether this is because the Court is "powerless to challenge any legal act issued by the president" as Richardson and Shterin suggest (*op.cit.* note 62, 257)—or whether restraint is connected to alignment of the Court and the legislature's overall goals as Trochev argues (*op.cit.* note 99, 54-188 and 207-300)—is an interesting question.

110 Richardson and Shterin, *op.cit.* note 62, 262-264.

111 Postanovlenie Konstitutsionnogo Suda Rossiiskoi Federatsii, "O svobode sovesti i o religioznikh ob"edineniiakh v sviazi s zhalobami religioznogo obshchestva svidetelei iegovy v gorode Iaroslavle i religioznogo ob"edineniia Khristianskaia tserkov' proslavleniia" (23 November 1999) No.16-P, *Rossiiskaia gazeta* (16 December 1999). Translation from Richardson and Shterin, *op.cit.* note 62.

112 Opredelenie Konstitutsionnogo Suda Rossiiskoi Federatsii, "Nezavisimyi Rossiiskii region obshchestva Iisusa" (13 April 2000) No.46-O, *Rossiiskaia gazeta* (16 May 2000); and the case of *Moscow Branch of the Salvation Army, op.cit.* note 82.

> with the problem of proselytising), if they are incompatible with respect for the freedom of thought, conscience and religion of others."[113]

Legitimacy is added by referencing Strasbourg decisions and Council of Europe documents (although conveniently avoiding reference to their actual content).[114] Deference to the state is a recurring theme throughout the Court's case law, as it performs legal gymnastics to avoid declaring provisions of the 1997 Law on Religion unconstitutional—even though, often, the logic that it puts forward regarding its interpretation of the Constitution and the 1997 Law suggest that this is, in fact, what it is doing.[115]

Thus, the protection offered by the Court comes in the form of an open interpretation of the articles of the law, onto which it then affixes a stamp of authority, claiming that any other interpretation is unconstitutional.[116] An example of this was the reasoning in the 1999 judgment in the *Jehovah's Witnesses in Iaroslavl' and the Christian Church of Glorification (in Abakan)* case. When considering Article 27(4) of the 1997 Law, the Court considered the article in accordance with the Constitution, as its interpretation must give primacy to the Constitution. It suggested that, as this was the case, the drafters could not have intended to remove pre-existing freedoms and, thus, that re-registration could not have been intended to involve extra conditions.

In this way, problematic issues were interpreted out of existence, leaving the constitutional principles and the principles of the 1997 Law intact and avoiding a clash altogether. This interpretation to reconcile the facts of the case with the article of the Law without strongly considering the structural quality of the article is the key to the Court's strategy of protection.

This interpretative protection comes with limits, however, and one can see political and social pressures on the Court within them. The Court can be seen to have protection of minority religions and certain forms of 'recognized foreign religions' as a goal, while stopping short of guaranteeing religious freedom to all. In the 2002 case of the *Church of Scientology in Izhevsk*, the Court made no reference to constitutional principles when it refused to hear the case but, rather, listed a number of reasons why a group could be banned (although this had nothing

113 *Ibid.* Translation by Richardson and Shterin, *op.cit.* note 62.

114 Postanovlenie No.16-P, *op.cit.* note 111; see, also, Richardson and Shterin, *op.cit.* note 62, 259-261 for commentary.

115 Postanovlenie No.16-P, *op.cit.* note 111. For example the dissenting opinion of Liudmila Zharkova. Zharkova disagreed on the issue of the constitutionality of Arts.27(3) and 27(4). On the one hand, she pointed to the lack of judicial logic since the decision referred to the primacy of the constitutional principles of freedom of religion but, on the other, agreed that these articles—allowing for restrictions on a whole category of religious associations—were in accordance with the Constitution.

116 Postanovlenie No.16-P, *op.cit.* note 111.

to do with the dispute).[117] Although the Court was technically acting within its jurisdiction, it showed none of the willingness to protect constitutional values in a case very similar to many in which it previously had done so.[118] Richardson and Shterin argue that:

> "The Russian Constitutional Court's decisions attempt to reconcile the constitutional principles of freedom of religion with the perception that newer faiths may abuse this freedom by engaging in 'socially unacceptable' activities [...] the rationale echoes 'cult controversies' in Russia and elsewhere [...] The rationale of the decisions is clearly designed to limit the application of their liberal interpretations to more 'recognizable' foreign faiths."[119]

Relationship of the Russian Orthodox Church to the State

To consider this system in a broader context, it is necessary to consider the relationship between the Russian Orthodox Church (ROC) and the Russian state. This relationship is key to understanding how freedom of religion as a model is perceived and how it operates in reality. It is also key to understanding how the other relationships in question operate.

The ROC is widely assumed to have become the *de facto* state church, but in public statements, the Church not only refutes this but claims that this would be undesirable.[120] In no official documentation or legal instrument is the ROC ever referred to as the 'state church', and this has never been confirmed by the authorities. Yet, there appear to be allusions to this throughout legislation and in the actions of certain authorities. It would be very difficult to openly proclaim the existence of a state church. To do so would openly violate constitutional principles, something the state has taken great efforts to avoid (Art.13).[121]

The ROC, for its part, sets forth in the 2005 "Bases of the Social Concept of the ROC" the view that it spiritually is the Church of Russia, at the center of its culture, and that its connection to culture and development ought to bestow certain rights on it. It claims that religious equality before the law is impossible

117 Opredelenie Konstitutsionnogo Suda Rossiiskoi Federatsii, "Ob otkaze v priniatii k passmotreniiu zhaloby grazhdan I.A. Zaikovoi, N.Kh. Nikitina, A.G. Prozorova, V.G. Rabotneva, N.P. Sergeevoi, N.R. Khalikovoi i F.F. Khalikova na narushenie ikh konstitutsionnykh prav punktom 1 stat'i 9 i punktom 5 stat'i 11 Federal'nogo Zakona 'O svobode sovesti i o religioznykh ob"edineniiakh'" (9 April 2002) No.113, *Vestnik Konstitutsionnogo Suda RF* (2002) No.6.

118 Richardson and Shterin, *op.cit.* note 62, 262.

119 *Ibid.*, 263.

120 Russian Orthodox Church, "Osnovy sotsial'noi kontseptsii Russkoi Pravoslavnoi tserkvi" (12 September 2005), available at <http://www.patriarchia.ru/db/text/141422.html>; English translation "Bases of the Social Concept of the Russian Orthodox Church" from the Department for External Church Relations of the Moscow Patriarchate available at <http://orthodoxeurope.org/page/3/14.aspx>. For the ROC's view on this, see Section III: "Church and State".

121 Codevilla, *op.cit.* note 71, 113-122.

and that secularity must be built considering the Orthodox foundation of the state. However, it stops short of claiming itself to be a state church, in fact, suggesting that in the modern secularity of the state it cannot exist as a state church.[122] Thus, the connection that exists, *de facto* or *de jure,* must be defined and implied from the evidence and movements of the parties rather than demonstrated through the legal status of the relationship.

The phrase 'state church' has a variety of meanings in different places. One common aspect of state churches is the two-way relationship that exists between them and the state. The existence of a state church implies an organizational synergy between state and church.[123] In this instance, there seems to be little state interference in the workings of the ROC or in its decisions. This is not to say that the ROC is not used for political purposes by the state; but, if this happens, it happens on the ROC's terms. For example, ministers in the employ of a state church in Western Europe may have significant restrictions on their actions due to government control, while cases such as these would not occur in relation to the ROC, as the clergy have no obligation toward the state outside what has been laid out for them by the hierarchy of the church itself. Equally, the Church has the ability to openly criticize the actions of the state, as it did with the 2006 NGO law—its lobbying pressure forcing reform of part of the legislation.[124] It is, thus, possible to assume that the ROC does not fit into the mould of a department of state. The two remain distinct entities.

On the other hand, the ROC does enjoy preference regarding its status. This is true, first, in terms of the law and its formation. For example, the 1997 Law on Religion contains language that raised its status above other religions (although the fact that some of this language is in the preamble makes its legal impact debatable).

This is also shown by the ability of the ROC to put pressure on legislators in a way that no other religion can. The 1997 Law was pushed through on the back of extensive lobbying by the more conservative elements of the Orthodox Church.[125] Orthodox legal scholars suggest that the state is fully entitled to create privileges for the Russian Orthodox Church as historically 'the' Church of Russia.[126]

122 "Osnovy sotsial'noi kontseptsii [...]", *op.cit.* note 120 (Secs.II and III).

123 See the section in the present work above on "Neutrality and the ECtHR" for examples and a description of the common functioning of a state church.

124 Geraldine Fagan, "RUSSIA: Religious Organisations' NGO Law Financial Accounting Simplified" (17 April 2007), available at <http://www.forum18.org/Archive.php?article_id=943>.

125 Astrid S. Tuminez, *Russian Nationalism since 1856: Ideology and the Making of Foreign Policy* (Rowman & Littlefield, Lanham, UK, 2000), 202.

126 A.M. Ivanov, "Russkaia Pravoslavnaia Tserkov' v kontekste osnovnykh prav cheloveka i grazhdanina v sovremennoi Rossii", 4(279) *Pravovedenie* (2008), 19-35, at 32.

An investigation into certain state policies also reveals an alignment and preference for the ROC. *First*, if we consider Orthodox documents such as the 2005 "Bases of the Social Concept of the ROC" or "Catholic Proselytism Among the Orthodox Population of Russia"[127] and compare them with state instruments such as the 2000 National Security Concept, one can find many Orthodox opinions and politics reflected in state doctrine. This is especially true concerning burning social issues that cross into the religious sphere, for example relating to sects and proselytism.

Second, it is suggested that terminology and ideas brought to the fore by Orthodoxy are often adapted for use by politicians, and that Orthodoxy plays a role in shaping the language and foundation of discourse, therefore shaping the foundations and direction of eventual action.[128] The issue of sects demonstrates this idea well. The phrase 'totalitarian sect' was created by hard-line traditionalists and soon taken up by the ROC, as it took up a strong position against new religious movements. This terminology was then taken up politically, largely on the back of Orthodox lobbying in the area. This was then used as a core term around which a discourse arose and thus eventually contributed to concrete action against specific bodies.[129]

Finally, Orthodoxy is directly privileged in the interpretation of the law and its development, as it is often used as an authoritative source relating to religion. For example, the reference booklet on sects in circulation among the Russian judiciary was written by the External Affairs Department of the Orthodox Church, and public displays offensive to the Orthodox Church have been received negatively by the judiciary, as in 2005, when an art exhibition (found distasteful by the ROC) was banned on blasphemy charges (masquerading as incitement-to-hatred charges).[130] Moreover, on 12 July 2010, the Tagan District Court of Moscow declared the organizers of the exhibition "Prohibited Art–2006" guilty of violating Article 282 of the Criminal Code ("incitement of hatred").[131] On 4 February 2011, the Council of Bishops, the highest body of the Russian Orthodox Church, adopted a document on blasphemy and defamation, arguing

127 "Katolicheskii proselitizm sredi pravoslavnogo naseleniia Rossii" (26 June 2002), available at <http://www.mospat.ru/archive/nr207011.htm>.

128 Willems, *op.cit.* note 63, 287-297.

129 Julie Elkner, "Spiritual Security in Putin's Russia", H&P *Policy Papers* (January 2005), available at <http://www.historyandpolicy.org/papers/policy-paper-26.html>.

130 Alexander Verkhovsky, "Intervention to the 2008 OSCE Human Dimension Implementation Meeting by the SOVA Centre, 2008. Working Session 'Freedom of Religion or Belief'", available at <http://religion.sova-center.ru/publications/194EF5E/BD440DB>.

131 Grigorii Revzin, "Tsena koshunstva", *Kommersant Vlast'* (19 July 2010), available at <http://www.kommersant.ru/Doc/1413070?isSearch=True>.

that both are criminalized within the existing Criminal Code. However, experts point out that blasphemy is not technically mentioned in the Criminal Code.[132]

In relation to organs of the state, the ROC also enjoys certain privileges. In 2006, the ROC signed an agreement with *Rospatent* so that any trademark related to religious associations first had to be agreed with the Patriarchate.[133] This form of agreement with state organs is widely evident and also can be seen with regard to the armed forces and prisons. Various commentators note that the ROC enjoys a *de facto* monopoly on sectors of the armed forces, even being asked to bless vehicles and conduct mass baptisms and has signed agreements with many agencies of the armed forces.[134] Museum directors must find a common language with the ROC under threat of being fired by *Roskino* (the Federal Agency for Culture and Cinematography), and in 2007 among many others *Rossviaz'okhrankul'tura* (the Federal Service for the Supervision of Legal Adherence in Mass Media, Communications and Cultural Heritage) signed an agreement with the ROC—there are no such agreements with other religions at the federal level (although parallels may be drawn at regional levels where other religions are in the majority).[135] Finally, the debate about Orthodox Culture courses in Russian schools and on state support for teaching Orthodox principles is too detailed to consider fully here; however, it further evidences a seeming preference on the part of the state for Orthodoxy and its principles.[136]

The ROC enjoys certain extralegal preferential treatment in aspects of religious life compared to other religions. This is evidenced firstly by the funding it receives. There is no federal legislation about funding distribution to religious organizations, but the ROC receives a disproportionate amount. In 2007, President Medvedev promised a total of 6 billion rubles to the Patriarchate over the period 2008 to 2010.[137] This is also evident in the transfer of property to religious organizations. Many organizations have had difficulty in recovering property since

132 Aleksandr Verkhovskii, "Religioznye organizatsii vyrabatyvaiut pravovoi immunitet", *Nezavisimaia gazeta* (16 February 2011), available at <http://www.sova-center.ru/religion/publications/2011/02/d20991/>.

133 Alexander Verkhovsky and Olga Sibireva, "Problems Relating to Freedom of Conscience in Russia in 2006", SOVA Center (2007), available at <http://www.sova-center.ru/en/religion/publications/2007/04/d10651/>.

134 Verkhovsky and Sibireva, *op.cit.* note 45. This can also depend on the locality and the individual commander; for example in Muslim areas, Muslim clerics may also be allowed to engage in these activities.

135 For many examples see *ibid.* and the US Bureau of Democracy, Human Rights and Labor, *op.cit.* note 85. See, further, Verkhovsky and Sibireva, *op.cit.* note 45.

136 Question-and-answer session by Vsevolod Chaplin, "Zachem uchit' shkol'nikov pravoslaviu?". See, also, Verkhovsky and Sibireva, *op.cit.* note 45; and the US Bureau of Democracy, Human Rights and Labor, *op.cit.* note 85, for examples of how Orthodoxy benefits from this.

137 Verkhovsky and Sibireva, *op.cit.* note 45.

the Soviet period or in obtaining possession of property promised to them; yet, the ROC has had very few issues in this regard. In fact, it has been granted possession of many non-ROC properties—particularly with regard to the property of non-ROC Orthodox communities' churches, as well as certain sites of cultural value such as the Solovki Museum.[138] As concerns construction of new religious buildings, the ROC not only receives the blessing of the federal administration, and often funding as well, but seldom meets the resistance encountered by other religious groups in seeking to construct places of worship.[139] In many instances, regional authorities have consulted the local Orthodox hierarchy before confirming permission for other religions to carry out their building plans.[140]

The ways in which the ROC enjoys favor could be seen as creating a close relationship of patronage and approval. However, the causes for these actions can be further analyzed to understand what motivates the relationship. A convergence in aims and principles is the first strand to consider. In many ways, it can be seen as a relationship of convenience for both parties, as their current views and standpoints lead to a convergence of aims and, consequently, to an alliance of convenience.[141] There has been a political trend, in the last few years, toward a recentralization of power.[142] This development parallels the view of how the state should operate held by the ROC in its 2005 "Bases of the Social Concept of the ROC" and other documents.[143] Further, the ideas of a strong nation and the rediscovery and protection of national values and culture—pushed by the Putin regime—find strong similarity in goals and ideology with the ROC.[144] This

138 *Ibid.* For example, the gifting of former Lutheran churches to the ROC in Kaliningrad *Oblast'*.

139 Verkhovsky and Sibireva *op.cit.* note 45; and US Bureau of Democracy, Human Rights and Labor, *op.cit.* note 85.

140 *Ibid.*

141 For more information on the convergence of views, see Codevilla, *op.cit.* note 71, 113-138; and Willems, *op.cit.* note 63, 287-297. See, also, Wallace L. Daniel, "The Children of Perestroika: Two Sociologists on Religion and Russian Society, 1991-2006", 35 *Religion, State & Society* (2007), 163-185, for a more sociological viewpoint about the convergence of aims of the ROC and the Russian state.

142 Kozlychin, *op.cit.* note 46, 70-75.

143 "Osnovy sotsial'noi kontseptsii [...]", *op.cit.* note 120 (Sec.III).

144 See, particularly, the Declaration on Human Rights and Dignity, adopted by the World Russian Peoples' Council (14 April 2006), available at <http://www.mospat.ru/archive/en/30728.htm>, with heavy Orthodox influence that closely mimics Kremlin views on various issues. See the concept of 'sovereign democracy' as outlined in a speech by Vladislav Surkov on 22 February 2006 to a gathering for the United Russia party as an example of this in the political theory of the Putin regime. See, also, Andrei Okara, "Sovereign Democracy: A New Russian Idea or a PR Project", *Russia in Global Affairs* (8 August 2007), available at <http://eng.globalaffairs.ru/numbers/20/1124.html>, where the nature of the Russian state is compared to that of the ROC.

convergence of goals and philosophies has been particularly visible in rhetoric and laws concerning newer foreign religions. The idea of Russian culture arguably contains the idea of a more collective identity, where the good of Russia must sometimes come before the individual. This has had an impact on the way that 'imported values'—such as human rights and other foreign identities (including foreign religions)—are seen to fit into society within Russia. This thinking, again, is theory found in Orthodox opinions on society.[145]

This convergence happened against the background of a transition period in which it is perhaps no surprise that the needs of the two came together. The ROC has massive popular support—over 70% of Russians claim to be Orthodox and support the ROC.[146] It is recognized as a traditional Russian institution, sets itself out as the keeper of Russian values[147] and legacy and puts itself at the foundation of the Russian entity as a nation-forming tradition.[148] However, it has faced increasing marginalization in a less religious Russia (a large portion of the 70-plus-percent being believers from a cultural rather than a religious viewpoint), as a new form of secular society is once again pushing religion out of the public sphere, and there is greater competition for believers on account of the increased numbers of religions, many of which are better funded by foreign sources.[149]

Concurrently, the state under Putin was looking for alliances to legitimate itself and its cause in popular opinion, at a time when the authenticity of the

145 See "Osnovy sotsial'noi kontseptsii [...]", *op.cit.* note 120; "Basic Principles of the Attitude of the Russian Orthodox Church Toward the Other Christian Confessions", adopted by the Jubilee Bishops' Council of the Russian Orthodox Church (14 August 2000), available at <http://www.orthodoxresearchinstitute.org/articles/ecumenical/roc_other_christian_confessions.htm>; and "Katolicheskii proselitizm", *op.cit.* note 127, as documents providing one with insight into the Russian Orthodox Church's conception of social organization, foreign religions, etc. See, also, the National Security Concept of the Russian Federation, *op.cit.* note 89, and cited legislation as well as the use thereof to gain a better appreciation of the Russian government's stance on foreign religions.

146 Vladislav Mal'tsev, "Tserkov' kak instrument sotsial'noi stabil'nosti", *Nezavisimaia gazeta* (16 June 2010), available at <http://www.ng.ru/ng_religii/2010-06-16/1_social.html>.

147 Andrei Nikolaev, "Russkaia tserkov' prevrashaetsia v 'ministerstvo pravdy'", *Nezavisimaia gazeta* (16 February 2011), available at <http://www.ng.ru/society/2011-02-16/2_min_pravdy.html>.

148 Sergei Filatov and Roman Lunkin, "Statistics on Religion in Russia: The Reality behind the Figures", 34 *Religion, State & Society* (2006), 33-49.

149 Alexander Verkhovsky, "The Role of The Russian Orthodox Church in Nationalist, Xenophobic and Antiwestern Tendencies in Russia Today: Not Nationalism, but Fundamentalism", 30 *Religion, State & Society* (2002), 333-345, at 335; and Peter Juviler, "Religious Human Rights: Constitution, Law and Practice in Post-Soviet Russia", in Robert Sharlet and Ferdinand Feldbrugge (eds.), *Public Policy and Law in Russia: In Search of a Unified Legal and Political Space*, in William B. Simons (ed.), *Law in Eastern Europe*, No.55 (Martinus Nijhoff, Leiden, 2005), 225-240, at 231.

state and its apparatus were under scrutiny.[150] Vladislav Mal'tsev suggests that the representatives of power understand that society does not trust them and consequently try to legitimize their situation with the help of the authority and trust the populace has for the Russian Orthodox Church.[151]

This idea of an alliance of usefulness is supported by observations of situations in which the Church is at odds with the direction or philosophy of state policy, or where it is seen to be acting outside its perceived sphere of influence.[152] In these situations, the Church's voice is not always taken above others and may even be ignored. Willems comments: "The ROC is in fact involved in a power struggle with other political and social actors, all the players have their own strengths and weaknesses, consequences of their positions in the social and historical context."[153] This was shown as the opinions of the ROC met those of politics and business in arguments about an ethical code for businessmen. In this discussion, the suggestions of the church were flatly ignored.

Thus, the relationship is that of an implied special status among religions. The ROC clearly enjoys benefits not given to other religions and enjoys a pre-eminence in issues of the non-secular. An interesting question is the dynamic of this alliance, Codevilla suggesting that the Church has such popular support that it is in a position to call all the shots, while others—such as Behrens—suggest the opposite is true and that the ROC is used as a political tool.[154]

Thus, *de jure,* there is no state church, although there is a very important *de facto* relationship.[155] This does not mean that a paradigm is not being created legally. The more the synergy and the goals of the institutions coincide, the more they will overlap and intertwine, and this may become irreversible. For example, the dependency of the ROC on state funds cannot be easily reversed. Thus, if the

150 Daniel, *op.cit.* note 141, 163-185.

151 Malt'sev, *op.cit.* note 146.

152 This alliance of convenience is shown in the temporal nature of the connection when considered in relation to the dynamics of the relationships in the past. Verkhovsky (*op.cit.* note 149, 335) discusses the strong connection which the ROC had—during the El'tsin era—with the communist opposition.

153 Willems, *op.cit.* note 63, 288.

154 Codevilla, *op.cit.* note 71, 115-122; and Kathrin Behrens, *Die Russische Orthodoxe Kirche: Segen fuer die 'neuen Zaren'? Religion und Politik im postsowjetischen Rußland* (Ferdinand Schöningh Verlag, Paderborn, 2002), 379. Behrens states: "The real influence of the ROC on political processes and political actors depends on how far its own interests coincide with those of the political classes and in particular with those of the decision makers within the state [...] the greater the convergence, the greater the evidence of the ROC's potential power [...] in cases where the ROC has not impinged on the political players [...] or where they have been in direct conflict with the politicians' plans, the ROC has not been able to influence events." Translation from Codevilla, *op.cit.* note 71.

155 Juviler, *op.cit.* note 149, 232.

present trend continues, a state church may come into existence.[156] This raises the question as to whether the relationship that exists breaches the constitutional principles of the neutrality and secularity of the state. In this regard, the breadth of support the ROC enjoys should be considered, as should the historical role it has played in shaping Russian culture. The government's behavior recognizes the ROC as the dominant religion and pays respect to its large base of support and contribution to Russian culture.[157] To do otherwise might be seen as denying historical truth. At the same time, it can easily be seen as undemocratic not to recognize the ROC's preeminence. That an organization with such a wide base of support would be treated the same as all others would be to ignore the confession of the vast majority of people.[158] "It is as unjust to handle equal legal relationships in an unequal way as it is to handle unequal legal relationships in an equal way."[159]

Pluralism

In theory, the constitutional principles of secularism and pluralism are very similar to those in the ECHR. In fact, other factors such as aspects of the 1997 Law, its interpretation, developments in the relationship between the ROC and the state—and various social and political developments—alter this model from its theoretical base. What does pluralism mean in the Russian system?

In the pluralistic system established in the Constitution, all religions should be equal before the law and enjoy equal rights in relation to what they are allowed to do and to the restrictions that are placed on them. Currently, this is not the case. The 1997 Law created the opportunity for the foundations of a system of 'preferential pluralism' legally, while developments in the relationship between the state and the ROC have developed the same idea extralegally. Thus, what exists is a hierarchy of religions. All religions are allowed to exist, but their legal and factual status differs greatly. At the top, there is the ROC. Owing to its relationship with the state, it occupies a privileged position; it suffers little interference and is even consulted for its views on the religious landscape. Below this, there are other traditional religions that operate relatively unrestricted (with the exception of Islam of certain codes and in certain areas) and occasionally enjoy local preference. Then there are religions that have existed for longer than fifteen

156 Codevilla, *op.cit.* note 71, 121. For the theory behind the intertwining of the church and the state, see A.C. Jemolo, *Premesse ai rapporti tra Chiesa e Stato* (Giuffre, Milano, 1965).

157 See Andrei Zolotov, Jr., "Why Russia Restricts Religions", *The Christian Science Monitor* (28 October 1997), available at <http://www.asylumlaw.org/docs/russia/RUS_3/Sec%20 II/Why%20Russia.pdf>. The argument is that Orthodoxy is Russia's national religion, and its place in society and Russia's specificity/*spetsifika* (exceptionalism) mean that foreign proselytism must be limited.

158 Codevilla, *op.cit.* note 71, 124-126.

159 Ruffini, *op.cit.* note 30. Translation from Codevilla, *op.cit.* note 71.

years in Russia. These should be afforded the status of equal legal protection with the other traditional religions but, equally arbitrarily, may not. Their treatment rests on various factors: how they are regarded in the eyes of the ROC, how they are regarded in the eyes of the public (this largely, also, depends on how they are portrayed in the media), how they conform and align with the philosophy of the government, and their perceived foreignness. Various religions (some of which even have claims to being traditional) have suffered because of different constellations of these factors. The Catholic Church, for example, has an ongoing dispute with the ROC concerning proselytism and, thus, despite centuries of presence in Russia has come up against measures preventing its functioning.[160] Jehovah's Witnesses, particularly, and various other branches of Protestantism have been demonized in the media, in various areas being labeled as dangerous sects—often at the behest and encouragement of the ROC—and have come up against opposition in achieving equality.[161] For example, the ROC led a campaign in the media and elsewhere using a particularly wide definition of extremism to close the Jehovah's publication *The Watchtower*.[162] In November 2007, an 'anti-sectarian' report about the Light of Awakening Evangelical Christian Church in Barnaul appeared on the federal TV channel '*Rossiia*' as part of a crime show. According to the Slavic Center for Law and Justice, the report "exceeded the traditional allegations of turning people into zombies and brainwashing, and took [the accusations] to a new level".[163]

Finally, there are new religious movements. These have a lower legal status that entails a more restricted sphere of activity and a weaker position that is open to more interference. Due to the prominence of the issue of sects and their supposed danger to Russian values, these new religions find themselves in a very precarious position.[164] The unfamiliarity of these NRMs to Russia, the consideration of them as foreign influences and the lack of differentiation between the terms 'new religious movement' and 'sect' make them an easy target—especially considering the influence of the ROC on the issue of sects. For example, anti-sect centers have been set up in various areas such as St. Petersburg, Adygeia and Chuvashiia, and local governments have been funding anti-sect conferences and initiatives such as the anti-sect conference sponsored by Riazan'.[165] These initiatives have

160 "Katolicheskii proselitizm", *op.cit.* note 127.

161 Emily B. Baran, "Contested Victims, Jehovah's Witnesses and the ROC 1990-2004", 35 *Religion, State & Society* (2007), 261-278.

162 Verkhovsky and Kozhevnikova, *op.cit.* note 95.

163 Verkhovsky and Sibireva, *op.cit.* note 45. The SCLJ is a Moscow-based non-governmental organization (<http://sclj.org>) the goal of which is to protect "religious rights and freedoms of individuals and associations in Russia". It has affiliates in the US and Europe.

164 Marat Shterin, "New Religions, Cults and Sects in Russia: A Critique and Brief Account of the Problems" (no date), available at <http://www.cesnur.org/testi/Shterin.htm>.

165 Verkhovsky and Sibireva, *op.cit.* note 45.

often been founded in collaboration with the ROC and have largely targeted new foreign religions (and un-favored religions) without particular differentiation or attention to the principles of differentiation between a religion and a sect.

Political leanings can also be associated with faiths, and it has been suggested that these play a role in defining state behavior toward a confession. For example, adherence to the ideals of liberal democracy can be found in protestant teaching and philosophy along with a leaning toward development together with the West. This has been cited as a reason (with development of a more authoritarian government) why the Protestant churches have begun to encounter difficulties.[166]

The trend toward re-Russification and the prominence of the ROC and its stance against 'non-Russian' religions has made securing rights for religions such as the Unification Church or the Hari Krishna Movement more difficult. For example, the building of the Krishna Consciousness Society Temple in Moscow has not started, (although land has been allocated and the building has been in planning for years) due to protests by local Orthodox movements. Unification Church leader Jack Corley was deported, and various foreign invitees have had visa problems, such as the Japanese member who was refused entry and forced to buy a ticket for himself and an accompanying *FSB* agent back to Japan (although he appealed and won the right to re-enter).[167]

Between religious and non-religious groups, this preferential pluralism also plays a key role. The issue of balance between freedom of expression and freedom of religion is an example of this. The RF Constitution asserts that freedom of speech and expression is a freedom that deserves special protection, even though what is said may offend certain people or groups. However, when it comes to religions, it depends on the position that a religion occupies in the hierarchy as to the level of protection it will receive and the way in which rights will be balanced. As seen above, there have been a number of negative newspaper articles and media broadcasts concerning the Jehovah's Witnesses.[168] These articles claim that the Jehovah's Witnesses are a totalitarian sect and that their texts can be seen as incitements to genocide and worse. It usually is quite difficult for them to defend their rights. In situations involving minor religions and other groups, a broader margin of appreciation of state action is applied by the courts and, indeed, in many cases the courts have declined to admit cases at all.[169] We can compare this to a situation involving an attack on (or threat to) the ROC; for

166 Filatov and Lunkin, *op.cit.* note 148, 5-16.

167 US Bureau of Democracy, Human Rights and Labor, *op.cit.* note 85.

168 Baran, *op.cit.* note 161, 261-268.

169 Case of the *Church of Scientology in Izhevsk, op.cit.* note 117, as an example of a wider margin given to authorities in a case involving a minority religion.

example, as already has been mentioned, the 2006 exhibition "Religion! Beware" was shut down following protests by the ROC.[170]

Thus, within the sphere of religion, the playing field is not level; instead, there is a hierarchy throughout every aspect of religious life. However, it has been argued that the positions occupied by the various religions are supposedly justified by their social and historical importance. Defense of Russian values is a commonly used argument by both the ROC and the government. It has also been proposed that the idea of a fifteen-year gestation and the skepticism at new and foreign religions come as a natural and sensible response to the influx of new religions in a transitional society. Morozov and Kyrlezhev consider the possibility of a spiritual free-for-all being created as a result of an unexpected overflow of new religions due to the liberal 1990 law after a long period of a totally secular state.[171] Their argument follows that of Berman, who also suggests that an amount of spiritual skepticism and uniformity is necessary in states in transition. As Codevilla suggests, the ranking system undoubtedly gives the government room to maneuver against new religious movements that were not genuinely religions but used the liberal law to exploit a society in transition.[172] However, arguments such as these were aimed at providing the best conditions in which nascent democratic values would be able to flourish. It is not certain whether the development of the current paradigm fits these conditions.

Therefore, the role of the state cannot be seen as that of a 'neutral moderator and creator of the framework' in which religion can flourish. The hierarchy of religions was deliberately created and allowed to develop. In some ways, the structure can be seen as an extension of state power—as a device to allow the state to control the penetration of religion into the public sphere and to justify control and observation of activities within the religious sphere, to control the impact of religion and religious organizations.[173] That a religious group cannot teach its philosophy to those outside its own group of followers is one example of the state preventing penetration by certain religions into the public sphere. However, once again, as we move up the hierarchy, these restrictions become less prohibitive until we reach the ROC. Rhetoric and reference to sects and

170 For the view of the Moscow Patriarchate's Department for External Church Relations concerning the exhibition, see Dimitri Ageev, "'Beware of Religion!': A Rebirth of Militant Atheism in Moscow", available at <http://orthodoxeurope.org/page/14/14.aspx#5>.

171 See Alexander Kyrlezhev, "The Postsecular Age, Religion and Culture Today", 36 *Religion, State & Society* (2008), 21-31 (translation of Aleksandr Kyrlezhev, "Postsekuliarnaia epokha", *Kontinent* (2004) No.120; Alexander Morozov, "Has the Postsecular Age Begun", 36 *Religion, State & Society* (2008), 39-44; and *id.*, "The Fourth Secularization", 36 *Religion, State & Society* (2008), 33-38.

172 Codevilla, *op.cit.* note 71, 127.

173 See Verkhovsky, *op.cit.* note 149, 337, for examples of state interference in the religious sphere (*e.g.*, interfering with the election of a rabbi).

foreign religions in the National Security Concept can also be viewed as part of this control. Linking security and faith can be seen as a justification for the state to observe or liquidate religious movements, particularly religious groups. The constant supervision and suspicion of the Jehovah's Witnesses receives justification when they are linked with the discussion concerning sects and security.[174]

Compliance and Compatibility

The most obvious starting point is to examine what Strasbourg has considered regarding Russia. However, Strasbourg has not had much comment on structural problems in the Russian model. Instead, it has treated most cases as isolated incidents. For example, in the cases of the *Moscow Branch of the Salvation Army* or the *Church of Scientology Moscow* (2006 and 2007 respectively), the Court considered the specific legal issues raised—such as minor areas of the 1997 Law requiring amendment—together arbitrary actions by government agencies, and how their interpretations of the law were incompatible with the Strasbourg system. However, the Court avoided making comments on fundamental aspects of the law that had been in question for their potential incompatibility with the Strasbourg system (such as the hierarchy of religions set up by the 1997 Law). Strasbourg did go a step further when, in 2009, it decided the 2009 case of *Nolan and K v. Russia* and alluded to potentially questionable sections of the National Security Concept.[175] However, it again veered away from passing judgment on systemic incompatibility. In fact, the Strasbourg jurisprudence shows a tendency for behavior that avoids questions on the nature of the Russian system of protection. Both cases directly involving the use of the 1997 Law on Religion and concerning the contentious state of the registration procedure were decided on the basis of Article 11 (the right to freedom of assembly) in relation to Article 9—even though both cases appeared to concern religious issues that could have (and might normally have) been dealt with under Article 9.[176]

Despite this, the Court is undoubtedly aware that further problems exist, and this is shown by the Court's citing of Council of Europe documents concerning Russia's obligations and Russia's Law on Religion.[177] In these documents and others from the Council of Europe, a broader perspective can be seen; however, the documents consider certain wider issues inconsistently. For

174 Elkner, *op.cit.* note 129. Also, for example, in Staryi Oskol, a Methodist prayer meeting was interrupted by *FSB* agents who claimed that the Methodist community was "an alien body for the city and agents of American interests". In Pskov *Oblast'*, the Chief of the *FSB* claimed that western missionaries had been trained by their domestic espionage agencies.

175 Case of *Nolan and K v. Russia* (12 February 2009) No.2512/04.

176 Cases of the *Moscow Branch of the Salvation Army, op.cit.* note 82; and the *Church of Scientology Moscow, op.cit.* note 101.

177 PACE (2002) Document 9396, *op.cit.* note 83; PACE (2002) Resolution 1277, *op.cit.* note 83; and PACE (2002) Resolution 1278, *op.cit.* note 65.

example, the tone of the documents is legal and considers issues legally; yet, in one document (although not referred to by the Court), the policies of the ROC and its opinion on canonical territory are highlighted as an issue.[178] Considering the legal focus, why the Church's opinion concerning proselytism (not its relationship with the state) should be considered is confusing. Many religions hold similar thinking about canonical areas, among other anti-pluralistic traits. Overall, the opinions and documents avoid confronting structural discrepancies by putting discrepancies down to arbitrary and local variations on the part of regional organs of governance or individual action. They hold the law (and, by proxy, the model—officially, at least) largely in conformity with Strasbourg and Council of Europe ideals.

There are various reasons why the Court may have withheld judgment on the Russian system up to now and why it has failed to consider many of the structural issues pointed out above. It may be that the case law is still too sparse to consider deeper problems, or perhaps the legal considerations and case-by-case approach of the Strasbourg model make structural issues in Russia difficult (considering their combined legal and extra-legal characteristics) to consider, appearing as isolated arbitrary action rather than complex structural cause and effect.

Likely, the most important reason, among several possibilities, is the general context in which Strasbourg meets Russia. All decisions made by Strasbourg regarding Russia have importance beyond the cases themselves—particularly in an area as convoluted and socially charged as religion. The Council of Europe and the Court represent one of the few forums in which to engage Russia concerning human-rights issues. They represent one of the only forums in which Russian citizens have the chance to have their grievances heard and remedies granted, and, from a legal point of view, they are one of the few breaches in Russia's closely guarded sovereignty.[179] These are issues that remain important to the relationship between the Council's member states and with Russia—and not only with respect to human rights.

However, with the importance its sovereignty holds for Russia and the stream of negative judgments and the embarrassing percentage of cases concerning Russia every year, there is a feeling in certain circles that this relationship constitutes a form of importing more foreign values that are detrimental to Russia.[180] A.M. Ivanov, an Orthodox legal scholar, argues that "instead of 'totalitarian Communism' there is now 'totalitarian liberalism'".[181] Yet, at the same time, for

178 PACE (2002) Document 9404, *op.cit.* note 65.

179 For details, see Jean-Pierre Massias, "Russia and the Council of Europe: Ten Years Wasted?" (2007), available at <http://www.ifri.org/files/Russie/ifri_CE_massias_ang_jan2007.pdf>.

180 See, for example, Zolotov's arguments about foreign values and the ROC's place in Russian society at *op.cit.* note 157.

181 Ivanov, *op.cit.* note 126, 34.

its membership and trust in the international community, the relationship with Strasbourg is equally as vital to Russia.

It is this frictional necessity that has given rise to a form of tit-for-tat relationship as concerns the Court. Russia feels under attack with the case load and responds through the power it has as a member of the Council, for example, through actions such as non-ratification of Protocol 14.[182] (Protocol 14 is the Court's reform protocol that was set up to allow the Court to process the current backlog and future cases faster.) For a while, this non-ratification prevented Protocol 14 from entering into force—effectively firing a warning shot across the bow of the Council of Europe and questioning the Court's authority. Coupled with this has been a lack of will on the part of Russia to effect the structural changes proposed by Strasbourg; rather, the fine has been paid, but no changes have been made.[183]

Cases concerning freedom of religion come against both a political and a legal backdrop. Perhaps it is the case that—in an area so uncertain and approached so differently (even across the member states of the European Union)—there is a hesitancy to make too proclaimed a judgment. Perhaps one reason accounting for the jurisprudence is that there is an understanding in this area that is so connected to the tender issue of Russian culture and values: a certain amount of restraint is required for the good of the bigger picture.[184]

A consideration of the models and their operation cannot be made without acknowledging certain similarities. From a legal point of view, the foundations of the systems and their current legal manifestation show great similarities. The Russian system has its foundations in its Constitution, which remains, in principle, the keystone and reference point of all law, one to which the state—despite its political maneuvering—still pays homage. The Constitution is designed on the same values and on the same principles as those that underpin the Strasbourg model. In addition, the RF Constitution proclaims the Russian state as monist and gives a high domestic priority to Russia's international obligations and the protection derived from them, therefore placing the ECHR and Strasbourg jurisprudence very high domestically.

Developments regulating freedom of religion have been publicized as unconstitutional and in violation of fundamental principles, although, from a legal

182 Christina G. Hioureas, "Behind the Scenes of Protocol 14: Politics in Reforming the European Court of Human Rights", 24 *Berkeley Journal of International Law* (2006), 718-759, at 725-745; and Burkov, *op.cit.* note 104, 68-75.

183 For further information, see Vladimir Kuchin, *Pretsedentnoe pravo Evropeiskogo suda po pravam cheloveka* (URGIUA, Ekaterinburg, 2004); and William Pomeranz and Max Gutbrod, "The Push for Precedent in Russia's Judicial System", 37(1) *Review of Central and East European Law* (2012), 1-30.

184 See, *e.g.*, the case of *Lautsi and Others v. Italy* (18 March 2011) No.30814/06. In this case, the Russian Federation was among the third-party interveners.

point of view, they have have defensible grounds under the Strasbourg system. For example, the 1997 Law on Religion can be defended by the need to protect Russia from cults and new religious movements.[185] Indeed, the compatibility of consequent laws and subordinate regulation has been generally confirmed by the Council of Europe in documents considering the 1997 Law, in particular, and Russia's obligations in the sphere of freedom of religion in general.[186]

Considering operation of the legal systems in a wider context and what shape protection takes also reveals similarities. Strasbourg attempts to create a regulatory system that gives religion its own space by regulating religion's place in a democratic society, developing protection not as protection of religion considering its nature, but as a special type of body—among other groups and bodies—in a general model encouraging political and social pluralism. Religion occupies a similar space in Russia, created around the principle of religion's function in society rather than around its specificity. When religion comes into contact with elements outside this space, a balancing act is demanded and acted upon in both systems. Furthermore, it can be asserted that Russia is not a confessional state. Further consideration of this—and evidence such as pointers denoting the limits of religious influence—leads to the conclusion that there is at some point a separation between church and state that falls short of a traditional state-church model.

Considering that much has been made of the relationship between the ROC and the state, it can be argued that this relationship has an effect on the protection offered. However, provision has been created for all religions to operate somehow in the religious space. Furthermore, this relationship can be justified under principles offered by Strasbourg. *First*, considering the public support the ROC has, it would not be unfair to afford it special recognition among religions; *second*, it is arguable that this level of relationship is also present in many other European countries where Strasbourg has already confirmed the acceptability of state churches. In essence, all the base principles composing the Strasbourg model can be detected in the Russian system.[187]

The proposition can be put forward that differences among the systems arise from the need (or willingness) in Russian society to find specific answers to the questions that Strasbourg avoids. For example, Strasbourg does not claim to define or judge religious manifestations. This is a contradiction in the idea of a system of freedom of religion and practically impossible in the creation of a model of protection in any real society (and, especially, in one with such a range of variables). Considering the role that religion has played in Russian

185 For an argument about the danger of sects, see Alexander Morozov, "The Fourth Secularization", 36 *Religion, State & Society* (2008), 33-38.

186 PACE (2002) Document 9396, *op.cit.* note 83; PACE (2002) Resolution 1277, *op.cit.* note 83; and PACE (2002) Resolution 1278, *op.cit.* note 65.

187 Zolotov, *op.cit.* note 157.

society, this may have led to a more restrictive interpretation.[188] As mentioned above, the debate concerning sects and other new religious movements—and the conceptual uncertainty within the Strasbourg model—has led, in Strasbourg, to calls for clearer definitions of many issues, including as to what a religion is and as to what proselytism means (issues that the Russian state and system have found themselves more comfortable in considering).[189] In considering the issue of greater protection granted to 'traditional religions', the argument is the same. The Russian system has seen fit to define and make clear its stance, while the Strasbourg system inevitably grants greater protection to traditional and familiar religions without expressly stating it.[190]

Differences and Incompatibility

Although the foundations of the systems may be similar and create a similar theoretical legal model, it is the distortions and differences that have developed that define the Russian model's deviation from the Strasbourg standard. A consideration of similarities is largely confined to a comparison of the letter of the law and the theoretical construction of space and protection for religion. Unfortunately, construction of a space and a legal model describes the framework but does not describe the reality of protection. The vast range of religious restrictions and limitations that have come into being—and the huge number of individual events—make suggestions of compatibility extremely difficult to support. Despite the above similarities, it is clear that the two systems have moved too far apart to be considered compatible any longer. This is true in two ways: functionally and foundationally. *Functionally*, the discrepancy in the systems as they function and the qualitative differences between the two mean that the Russian system, in its derivative state, no longer fits the Strasbourg model. *Foundationally*, there are certain prerequisites for a model of protection to fit into the Strasbourg model that have not been achieved by the Russian model: namely, the quality and position of the law and legal system and its place and role in the functioning of protection.

Even legally, there are small anomalies that can be observed and have been commented on by the Court. For example, it is unclear why a distinction should be drawn between foreign and local founders of religions, as was pointed out in the 2006 case of the *Moscow Branch of the Salvation Army v. Russia*.[191] Further,

188 Evans and Petkoff, *op.cit.* note 31, 206-213.

189 Clare Ovey and Robin White, *Jacobs and White: The European Convention on Human Rights* (Oxford University Press, New York, NY, 2006), 304; and Renata Uitz, *Freedom of Religion in European Constitutional Case Law* (Council of Europe Publishing, Strasbourg, 2007), 164-170.

190 Ovey and White, *op.cit.* note 189.

191 Case of the *Moscow Branch of the Salvation Army, op.cit.* note 82. At the same time, the principle of legal regulation created by the 1997 Law on Religion seems to have been considered, in

in the 2002 case of the *Metropolitan Church of Bessarabia and Others v. Moldova*, it was made clear that any hierarchy of religious movements by the government was in violation of basic principles—such as neutrality of the state and equality of religious movements—yet a hierarchy is widely what is seen as being created by the 1997 Law.[192] Equally, while the legal system may appear sound in principle, it has within it many uncertainties. These create the opportunity for manipulation of the law by other factors. For example, the preamble and the 1997 Law create the principle of traditional religion; yet, they do not define which factors create a traditional religions. This has left room for the opportunity to distort definitions in order to achieve certain goals. This is precisely what has been done by the ROC and by state agencies: *first*, when giving efficacy to the preamble; and, *second*, in the redefinition of terminology as to what traditional religions are so as to suit specific purposes and agendas.

Considered in a broader context as to the model created, while the overall features of the system retain the same foundation, the Russian system is a distorted version. The link between the ROC and the state, as has been illustrated above, now is a key factor in influencing the shape of freedom of religion in Russia, as are the relationships created by factors such as the Russian state's power centralization and encroachment into the religious sphere. These relationships—particularly the power and influence of the ROC over the sphere of religion and the extent of its influence over matters that would have been considered outside the sphere of influence of religion by those who created the foundation of the model—have seriously distorted the image of the religious-space model. Religion and state are now far more linked than the secular principles suggested in the legal foundations. This has knock-on effects in all areas. Apart from having made the membranes of religion-state separation increasingly permeable, the close relationship and the power and influence have afforded to one denomination, to one church, the means for making the principle of neutrality of the state no longer possible. This—as well as encroachment by the state into aspects of religion—has led to a diminishing of the idea of equality of religions. One religion has been given dominion in the sphere of religion and has used this to establish its dominance and to restrict the activity and the presence of others, while politics asserts influence on the matter of which religions thrive and which do not. Extension of these influences outside religious bounds has had the same unbalancing effect on the relationship between religions and other (non-religious) groups when they come into contact.

principle, acceptable by certain Council of Europe documents on the matter. Commentary on the law and a comparison with certain Strasbourg jurisprudence raises other legal issues. For example, PACE (2002) Document 9396, *op.cit.* note 83; PACE (2002) Resolution 1277, *op.cit.* note 83; and PACE (2002) Resolution 1278, *op.cit.* note 65.

192 Case of the *Metropolitan Church of Bessarabia, op.cit.* note 23.

In considering the role of the ROC and its potential legitimization by comparison with the existence of state churches in Europe, it must be concluded that, qualitatively, they are different entities in two significant ways. *Firstly*, the established state churches were accepted parts of the model envisaged by the Council of Europe in its conception of a democratic society because they were part of the models of the states founding and developing the idea of the ECHR.[193] Therefore, they were legally regulated and predictable parts of Strasbourg's conception and machinery. This is not the case with an extralegal model developing as quickly and haphazardly as the relationship between the ROC and the Russian state. This relationship was not a considered part of the conception of freedom of religion in Russia as Russia joined the Council.

Secondly, the state churches of Europe function essentially as religious entities within the apparatus of the state. In this way, they are (to an extent) directed and controlled by the needs of the state as well as its restraints. Thus, the very nature of the state church is subject to the model of control advanced by Strasbourg unless the state itself veers from this path. For the traditional state church, the possibility of disrupting relational formats—or pushing its own goals outside these formats—is severely diminished by the necessity to follow not only its own religious goals but, also, the needs and structure of the state. Through this, conflict between the existence of a state church and Strasbourg principles is automatically minimized.[194] This is a key aspect of maintaining the balance of pluralism in a system permitting state churches. On the presumption that all states in the Council of Europe model work on secular governance principles, a state church does not violate principles laid down for a democratic society, as it itself is regulated from negatively affecting those core principles. This cannot be compared with the relationship in Russia in which the ROC occupies not a place within the state apparatus but, rather, a place outside it. In essence, it operates as a sort of partner to the state apparatus. While still practically playing a large role in forming the standard of protection and enjoying many of the benefits of being a state church, its goals and means can be far outside the means of the traditional state-church model and, short of criminality, also outside state control.

The above unbalancing of equilibrium has led to a loosening of theoretical principles, as well as having practical results in distortion of the model. As religion has come closer to the state, and as it plays a bigger part in the essence of governance, it has found the ability to distort the boundaries of its involvement with the state and, through this, also its place and theoretical presence in governance. Religion in the Strasbourg system is regulated in secular terms. Religion in the Russian system has moved toward regulation as to its own unique

193 Carolyn Evans, *Freedom of Religion under the European Convention on Human Rights* (Oxford University Press, New York, NY, 2001), 4-5.

194 For examples, see *Karlsson v. Sweden, op.cit.* note 25; and *Knudsen v. Norway,, op.cit.* note 25.

essence (it is no longer one form of group regulated within a secular model of pluralism). This can be seen with reference to binding state obligations and the 'spiritual security' of the Russian people in the National Security Concept or, more practically, in the closing of an art exhibition on blasphemy charges. Essentially, it has moved ideologically away from its conception in the principle of regulation concerning religion's place as part of a wider system of pluralism in a democratic society.[195]

As the relationship with the ROC has developed, we can observe a change in the position of the state's willingness to judge religion and manifestations of religion. With the further perceived clarity of what religion is, which religion has preference and the power afforded to one religion in relation to others, the state can and has moved theoretically away from an open inclusive approach creating a religious playing field conducive to the development of religion, toward an approach in which religion is increasingly exclusively defined. Although theoretical space is given to all religions to operate, this freedom is made illusory by the suffocating demands and restrictions placed in the way of enjoyment of religious rights for certain religions.[196]

Finally, freedom of religion is so important in the ECHR model of a democratic society due to the fact that it represents the essence of the relationship between the individual and the state. In molding and altering the philosophical foundations, and in the practical manipulation of the ideas of state neutrality and pluralism, the Russian state has begun to come close to infringing on the *forum internum*. This includes controlling what people are, and are not, allowed to spiritually have access to and making decisions about what is good and what is not for the individual. This is in contradiction to what the ECHR stands for.

In summary, the systems—when compared in function—are no longer compatible. The constituent parts of the Strasbourg and constitutional model have been progressively altered (often deliberately) on a practical and philosophical level. This has led to a system in which elements of the original framework are recognizable but have been emptied of much of their original purpose. This has, in turn, led to situations in which religions do not always receive protection and, in certain circumstances, are actively persecuted.

The reasons for the discrepancies considered above may be found, partially, in the altered nature of the legal foundation for protection of freedom of

195 See the commentary in Joera Mulders, "The Debate on Religion and Secularization in Russia Today: Comments on Kyrlezhev and Morozov", 36 *Religion, State & Society* (2008), 5-20.

196 Case of the *Moscow Branch of the Salvation Army, op.cit.* note 82 (the state had suggested that the obstructions to registration and operation did not hinder the activity or status of the organization; see para. 51 of the judgment: "The Government claimed that the applicant branch was not a 'victim' of the alleged violations because it had continuously held the status of a legal entity" and, also, that "there could be no doubt that the applicant branch had continued to operate without any hindrance").

religion. Logically, if the Constitution would have retained its initial principles and intended efficacy in practice, many of the above discrepancies could not have occurred. Perhaps from the start, it never represented a possible option in a transitional country such as Russia. Berman makes specific reference to this idea in relation to religion—considering that a certain amount of faith variety restriction and traditionalism is necessary in transition.[197]

With this discrepancy between law and reality in mind, we can see two trends in Russian protection. *One* lays the foundation and suggests what the situation should be on paper. The *other* distorts this picture through historical relationships and social interactions between the actors relevant in the model at the moment. It is here where one can observe the fundamental difference between the two models. The key relationship is that of the alliance between the state and the ROC and the confluence of their goals and reasoning. This has occurred for various reasons outside the sphere of law; when considered from a legal point of view, this relationship is never expressly mentioned and has never been codified. Yet, it has developed to be a major factor in the shaping and functioning of the model as it exists. Reflections of the relationship manifest themselves legally in certain places, such as in the preamble to the 1997 Law on Religion. Its reflection also can be seen in the manifestation of religion in certain previously non-religious laws, policy documents (such as the National Security Concept) and further cooperation among agencies of the government, the Russian Orthodox community and the Patriarchate and the ROC's consultative power in the area of religion. *Finally*, the effects of this relationship can be seen in the practical effects it has had on the shape of the religious-protection model. The threats to Jehovah's Witnesses parishes using the NGO law are undoubtedly examples of Orthodox influence—whether directly, as they stand publicly against the Jehovah's Witnesses, or indirectly, as they shape the dialogue concerning sects and foreign religions.

In essence, two systems exist: a legal system and a social system. Both are important aspects of how the overall model works but, considered individually, they fail to explain the whole. This dual-track system makes the Russian system of protection foundationally incompatible with the Strasbourg model.

It is this reality that sets the Russian system apart from many other Council of Europe states despite the unique place and form of religion in each society. In 2011, Patriarch Kirill reiterated that the ROC would not accept the Western concept of religion becoming only a private matter, as he stated that, in the societal sphere, all citizens must live by similar civic rules.[198]

197 See Harold Berman, "Freedom of Religion in Russia: An Amicus Brief for the Defendant", in John Witte and Michael Bourdeaux (eds.), *Proselytism and Orthodoxy in Russia: The New War for Souls* (Orbis Books, New York, NY, 1999), 265-284; and Kozlychin, *op.cit.* note 46, 74.

198 "Kokteil' tolerantnosti", *Nezavisimaia gazeta* (14 March 2011), available at <http://www.ng.ru/editorial/2011-03-14/2_red.html>.

The Strasbourg system protects freedom of religion under the framework of the ECHR and attempts to establish a set of minimum standards under which no protection can fall and thereby forms the foundation for a certain model of democratic society with which all states must comply. A feature of this, undoubtedly, is that a certain level of rule of law must have been achieved.[199] Apart from the obvious instances of arbitrary and *ultra vires* acts that are not representative of structural forces (if they cannot be seen as permissive proof of a dual system (*Kuznetsov and Others v. Russia*)), freedom of religion in Russia itself—and the factors by which it is defined—now exist partially outside the legal framework.[200] In light of principles fundamental to the Strasbourg system—such as a certain solidity of effective framework based on the clarity, certainty, foreseeability and availability of the law—this clearly does not match the basic requirements needed. To map and compare systems, the systems must be chartable and be of the same reference material.

As we consider the structure of Article 9 ECHR, we can see the reliance directly placed upon these basic principles. The provisions for the state to have legitimately interfered with a right as prescribed by Article 9(2) immediately consider whether the interference was prescribed by law. Should the interference have been the result of an act based on a structure that is only half codified and whose codifications are seriously altered by other factors, this question becomes extremely difficult to answer conclusively. This is particularly true because consideration of whether as act has been prescribed by law will take into account whether the foreseeability, accessibility and quality of the law meet Strasbourg standards. Quality, in this respect, refers not only to how good the law itself is on paper but, also, presumes that it functions within a system where the law as written can be considered legitimately as it stands. Quality of law also means that the law itself must have fulfilled certain criteria as laid out by democratic principles and the rule of law.[201] Considerations in the context of Russian legislation on freedom of religion fail on these grounds, as the law as written forms only half the image that is necessary to evaluate the law. On the one hand—as these criteria are impossible to judge on the basis of the law alone—the conclusion could be reached that infringements should inevitably be found in all cases of state intervention, on the grounds that the law, and the system in which it exists, are not of sufficient quality. On the other hand, should the law be considered in isolation, interference would simply appear as an arbitrary act, separable from structural deficiencies, which would not show up at all.

199 Statute of the Council of Europe, ETS 1, Chapter II, Art.3, available at <http://conventions.coe.int/Treaty/en/Treaties/html/001.htm>

200 Case of *Kuznetsov and Others v. Russia, op.cit.* note 100.

201 Ovey and White, *op.cit.* note 189, 223-240.

We can also see the relevance and necessity of a sound legal base when considering the margin of appreciation. The margin-of-appreciation principle takes into account that the system as perceived by Strasbourg is always subject to the social and historical context of each state. Issues of structural protection raised by a case are considered in light of the peculiarities of a society. Numerous factors are taken into account and are compared with the principles of the Strasbourg model; together, they are used to decide how much leeway a state should be given in its behavior. However, consideration of the margin of appreciation that a state is accorded is impossible in general (considering its specificity in individual cases) without the foundation of the rule and the quality of law.

When considering the margin of appreciation granted and how it is evaluated, the markers used to consider these social specificities are predominantly legal. Considering the relationship between the state and the ROC, it is clear to see that the extralegal factors affecting the system of protection make it impossible to consider what the Russian margin of appreciation should be since the relationship has no legal markers. Strasbourg has created a paradigm within a paradigm related to the functioning of state churches (as is the case with most aspects of issues that may alter or diminish a standard of protection) based on the principle that they may exist but that they are subject to certain rules and regulations such that they must not endanger pluralism, minority protection or other principles of the model. Within this framework, certain limits have been set. This jurisprudence demands that there be legal recognition of the relationship and its functioning within a state so that it can be aligned and compared with the Strasbourg model. The fact Strasbourg has felt that it may begin to establish a rough paradigm for this aspect of protection of religion means that it is also an obligation for states to codify—if, and when, a state-church relationship exists. For example, when considering the Greek Orthodox Church and its potential negative impact on freedom of other religions, Strasbourg was considering a codified relationship and national legislation putting this relationship into practice. The uncodified and legally invisible relationships that have such a large impact on the Russian system make their consideration in relation to the relevant margin of appreciation impossible. Essentially, they do not compose the raw material for Strasbourg to work with.

In the same motion, the argument could be made that lack of codification of such a relationship itself falls outside allowable bounds, as it creates a 'legislative hole'. Strasbourg relies on a certain solidity of legal framework that allows the Court to weigh trends and effects of a certain infraction or situation before it. As a delicate and interconnected system—without the required solidity of a legal framework or with elements of it missing—the Court cannot assess the consequences for other aspects of the system; therefore, it cannot consider whether or not the issues at hand reach the required level of protection.

The Court also depends on an evaluation of whether the laws and measures in the specific case were justified in principle and whether they were proportionate in order to consider the margin of appreciation. Thus, on a case-by-case basis, the partial representation that the legal system gives of the reality of the standard of protection makes this very difficult to judge. Arguably, where the law would be considered for justification and proportionality on rule-of-law principles—in conjunction with the factors affecting it and manipulating its effect—this potentially would substantially narrow the margin of appreciation.[202]

It could be argued that, throughout Europe, there are social and relational dynamics to all systems of protection not specifically regulated by law. For example, public opinion on a religion clearly plays a role in how protection works in fact and, yet, should not necessarily always find expression in the law. However, in relation to Russia, the quantity of extralegal influence in the model is arguably considerably wider and consistent to the point where it forms a structure itself. In no other state do social relationships among actors, and specifically between one church and the state—existing predominantly outside the legal sphere—have such an impact on the realities of freedom of religion.[203]

Thus, on a basic level, the systems are not compatible—like two operating systems that can be compared as to what they do for advantages and flaws; but, essentially, they are the results of two different programming languages. The Russian system cannot be compatible with the Strasbourg system because it fails to meet the initial requirements to be recognized by the Strasbourg system.

Expansions and General Conclusions from the Russian Model

Concerning freedom of religion, the Court has claimed that "freedom of religion and belief is one of the foundations of a democratic society and is a vital element for the identity of believers and vitally important for non-believers and the unconcerned". Thus, fundamental issues with respect to protection of freedom of religion also mean fundamental flaws in one of the cornerstones of a democratic society.[204]

In this respect, we can consider how religious-protection functions have a direct impact on other rights and, therefore, a defining role in any approximation to the ideal model. Not only because it forms part of a delicate governance framework but, also, because it is directly connected with protection of the

202 Michael R. Hutchinson, "The Margin of Appreciation Doctrine in the European Court of Human Rights", 48 *International and Comparative Law Quarterly* (1999), 638-650, at 640-641.

203 For very broad consideration of the conflict with rule-of-law principles in Russian society, see Ronald R. Pope, "The Rule of Law and Russian Culture: Are They Compatible?", 7 *Demokratizatsiya* (1999), 204-213.

204 Case of *Kokkinakis v. Greece, op.cit.* note 9.

individual's freedom (to think, shape her personality, or believe what she wishes) and, therefore, other freedoms. In turn, this represents an interference with the concept of 'the individual' (arguably, the very core of the ECHR) within the community of rights as laid out by the ECHR. It is, therefore, impossible to isolate religious protection from other rights. As a demonstration of this, all the main Strasbourg cases dealing with Russia mention other rights in relation to Article 9 infringements. In addition, religion is often a deep part of the composition of a person. Thus, to interfere with the balance and place of religion in a model is indicative of an alteration in the relationship between individual and state.

On a more fundamental level, many of the flaws considered in the compatibility of the two models stem from rule- and from quality-of-law issues relating to protection of freedom of religion. The rule of law is also a founding principle and of vital importance to the model of a democratic society protected by the ECHR. As mentioned above, the question of the Russian legal system's preparedness for accession to the Council of Europe arose before Russia's accession—both internally in Russia and in Council of Europe considerations. This happened at a time when liberal democratic values were still the order of policy. A trend that has arguably ceased, in recent years, leading some observers to generally comment on the democratic backslide and inward turning of Russia.[205] In relation to freedom of religion, there are rule-of-law issues that can be traced to founding principles and can be seen as indicative of wider rule-of-law flaws.

It is not possible that isolated issues relating to freedom of religion in Russia are solely connected to freedom of religion. The range of state organs involved, the consistency of activity and the pervasiveness of problems is marked by a consistency that cannot be restricted solely to religion. For example, trends can be spotted across the state apparatus from the Constitutional Court to the *FSB* to local state media. It is clear that an uncodified system regulates the behavior of diverse bodies on a scale beyond just religion.

In regulation of religion, the founding principles still place religion within a greater form of political pluralism (although we are perhaps now seeing an alteration of this on a philosophical level). The secular legal positioning of religion means that we can theorize a similar range of issues affecting many other relationships and areas of governance. The delicacy of the balance of a pluralistic system was demonstrated above and can be expanded to suggest that it is highly unlikely that the religious sphere has been solely affected by the extralegal regulation system and that this trend cannot be detected elsewhere. In fact, the relationships that were allowed to develop in relation to religion could only have done so as a reflection of how things operated in more general contexts.

Issues in Russia, and discrepancies between the Russian and Strasbourg models, have not affected the right as understood and applied by Strasbourg for two reasons. *First*, in its case law referring to all states, Strasbourg has consistently

205 Burkov, *op.cit.* note 104, 68-75.

retained an idealistic system based on a secular model of governance that truly exists nowhere in Europe.[206] This model is admittedly molded to local circumstances, with only certain fundamental principles being held firm in all cases. Thus, unlike certain other rights, deviation from a standard leading to a judgment in Russia will not necessarily be applicable in other situations.

Second, the standard of protection—as regards the right—will remain unaltered as a result of issues in Russia due to the way that cases have been dealt with by Strasbourg. In essence, by ruling on a case-by-case basis, withholding judgment on deeper issues, dealing with each case cautiously and apparently by attributing blame to arbitrary acts, the above conclusions—concerning the specifics of the model in Russia and how it operates—have not been allowed to enter into active Strasbourg jurisprudence. Thus, they have not played a role in diminishing standards of protection. Situations in which reference could be made by other states to a Russian case and the specific issues it concerned have been avoided.

However, this strategy cannot be maintained indefinitely. Strasbourg and the Council of Europe have shown their awareness of the deeper structural issues already; should there be a continuation in the trends pointed out above, and should the discrepancies continue to grow, it may become unrealistic to avoid them any longer. Likewise, the growth of a body of case law will inevitably yield its own truths. In essence, the current strategy may have a short life-span. This is possibly already becoming legal truth, as a reading of certain Strasbourg cases concerning Russia reveal the necessity for significant legal gymnastics to come to an unproblematic conclusion. It will be interesting to see which route is taken by Strasbourg: whether it decides to tackle the deeper issues and risk a backlash or whether it is meeker and potentially jeopardizes the integrity of its own model.

The relationship between Russia and the Council of Europe is a difficult one. It is desired on both sides, but is subject to an awkward friction, as certain issues are not seen eye-to-eye. Differences in the operation of systems in relation to freedom of religion—extrapolated to a general level—form a large part of this awkwardness. Friction is created as two different entities with different perceptions and desires try to fit together.

However, the Council has been aware of issues within the Russian legal system since it accepted its membership and has always acted on the principle that socializing Russia through inclusion was preferable to exclusion. As can be seen with the Protocol 14 issue, the Council took a cautious and considered stand toward Russia; but with Protocol 14*bis* and other recent declarations suggesting sanctions, it has shown a policy of 'this far and no further'—thus preventing

206 Willaime, *op.cit.* note 4, 24-26.

Russia from having an adverse effect on the operation of the Council, its goals, and the protection its organs offer.[207]

In light of what has been said above considering freedom of religion in Russia, there are clearly current questions about Russia's compatibility with the Strasbourg system, which may lead the Council to ask itself wider questions about what Russia's membership means, such as, 'if Russia is allowed to be a member, then where do the principles and limits of the Council actually reside—what does it really stand for?' However, taken in light of the goals of encouragement and socialization, the issues have never been otherwise (although the projected result seems to be taking longer to achieve than expected). Indeed, it cannot be said that membership in the Council has had no effect at all—certain issues involving religion having improved as a result of Council and Court intervention in recent years.[208]

Thus, the current policy based on cautious interaction—allowing Russia influence to a point but no further—seems sensible. The Council behaves with a wariness of Russia that prevents it from negatively impacting too much on its goals and operations.

However, considering issues related to freedom of religion as a measuring stick, the current point is a particular low in the relationship and the situation should change for the better over time—if not leading to more compatibility, then certainly leading to a better atmosphere in which to try and align the models and undoubtedly to a halt in the momentum forcing the models apart.

The *first* reason for this is that the main actors and relationships in this model are governed by political forces. For example, the state and ROC have found a recent political alignment that has developed the model in a certain direction. However, Russia has shown that the opinion of the international community and its membership in the Council of Europe are also important political motivators. In this respect, trends toward traditionalism and the goals of the ROC will inevitably come into direct contact with external influences that mean its influence politically will be curtailed and balanced further against other concerns.[209] As has been seen, when this has happened in the past, the ROC has not always had its way. This can already be seen in the behavior of the Constitutional Court, which acts with one eye on external influences and requirements. The development of the current system relies on the alignment of the goals of the ROC and the state. As current trends continue, other factors will

207 Yanina Savenko, "Russia Slows the European Court's Human Rights Work" (28 December 2006), available at <http://humanrightshouse.org/Articles/686.html>.

208 US Bureau of Democracy, Human Rights and Labor, *op.cit.* note 85.

209 Elena A. Lukasheva, "Prava cheloveka: konflikt kul'tur", in Grafskii, *op.cit.* note 46, 245-255.

grow in comparative importance, and the state will change direction, splitting the convergence of goals and means and minimizing the influence of the Church.[210]

Second, the law is subject to significant manipulation and external forces, but it is not a completely dead letter. Acts still go through its channels, and the government still avoids openly denying or abusing the Constitution; as considered, the legal framework is quite good. Thus, in its establishment of the system on democratic principles—and in the fact that the framework has been laid by the Constitution—there are limits built in as to how far it can be manipulated. In essence, the fundamental shape of the space can only be manipulated within certain bounds, considering the nature of its foundations. This is particularly relevant to freedom of religion, which has a unique and influential position in the construction of a pluralist system.

Finally, the relationships and extralegal factors that have such a great impact become more evident and predictable over time. As they define their boundaries more clearly in relation to one another, the limits of their influence also become clearer. As this happens, they become easier for external entities to observe and assess. In the case of the ROC, this is already in effect.[211] As it becomes more connected with the state, a state-church model will develop in a more concrete form—and, with this, should come ever increased regulation and clarity. This will form the groundwork for compatibility and consideration at the hands of the Strasbourg organs.

210 Lauri Mälksoo, "The History of International Legal Theory in Russia: A Civilizational Dialogue with Europe", 19 *European Journal of International Law* (2008), 211-232, shows a historical tradition of Russian legal theory turning away from, and then back toward, Europe.

211 Codevilla, *op.cit.* note 71, 121.

Assessing Human Rights in Russia: Not to Miss the Forest for the Trees A Response to Preclik, Schönfeld and Hallinan

Vladislav Starzhenetskii

First of all, I would like to congratulate my European colleagues—Petr Preclik, Dorothea Schönfeld and Dara Hallinan—on preparing such solid and interesting papers that are included in this volume. The topics chosen and the way legal and social issues have been presented by these talented scholars reflect many current dilemmas in Russian law and politics. I am especially pleased by the broad approach taken by the authors in analyzing the interaction of the Russian Federation with the European Court of Human Rights (ECtHR). Their focus is not only on the legal part of this interaction; they have also sought to embrace the social, political, cultural, and historical background of this process.

Although I really enjoyed reading these works, I found myself in the strange and awkward position of a person looking through the same window but having a different view. Some of these authors tend to explain the existing problems of Russia in the ECtHR and the Council of Europe ("the Council") in terms of fundamental differences between Russian and European values, or suspicion/contestation/challenge by the Russian government or nation of the human rights contained in the European Convention on Human Rights ("the Convention"). Probably, that is the reason why they remain so pessimistic in their conclusions; sometimes (from my personal perspective), even overly pessimistic about Russian progress in the sphere of human rights. Here, we are presented with the image of a bear in its imaginary cage—or of an authoritarian country being outside of the dominant (Western) world order and the most civilized (European) region with a hesitant and unsecured national identity.

It is difficult to agree with this perception of Russia and its attitude towards human rights. Placing Russia in line with 'evil', 'authoritarian' countries with non-European values and no civilized perspective will hardly help us to understand the existing state of affairs or to explain the reasons for the difficulties that Russia has had in the field of human-rights protection. And concentration on particular problems of human-rights realization in Russia should not distort the general picture of developments that have been achieved and current activity that is so much work-in-progress. Otherwise, we risk missing the forest for the trees.

Does Russia protect human rights? Are human rights a foreign notion to the Russian people and Russian culture? Is the Russian government doing anything to respect its international obligations under the Convention? Do we have full and objective answers to these questions?

Lauri Mälksoo, ed.
Russia and European Human-Rights Law: The Rise of the Civilizational Argument 207-215

At the moment, Russia indeed has numerous problems in the ECtHR. Every year, the ECtHR finds hundreds of violations and obliges the Russian government to pay millions of euros in compensation for violations of the Convention. At the same time, I am hesitant to explain this phenomenon solely by fundamental differences between Russian and European values or by the lack of a political will—or a governmental strategy to disregard protection of human rights.

Looking more than a decade into the past (when Russia ratified the Convention in 1998), we cannot ignore the enormous progress that Russia has made in reforming its legal system in order to ensure human-rights protection under the Convention. The list of all legislative and other changes is itself too long to reproduce here. But some of them are still worth mentioning so as to illustrate the considerable improvement in human-rights protection in Russia. In particular, I would point out judicial, procedural, civil and criminal law reforms that have introduced numerous necessary and important safeguards of human-rights protection and have extensively changed the Russian legal landscape. All of these reforms have been based on international (including European) human-rights standards and have been implemented in close cooperation with the Council.

Furthermore, this process of reform is still ongoing. For instance, reform of supervisory review in Russian courts of general jurisdiction,[1] reform of the system of state responsibility for damage caused to private persons by lawful and unlawful acts,[2] openness and transparency of judicial[3] and governmental systems,

1 For example, a 2007 landmark judgment of the RF Constitutional Court: Postanovlenie Konstitutsionnogo Suda Rossiiskoi Federatsii "O proverke konstitutsionnosti polozhenii statei 16, 20, 112, 336, 376, 377, 380, 381, 382, 383, 387, i 389 Grazhdanskogo Protsessual'nogo Kodeksa Rossiiskoi Federatsii v sviazi s zaprosom Kabineta Ministrov Respubliki Tatatarstan, zhalobami otkrytykh aktsionernykh obshchestv 'Nizhnekamskneftekhim' i 'Khakasenergo', a takzhe zhalobami riada grazhdan" (5 February 2007) No.2-P, *Rossiiskaia gazeta* (14 February 2007); and 2007 amendments to the RF Code of Civil Procedure: RF Federal'nyi Zakon 'O vnesenii izmenenii v Grazhdanskii Protsessual'nyi Kodeks Rossiiskoi Federatsii'" (4 December 2007) No.330-F3, *Rossiiskaia gazeta* (8 December 2008). See, *e.g.*, William E. Pomeranz, "Supervisory Review and the Finality of Judgments under Russian Law", 34(1) *Review of Central and East European Law* (2009), 15-36.

2 RF Federal'nyi Zakon "O kompensatsii za narushenie prava na sudoproizvodstvo v razumnyi srok ili prava na ispolnenie sudebnogo akta v razumnyi srok" (30 April 2010) No.68-FZ, *Rossiiskaia gazeta* (4 May 2010) available at <http://base.garant.ru/12175400/>.

3 RF Federal'nyi Zakon "Ob obespechenii dostupa k informatsii o deiatel'nosti sudov v Rossiiskoi Federatsii" with subsequent amendments (22 December 2008), No.262-FZ, *Rossiiskaia gazeta* (26 December 2008) available at <http://base.garant.ru/194582/>. For the implementation of this law in Russian arbitrazh (state commercial) courts, access to all judgments and decisions rendered, and numerous online services, see the RF Arbitrazh Court website at <www.arbitr.ru>.

reform of the criminal and penitentiary systems,[4] and the rise of the doctrine of precedent in the Russian legal system.[5]

Russian legislators and courts are making use of the legal positions of the ECtHR and of principles of Strasbourg law (such as the balance of private and public interests, proportionality, legal certainty and predictability, effective interpretation). For this reason, I am unable to agree with the proposition that, in general, Russian jurisprudence—in terms of its implementation of the Convention and of ECtHR practice—can be summed up as 'non-existent'. Contextual studies show that Russian courts borrow much from the Convention and ECtHR practice; in a substantial number of cases, they are frequently use the same language, legal tools and approaches as the ECtHR.[6] This is reflected in

4 *E.g.*, the further embedding of the presumption of innocence principle in law and practice and of jury trials, of guarantees concerning equality in criminal proceedings and restriction of the powers of prosecutors, and in particular the humanization of criminal law and the abolishment of antiquated criminal offenses.

5 Judgment of the RF Constitutional Court, No.1-P (21 January 2010) Postanovlenie Konstitutsionnogo Suda Rossiiskoi Federatsii "O chasti 4 stat'i 170, punkta 1 stat'i 311 i chasti 1 stat'i 312 Arbitrazhnogo protsessual'nogo kodeksa Rossiiskoi Federatsii v sviazi s zhalobami zakrytogo aktsionernogo obshchestva 'Proizvodstvennoe ob"edinenie 'Bereg', otkrytykh aktsionernykh obshchestv 'Karbolit', 'Zavod Mikroprovod', i 'Nauchno-proizvodstvennoe predpriiatie 'Respirator'", *Rossiiskaia gazeta* (10 February 2010); and Decision of the Plenum of the RF Higher Arbitrazh Court (14 February 2008) No.14 Postanovlenie Plenuma Vysshego Arbitrazhnogo Suda Rossiiskoi Federatsii "O vnesenii dopolnenii v postanovlenie Plenumy Vysshego Arbitrazhnogo Suda Rossiiskoi Federatsii ot 12.03.2007 No.17 'O primenenii Arbitrazhnogo protsessual'nogo kodeksa Rossiiskoi Federatsii pri peresmotre vstupivshikh v zakonnuiu silu sudebnykh aktov po vnov' otrkyvshimsia obstoiatel'stvam'", available at <http://www.arbitr.ru/as/pract/post_plenum/18671.html>. See, also, Ol'ga Pleshanova, Anna Pushkarskaia, "Sudebnyi pretsedent stal konstitutsionnym", *Kommersant* (22 January 2010) available at <http://www.kommersant.ru/doc.aspx?DocsID=1307870>; and Anton Ivanov, "Grazhdanskoe pravo: Rech' o pretsedente", *Vedomosti* (19 March 2010), available at <http://www.vedomosti.ru/newspaper/article/2010/03/19/228520>. See, also, William Pomeranz and Max Gutbrod, "The Push for Precedent in Russia's Judicial System", 37(1) *Review of Central and East European Law* (2012), 1-30.

6 One such example is the practice of the RF Higher Arbitrazh Court. See judgments of its Presidium based on the principles mentioned: (20 July 2010) No.2142/10; (1 June 2010) No.3342/10; (13 April 2010) No.17752/09; (9 February 2010) No.15353/09; (8 December 2009) No.12523/09; (8 September 2009) No.10750/07; (1 September 2009) No.1395/09; (28 July 2009) No.3703/09; (14 July 2009) No.3057/09; (28 April 2009) No.13798/08; (10 March 2009) No.13940/08; (17 February 2009) No.13356/08; (7 October 2008) No.5853/08; (30 September 2008) No.5263/07; (16 September 2008) No.6264/08; (1 July 2008) No.3431/08; (1 April 2008) No.16034/07; (18 March 2008) No.13084/07; (20 November 2007) No.3151/07; (5 June 2007) No.1650/07; (20 March 2007) No.4937/05; (27 February 2007) No.13584/06; (13 February 2007) No.12264/06; (5 December 2006) No.11801/06; (5 December 2006) No.11781/06; (5 September 2006) No.4375/06; (20 June 2006) No.3082/06; (22 February 2005) No.14548/04; (15 February 2005) No.13623/04; (21 December 2004) No.9366/04; and (21 September 2004) No.9486/00.

the texts of judgments, particularly those of the arbitrazh courts due to the legal reasoning of the RF Higher Arbitrazh Court.[7] However, it is true that Russian judges are hesitant to cite judgments and decisions of the ECtHR directly and on a regular basis, although this is due in no small part to the lack of official translations and similar reasons.

I regret that this positive process of reform has fallen mostly outside of the studies presented in this volume. Perhaps this was not their primary object and purpose; but this remark still needs to be added in order to offer the reader an assessment that is as objective as possible.

In reviewing the causes of the difficulties that Russia is facing in the area of human-rights protection—including those that my European colleagues have touched upon in their chapters in this volume—I am inclined to explain them in terms of difficulties with implementation of standards into the Russian legal system rather than any antagonism between Russian and European attitudes toward human rights. The 1993 Russian Constitution, which is based on the idea and supreme character of human rights, and Russian's fourteen-year participation in the Convention and other international human-rights instruments[8]—provide ample evidence of this and leave little room for such debates. I also would suggest that more attention be paid to the social context of human-rights implementation because it highlights those practical obstacles and existing conflicts that hinder the process in Russia.

To illustrate this approach, let me turn to the ECtHR. Judgments of the Court against Russia may be divided into several groups depending on the different grounds that led to a particular violation.

The *largest group* of judgments concerns repeated violations of the right to fair and public hearings in a court of law (non-enforcement of judgments, excessive length of proceedings in domestic courts, lack of legal certainty in supervisory proceedings), embodied in Article 6, as well as the right to property (Art.1 of Protocol No.1). Violation of the right to liberty and security (unlawful arrests), inhuman and degrading treatment in Russian prisons, etc. belong to the same group.

These violations reflect structural and practical problems of the Russian legal system immanent in a transition period of reforms and of the dismantling of old regulations and attitudes rather than ideologically based controversies with European values. This explains why the Russian authorities recognize existing

7 The fact that Russian arbitrazh courts are rarely criticized by the European Court of Human Rights may serve as evidence. There are only a few (about ten) judgments of the Court recognizing violations of the European Convention on Human Rights with regard to Russian arbitrazh courts.

8 *Inter alia*, the 1961 European Social Charter, the 1966 International Covenant on Civil and Political Rights, and the 1966 International Covenant on Economic, Social and Cultural Rights.

shortcomings and demonstrate a willingness to take legislative and organizational measures in order to comply with European standards on human-rights protection. Examples can be seen in the adoption of the 2010 Federal Law on Compensation for Violations of the Right to Trial Within a Reasonable Time or of the Right to Enforcement of a Judgment within a Reasonable Time[9] as well as in a significant number of other initiatives to improve compliance with the provisions of the Convention.[10]

The *second group* of violations may be accounted for by the lack of proper (efficient, adequate and balanced) measures and solutions to address the numerous new challenges that Russian society has been facing since the collapse of the Soviet Union. These challenges include, for example, economic development, terrorism, extremism, separatism, nationalism, and other problems arising out of the multinational and multicultural structure of Russian society, as well as preservation of social stability, security and traditional values. The Russian government time and again has been criticized by the ECtHR with regard to the situation in the North Caucasus; violations of the freedoms of expression, religion, assembly, and association are other examples. All these judgments demonstrate vital problems with human-rights protection in Russia.

But again, this is not a question of incompatibility between European and Russian values. Basically, this is a matter of balancing different conflicting values and the proportionality of measures taken to protect public interests. From my point of view, this is the most sensitive and problematic area of interaction between Russia and the ECtHR.

One would hardly doubt that Russia has a strong public interest in resolving these challenges, which cannot be ignored. Moreover, Russia has a positive responsibility to do so according to human-rights law and theory.

On the other hand, there are no 'one-size-fits-all' solutions that Russia can borrow from the West. Russia is the largest country in the world, with the largest population in Europe, with a great number of highly specific internal and external problems (starting from the economy and the demographic situation to sharing borders with some highly unstable and authoritarian states). Russia is a country with one of the most dramatic histories in the twentieth century, with almost irreconcilable contradictions, which it is still trying to overcome. Blind replication of Western models—disregarding the context of the Russian situation—has already led to dramatic consequences in the immediate past.

9 RF Federal'nyi Zakon No.68-FZ, *op.cit.* note 2.

10 "Doklady o sostoianii zakonodatel'stva v Rossiiskoi Federatsii". These annual reports have been compiled by the RF *Sovet Federatsii* (the upper chamber of the Russian parliament) and monitor the implementation of broad goals in the domestic and foreign policy spheres which have been embodied in Russian legislation. *E.g.*, the 2012 Report (dated 18 April 2013) is available at <http://council.gov.ru/activity/analytics/publications/590>.

Does this *per se* mean that Russia has its own unique notion of human rights and is trying to contest them? Or that its national identity does not include a human-rights component? Of course not. The mere fact that Russia is not following some traditional paths cannot be sufficient grounds for such allegations. There must be room for a 'margin of appreciation'.

At the same time, there have been many instances demonstrating a failure to strike a proper balance between public and private interests in trying to combat terrorism, extremism, and separatism, and to preserve social stability and traditional values. It has turned out to be (much) more difficult for Russia than for other European countries to cope with such tasks for a variety of reasons. This point alone could be the subject of separate and interesting research.

Proper solutions to address the challenges that Russia (as well as many other countries) is facing have yet to be worked out. They are of crucial importance; yet, they are not particularly easy to formulate. The good news is that judgments of the ECtHR serve as an effective inducement for Russia to reconsider its policy and regulations in problematic spheres of human-rights compliance.[11]

The above-mentioned are the two main categories of violations that can be traced in the practice of the ECtHR with regard to Russia; but, there are some others as well. For instance, there are ordinary violations that the Russian legal system has not been able to remedy itself due to the fact that the highest Russian courts (the Constitutional Court, the Supreme Court, and the Higher Arbitrazh Court) were not regarded by the ECtHR as constituting the effective remedy that applicants needed to exhaust prior to lodging their applications with the ECtHR.[12]

This situation started to change only after the ECtHR rendered two 2009 decisions in the cases of *Kovaleva v. Russia*[13] and *OOO Link Oil SPb v. Russia*[14] in which it expressly stated that an application for supervisory review before the RF Higher Arbitrazh Court must be considered as an effective remedy capable of preventing and putting right possible violations of the Convention at the domestic level and that the decisions of the Higher Arbitrazh Court constituted a 'final decision' within the meaning of Article 35(1) of the Convention and the starting point for calculating the six-month statute of limitations laid down by that provision. That ruling of the ECtHR became a reality only after substantial

11 See, for example, information provided by the Committee of Ministers of the Council of Europe concerning the execution of ECtHR judgments, including information about individual and general measures taken by states: <http://www.coe.int/t/dghl/monitoring/execution/default_en.asp>.

12 See cases of *Denisov v. Russia* (6 May 2004) No.33408/03; *Berdzenishvili v. Russia* (17 September 2003) No.31697/03; and *AO "Uralmash" v. Russia* (10 April 2003) No.13338/03.

13 Case of *Kovaleva v. Russia* (25 June 2009) No.6025/09.

14 Case of *OOO Link Oil SPb v. Russia* (25 June 2009) No.42600/05.

amendments had been made to the Arbitrazh Procedure Code of the Russian Federation concerning supervisory review proceedings (Art.304 and others). Now, similar amendments are expected to be made to the RF Civil Procedure Code so as to ensure that the rights and freedoms set forth in the Convention are fully secured at the national level and to strengthen the domestic remedies available in the Russian Federation.

There is also a group of so-called high-profile cases that Petr Preclick has used—along with other facts and statements—to illustrate his argument about Russia's refusal to accept the European human-rights regime fully and immediately (*Ilaşcu and Others v. Moldova and Russia*,[15] Chechen cases, *Shamayev and 12 others v. Russia and Georgia*[16]). I would also add to this list, *inter alia*, *Gusinskiy v. Russia*,[17] *Konstantin Markin v. Russia*,[18] and *Alekseyev v. Russia*.[19]

It is true that all these cases were rather sensitive for Russia for various reasons, and in its judgments the ECtHR found serious violations of the Convention. I also presume that it was not easy for the Russian government and the Russian courts (including the Russian Constitutional Court in the *Markin* case) to accept them and the mistakes made and to enforce the judgments that had been handed down.[20]

But this situation is not unique in the history of the Council and the ECtHR. Interaction between these institutions and European countries has, from time to time, produced similar examples where national authorities disagreed or were reluctant to accept judgments of the ECtHR that concerned highly sensitive internal policy issues. There are such cases as *Ireland v. United Kingdom*[21] (recourse to the five techniques of interrogation amounted to a practice of inhuman and degrading treatment and violated Art.3 of the Convention), *Lautsi v. Italy*[22] (crucifixes in Italian public school classes were regarded as contrary to parents' right to educate their children in line with their convictions and to children's right to freedom of religion), *GÖRGÜLÜ v. Germany*[23] (refusal to grant custody to the biological father of a child in violation of Art.8 of the Convention), and

15 Case of *Ilaşcu and Others v. Moldova and Russia* (8 July 2004) No.48787/99.

16 Case of *Shamayev and 12 others v. Russia and Georgia* (12 April 2005) No.36378/02.

17 Case of *Gusinskiy v. Russia* (19 May 2004) No.70276/01.

18 Case of *Konstantin Markin v. Russia* (7 October 2010) No.30078/06.

19 Case of *Alekseyev v. Russia* (21 October 2010) No.4916/07, No.25924/08, and No.14599/09.

20 For instance, see Valerii Zor'kin, "Predel ustupchivosti", *Rossiiskaia gazeta* (29 October 2010), available at <http://www.rg.ru/2010/10/29/zorkin.html>.

21 Case of *Ireland v. United Kingdom* (18 January 1978) No.5310/71.

22 Case of *Lautsi v. Italy* (3 November 2009) No.30814/06; however, the judgment was subsequently reversed by the Grand Chamber (18 March 2011).

23 Case of *GÖRGÜLÜ v. Germany* (26 May 2004) No.74969/01.

Cyprus v. Turkey[24] (numerous violations of human rights in Northern Cyprus after the 1974 partition of the island for which Turkey was held responsible).

All these high-profile cases confirm that interaction between European institutions and the member states is not an easy or a one-way road.[25] Russia has joined a permanent dialog in which it has become an active participant.

It is a huge advantage of the Strasbourg law that the Convention is a 'living instrument' and that the ECtHR remains open to different views in national legal systems, maintaining a dynamic and evolutionary approach without which it would risk engendering a bar to reform and improvement.[26]

The critical remarks by some Russian politicians, public figures, scholars, representatives of the Russian Orthodox Church and other religious people—that human rights are becoming excessively individualistic, selfish and egoistic; that 'rights talk' is confrontational, antagonistic, allowing no room for compromise and making contextual judgments about priorities in a situation of cultural diversity; that such values as solidarity, and the importance of family and community to which more attention needs to be paid—reflect public concern about the development of human rights. And this criticism had become part of the human-rights discourse long before Russia joined the Council of Europe and ratified the Convention.[27]

This brief analysis brings me to the conclusion that there is no genuine conflict between Russia and the Council, between Russian and European values or notions of human rights. This is not the view that I see through my window. Russia is undoubtedly moving toward European standards of human-rights protection; it is trying to accommodate its legal and political systems to the requirements of the Convention. Yet, there is no doubt in my mind that there are various difficulties in the implementation process and in the slow pace of

24 Case of *Cyprus v. Turkey* (10 May 2001) No.25781/94.

25 National legal systems sometimes tend to protect their sovereignty and even attempt to limit the binding effect of the Convention and judgments of the ECtHR. For instance, Leitsätze zum Beschluss des Zweiten Senats (14 Oktober 2004), Das Bundesverfassungsgericht 2 *BvR* 1481/04 (Order of the Second Senate of the German Constitutional Court (14 October 2004)), available at <http://www.bundesverfassungsgericht.de/entscheidungen/rs20041014_2bvr148104.html?Suchbegriff=1481%2F04>. See, also, Christian Tomuschat, "The Effects of the Judgments of the European Court of Human Rights According to the German Constitutional Court", 11(5) *German Law Journal* (2010), explaining why German authorities were reluctant to abide by the judgment of the Strasbourg Court in the *GÖRGÜLÜ* case.

26 See case of *Vilho Eskelinen and Others v. Finland* (19 April 2007) No.63235/00, §56. See, also, George Letsas, *A Theory of Interpretation of the European Convention on Human Rights* (Oxford University Press, Oxford, 2007).

27 William Twinning, *General Jurisprudence, Understanding Law from a Global Perspective* (Cambridge University Press, Cambridge, 2009), 173-217.

reforms in some vital areas of human-rights protection—combined with strong social inertia.

Concluding Observations. Russia and European Human-Rights Law: Margins of the Margin of Appreciation

Lauri Mälksoo

The title of this volume suggests a focus on three different aspects of Russia's recent interaction with European human-rights law: progress, tensions, and perspectives. In conclusion, let us now look at each of these dimensions separately.

I

Perhaps the previous chapters have not emphasized strongly enough that, undoubtedly, there has been considerable progress in Russia's acceptance of, and interaction with, European human-rights law. Twenty years after the dissolution of the USSR in 1991, Russia is a very different country from what it used to be during the Soviet period—and, mostly so, in a positive sense. Its compliance with European human-rights law leaves much to be desired if we compare it with Sweden or Poland. Yet, if we compare Russia's attitude towards human-rights law with, for example, that of China, Russia's post-Soviet transformation has been spectacular. Notwithstanding all the backlashes and irritations, Russia *does* in principle accept human-rights norms on both the level of its own constitutional law and of its international legal commitments. Seen from the perspective of the Russian history of state-centrism, the Constitution of 1993 with its natural-law approach to human rights is revolutionary.[1] Moreover, also revolutionary was the 1998 decision to accede to the European Convention on Human Rights. The revolutionary nature of the latter decision lay in the fact that the Strasbourg system offered a real and working mechanism for protection of human rights that penetrated the veil of state sovereignty.

Already during the late Soviet period, Russia had become a member of a number of multilateral treaties protecting human rights. Yet these United Nations treaties—due to insufficient or absent implementation mechanisms—were unable to change things on the ground significantly. The Soviet leaders could ignore them. A faithful reading of the writings of Karl Marx supported that attitude—Marx had made ironical comments about 'so-called human rights' in a bourgeois society.[2] Soviet doctrine rejected the idea that UN human-rights treaties could have been directly applicable. State sovereignty had clear predominance over human rights.

1 Natural-law aspects in the interpretation of European human-rights law as opposed to traditional positivism are emphasized in Tatiana N. Neshataeva, *Uroki sudeb'noi praktiki o pravakh cheloveka: Evropeiskii i Rossiiskii opyt* (Gorodets, Moscow, 2007), 17-40.

2 Elena Lukasheva (ed.), *Prava cheloveka. Uchebnik* (Norma, Moscow, 2009, 2nd ed.), 249.

Lauri Mälksoo, ed.
Russia and European Human-Rights Law: The Rise of the Civilizational Argument 217-227

Thus, in practice, internationally protected human rights remained largely on the level of high-minded yet empty declarations and slogans—as far as the USSR was concerned. The Russian Federation's accession to the European Convention on Human Rights in 1998 changed that; the Convention's back-up system finally provided the necessary teeth for human-rights protection.

We will never know to what extent Russian policy-makers—in the final years of the presidency of Boris El'tsin—were able to predict what consequences accession to the ECHR would bring for Russia. Had they have been able to foretell future Strasbourg case-law concerning Russia, some decision-makers might well have been more reluctant to approve the decision to join the Strasbourg system. In a way, by signing and ratifying the ECHR, Russian policy-makers jumped in the water in a somewhat unknown place. Most likely, they dared or perhaps needed to make this decision because they realized that Russia could not do without European human-rights law in the process of modernization. The Strasbourg system of human-rights protection became a supportive pillar provided from the outside—a pillar that could be used to support the country's transition from a state-centric history to a future more focused on the individual.

As Vladislav Starzhenetskii points out in his contribution to this volume, the ECHR and Strasbourg jurisprudence have already had a positive impact on reform of Russian domestic law, for example in the field of criminal procedure. Moreover, it seems that at least judges in the highest courts of the country seem to have benefited from the existence of the ECtHR. The judiciary has historically succumbed to the will of the executive in Russia. Having the ECtHR watching over Russia's domestic legal process has been occasionally uncomfortable—for example, for the Russian Constitutional Court in the *Markin* case (now settled by the Grand Chamber in Strasbourg)—yet it has simultaneously supported those in the Russian political elite who favor 'rule of law' over the traditional authoritarian 'vertical of power'.[3]

When talking about 'progress', one inevitably needs to ask: progress toward what? Russians education in the Post-communist period usually cannot be blamed for exaggerated political naivité and blind idealism. Rather, having experienced the failure of the grandest utopian project of the twentieth century—the USSR—they are unlikely to accept new dogmas easily. Instead, many tend to cynicism toward high-minded political idea(l)s, both old and new. This inevitably also applies to ideas connected with human rights and democracy. Polls suggest that Russians are much more skeptical about democracy than respondents in the rest of Eastern Europe—in 2009, 55% of Russian respondents considered a 'strong

3 For extensive criticism by a former justice of the Russian Constitutional Court regarding Russia's history system-centrism, see, *e.g.*, Boris S. Ebzeev, *Lichnost' i gosudarstvo v Rossii: vzaimnaia otvetstvennost' i konstitutsionnye obiazannosti* (Norma, Moscow, 2008), 157ff.

hand' to be a more efficient form of government than democracy.[4] Some results of such polls are quite shocking: in 2009, a slight majority of Russians held the opinion that there was more positive than negative in Joseph Stalin's activities.[5]

At the same time, Russians are also dissatisfied with the state of their country's judiciary; most people consider it corrupt and untrustworthy.[6] It is unlikely that acceptance of Strasbourg jurisprudence is semi-automatic among the educated Russian elites. Yet it is fascinating to see that the jurisprudence of the ECtHR concerning Russia is closely followed and covered by the leading Russian daily non-tabloid newspapers, such as *Kommersant*. It is not rare that a Strasbourg judgment or contentious development concerning Russia has been presented as the main news or one of the main news items in the paper (this in addition to special collections and analyses of Strasbourg cases concerning Russia, mostly accessible to specialists).[7] This is an entirely new informational situation, and we will learn only in the future what its impact will be. What will a young law student who reads *Kommersant* think of such cases and controversies and what opinions will s/he hold in the future? It is possible that a new type of informed and critical thinking toward state power and human rights will evolve. While most people may not yet refer to 'human rights' in terms of political language, they are worried about human rights in Russia in terms of substance.

Russia's accession to the ECtHR has also had a positive impact on Russian scholarship on human-rights law. Judging based on textbooks, monographs, and journal articles, the discipline of human rights is currently quite booming in Russia.[8] Here we should not overlook the fact that the reach of the Russian

4 Il'ia Kriger, "Instituty sil'nee reform", *Novaia gazeta* (27 January 2010), available at <http://www.novayagazeta.ru/data/2010/008/13.html?print=201104050527>.

5 Viktor Khamraev, "Stalin poluchil bolshinstvo k 130-letiu", *Kommersant* (19 December 2009), available at <http://kommersant.ru/doc/1296300>.

6 For a systematic and ideological critique of the Russian court system, see Mikhail Khodorkovskii, "Rossiia v ozhidanii suda", *Kommersant Vlast'* (15 June 2009), available at <http://www.kommersant.ru/doc/1185516>.

7 See, *e.g.*, Iu. Berestenev (ed.), *Evropeiskii Sud po pravam cheloveka i Rossiiskaia Federatsiia. Postanovleniia i resheniia, vynesennye do 1 marta 2004 goda* (Norma, Moscow, 2005).

8 See, *e.g.*, A.N. Golovistikova, L.Iu. Grudtsyna, *Prava cheloveka. Uchebnik* (Eksmo, Moscow, 2006); Vladimir Kartashkin, *Prava cheloveka: mezhduarodnaia zashchita v usloviiakh globalizatsii* (Norma, Moscow, 2009); Aslan Abashidze, Ekaterina Alisievich, *Pravo Soveta Evropy. Konventsiia o zashchite prav cheloveka i osnovnykh svobod* (Mezhdunarodnye otnosheniia, Moscow, 2007); Iurii Il'in, *Pravo cheloveka i gosudarstva na bezopasnost' v sovremennom mire* (Norma, Moscow, 2007); Aleksei Stemoukhov, *Pravovaia zashchita cheloveka* (Norma, Moscow, 2006); Nataliia Kolesova, *Prava cheloveka i demograficheskie protsessy* (Norma, Moscow, 2009); A.S. Avtonomov, *Pravo cheloveka, pravozashchitnaia i pravokhranitel'naia deiatel'nost'* (Novoe Literaturnoe Obozrenie, Moscow, 2009; Revol Valeev, *Mezhdunarodnaia i vnutrigosudarstvennaia zashchita prav cheloveka* (Statut, Moscow, 2011); Feliks Rudinskii, *Nauka prav cheloveka i problemy konstitutsionnogo prava* (MIR, Moscow,

language—one of the six official languages at the United Nations—goes much further beyond the borders of the Russian Federation. Thus, some of the scholarly literature on human rights in the Russian language is also read in other parts of the former USSR—nowadays, countries belonging to the Commonwealth of Independent States—and can contribute to the emergence of new ideas there.[9]

Finally, talking about progress, leading Russian politicians and high-ranking officials have in some high-profile cases criticized the 'politicization' and anti-Russian bias of Strasbourg practice—yet, so far at least, Russia has dutifully paid compensation awarded by the ECtHR. It is true that, while Russia pays for damages, it so far does not do enough in terms of revision of domestic judgments,[10] not to speak of more ground-breaking legislative changes. In this broader sense, Russia's compliance with Strasbourg jurisprudence has been unsatisfactory. Yet again, the situation can only be judged fairly if we take into account the historical legacy. Having to do what an international body says is a new thing for Russia. Again, paying damages the way Strasbourg determined them, especially in controversial cases where the government lost the case, is better than the clear '*nyet*' that the country's representatives would have expressed in similar circumstances in the past. By comparison, the big competitor of the Cold War era—the US—does not accept the jurisdiction of the Inter-American Court of Human Rights.

Russia's ride in the European system of human-rights protection has been quite similar to a ride on a roller-coaster; perhaps the biggest achievement so far has been that the weighty passenger has not fallen out; that the country continues to hold on.

II

The main focus of this volume has been on tensions created by accession of the Russian Federation to the Strasbourg system. 'Tension' can, of course, be a vague word—and certainly it is a word that has characterized not just Russia's relationship with the ECtHR but that of a number of other countries, including Turkey, for example, and more recently, the United Kingdom as well. Yet Russia's

2006); N.A. Pridvorov, E.V. Tikhonova, *Institut svobody sovesti i svobody veroispovedaniia v prave sovremennoi Rossii* (Iurisprudentsiia, Moscow, 2007); and Valerii Zor'kin, *Konstitutsiia i prava cheloveka v XXI veke. K 15-letiu Konstitutsii Rossiiskoi Federatsii i 60-letiu Vseobshchei deklaratsii prav cheloveka* (Norma, Moscow, 2008).

9 In fact, some of the most 'pro-Western' and cutting-edge literature on human rights in the Russian language has been published outside the Russian Federation, *e.g.*, in Belarus: Nadezhda Beliakovich, *Prava cheloveka i politika. Filosofsko-pravovye osnovy* (Amalfeya, Minsk, 2009).

10 Aleksandra Samarina, "Uklonchivoe pravosudie", *Nezavisimaia gazeta* (12 October 2010), available at <http://www.ng.ru/politics/2010-10-12/1_judgement.html?insidedoc> (referring to the expert opinion of Tamara G. Morshchakova, former justice at the RF Constitutional Court).

size and history determine that the tensions that we are talking about here are relatively unique in quantity and quality. It is sufficient to take, for example, the overwhelming number of complaints arriving in Strasbourg from Russia or the nature of some of the human-rights violations—such as those related to the war in Chechnia[11]—and one understands the *sui generis* situation that the Russian Federation is currently experiencing in the Strasbourg system.

One needs to be reminded that when Russia entered the Strasbourg system, neither the Council of Europe nor Russia itself considered the country to be in compliance with Council of Europe standards relevant for accession. For a positivist lawyer, that would already count as a challenging starting point. If even, at the time of accession, the country fell short of legal and political standards, how does one treat the issue of compliance later on? The reproach "you *still* do not comply!" can be psychologically or rhetorically confronted with the attitude "we *even then* did not comply and yet you let us in; so what are you going to do now?"

When this volume goes to print, Russia will already have been a member of the Strasbourg system for sixteen years. Reading newspaper headlines and studying their background further, one gets the impression that Russia's interaction with Strasbourg has often been more similar to a duel than to a duet.

Let us look at some high-profile examples. *First*, the question of abolition of the death penalty has not found a final solution. When ratifying the ECHR in 1998, Russia also acknowledged the obligation to ratify Protocol 6 to the Convention, abolishing the death penalty as punishment. Yet Russia has not taken this final step. Boris Gryzlov, the then-speaker of the State *Duma*, explained:

> "Indeed, we have not ratified the 6th Protocol. The question will be resolved differently but it will be resolved."[12]

On some level, this statement by Mr. Gryzlov is characteristic of the current Russian attitude toward European human-rights law. It is true that, at the end of 2009, the Russian Constitutional Court established a moratorium on the death penalty and that this penalty is no longer carried out in the Russian Federation. Yet legislators have rejected formal abolition of the death penalty; it is still enshrined in the Criminal Code of the Russian Federation. In this way, Russian legislators are showing resistance to the European consensus that the death penalty is in any case an unacceptable form of punishment. A mere moratorium as opposed to abolition is conditional, can be reversed, and thus ultimately leaves the door open. According to a 2009 poll carried out by the Levada Center, 53% of Russians support the death penalty.[13] Yet such polls can come to surprisingly

11 See Emma Gilligan, *Terror in Chechnya: Russia and the Tragedy of Civilians in War* (Princeton University Press, Princeton, NJ, 2009).

12 Aleksandra Samarina, "Bor'ba za prava cheloveka do poslednego patrona", *Nezavissimaia gazeta* (24 March 2010), available at <http://www.ng.ru/politics/2010-03-24/1_kazn.html>.

13 Boris Vishnevskii, "Verkhovnyi sud ne uveren", *Novaia gazeta* (2 November 2009), available at <http://www.novayagazeta.ru/data/2009/122/12.html>.

varying results—in another 2009 poll, this time carried out by *VTSIOM*, 79% of respondents supported the death penalty for rapists of minors.[14]

Second, the very high number of complaints coming in from some new member States of the Council of Europe, in particular from the Russian Federation, triggered a reform process in the Court. In 2004, Protocol 14 was created to solve or ease at least some of these problems—yet Russia actively refused to ratify Protocol 14 until it finally did so only in January 2010. Leonid Nikitinskii, a journalist at *Novaia gazeta*, has argued that, by that time, Russian parliamentarians had understood that the ECtHR functioned differently from Russian courts: no deals can be made with judges about controversial cases.[15] During the period of non-ratification, Russia even risked being suspended from the Council of Europe. What seems noteworthy is that Russia only gave in and finally ratified Protocol 14 after the other member states of the Council of Europe mobilized themselves and were willing to bypass Russia via Protocol 14*bis*, an initiative similar in effect to Protocol 14 that would effectively have left Russia behind. Yet the fundamental procedural issues facing the ECtHR have not been solved until today; it is unlikely that they can be solved easily. In early 2012, it seems that the two most vocal criticizers of the ECtHR are Russia and Tory-led Britain. Of course, the reasons why the two countries criticize the ECtHR are quite different: one (Britain) thinks it knows better; the other (Russia) does not want to be told that it knows worse.

Third, in October 2010, an open confrontation took place between the ECtHR and the Constitutional Court of the Russian Federation. In the case of *Markin v. Russia*, Strasbourg overruled the Constitutional Court's judgment regarding discrimination based on sex in the social-security system of the Russian Army. Valerii D. Zor'kin, the head of the Constitutional Court of the Russian Federation, even did not rule out that Russia might leave the Strasbourg jurisdiction.[16] In June 2011, Grand Chamber hearings were held in the *Markin* case in Strasbourg, and some Russian politicians seized the opportunity to 'retaliate' against the ECtHR. Aleksandr Torshin, a member of the upper house of the parliament, the Federation Council, initiated a draft law that would establish the priority of Russia's Constitutional Court over the ECtHR. Russia's media had already suggested that the presidential administration probably did not support Mr. Torshin's initiative.[17] However, there may be elements of the classic

14 Viktor Khamraev, Maksim Ivanov, "Dumskoe bol'shinstvo skloniaetsia k menshemu zlu", *Kommersant* (8 December 2009), available at <http://www.kommersant.ru/doc/1288374>.

15 Leonid Nikitinskii, "Ne dlia protokola", *Novaia gazeta* (18 January 2010), available at <http://www.novayagazeta.ru/data/2010/004/11.html>.

16 Anna Pushkarskaia, "Valerii Zor'kin gotov k oborone natsional'nogo pravovogo suvereniteta", *Kommersant* (22 November 2010), available at <http://kommersant.ru/doc/1544077>.

17 Maksim Ivanov, Vladimir Solovev, Kristina Volobueva, "Aleksandr Torshin otlozhil Evrosud na osen'", *Kommersant* (18 July 2011), available at <http://www.kommersant.ru/doc/1681064>.

'good cop-bad cop' game on display here, with the purpose of putting additional pressure on the Strasbourg system. The positive moment was that segments of Russia's intellectual elite—including the Russian Association of International Law—protested against Mr. Torshin's legislative initiative. In any case, quite an amount of hostile political energy is spent on such initiatives, which are designed to resist the normalization of Russia's presence in the Strasbourg system.[18]

Fourthly, a number of contested ECtHR cases have upset Russia's political elite and made it use harsh words about the 'politicization' and 'double standards' of the ECtHR. Some of these cases have had something to do with the former territory of the USSR, the historical 'sphere of influence' in which Russia has *de facto* claimed special rights. In *Ilaşcu and Others v. Moldova and Russia*, the ECtHR considered Russia to be co-responsible for human-rights violations committed in Moldova's breakaway region of Transdnistria. The breakaway territory existed and still continues to exist thanks to Russia's military and economic aid; yet Russia has not exercised direct control over it. Russia's leaders considered the verdict that Russia was co-responsible for human-rights violations committed in Transdnistria to be the result of the Court's 'anti-Russian' bias. Another case where harsh criticism towards Strasbourg has been expressed was *Kononov v. Latvia* (2010) in which the Grand Chamber of the ECtHR upheld a Latvian court judgment convicting a Soviet partisan of war crimes committed in a Latvian village during World War II.

Some other recent cases not well received in the Russian government have concerned restrictions in Russia's political system, *e.g.*, the 2011 *Republican Party of Russia* case[19] and another 2011 case involving high treason.[20] This is not even to mention the most prolonged, emblematic and high-profile cases where Russian and European perceptions of criminal justice have clashed, *e.g.*, the Khodorkovskii criminal case and the expropriation of the Yukos company. Tensions can also be witnessed in the European Parliament (an organ of the EU, not of the Council of Europe), which has criticized the Russian government for its suppression of

18 Svetlana Sukhova, "V PASE protiv popravok Torshina", *Nezavisimaia gazeta* (24 June 2011), available at <http://www.ng.ru/world/2011-06-24/2_pase.html>.

19 Case of the *Republican Party of Russia v. Russia* (12 April 2011) No.12976/07. See, also, Maria-Luiza Tirmaste, Ol'ga Pleshanova, Seda Egikyan, Tamila Dzhodzhua (Geouga), "Evropeiskii sud vypolnil partiinoe sozdanie", *Kommersant* (13 April 2011), available at <http://www.kommersant.ru/doc-rss/1620520>.

20 Case of *Sutyagin v. Russia* (3 May 2011) No.30024/02. See, also, Iurii Senatorov, Alena Mikhlashevskaia, "Kandidat nauk zashitilsia *v.* Ervopeiskom sude", *Kommersant* (4 May 2011), available at <http://www.kommersant.ru/doc/1634540>.

freedom of assembly[21] and its handling of the case of the death of anti-corruption lawyer Sergei Magnitskii.[22]

What is the significance of these tensions? What explains them? Is it because the Russian Federation is too big a country for the Council of Europe to 'digest'? Or is it because Russia is only partially and liminally a 'European' country, whatever exactly this means nowadays? Considering the number and magnitude of 'normative skirmishes' between Moscow and Strasbourg, the word 'tension' may almost sound like an understatement. The real question is: will Russia ever truly fit in the European system of human-rights law?

This question is not alien to Russian human-rights theoreticians. In order to deal with the question, Russian scholars writing on human rights have turned to history. A number of them point out that, already in history, Russia has had a difficult relationship with ideas of liberalism.[23] Elena Andreevna Lukasheva, a leading Russian human-rights scholar and "founder of contemporary Russian theory of human rights"[24] from the Institute of State and Law of the Academy of Sciences in Moscow brings to the debate the notion of 'civilization'. She argues that, historically, Russia is an independent civilization,[25] a civilization that is different from European civilization.[26] The interesting thing is that Lukasheva does not use this as a normative apology for Russian exceptionalism but, rather, as explanation for why Russia is yet unable to match up to its human-rights commitments—both in terms of constitutional and international/European law. In terms of human-rights protection, Lukasheva does not have much good to say about the history of Russian civilization:

> "Unfortunately, the main traditions of Russian civilization that have developed throughout the centuries cannot make its people proud, first of all the anti-individualistic direction of the whole system [...]."[27]

21 Elena Chernenko, Maria-Luiza Tirmaste, "Vygovornye obiazatel'stva. Evroparlament gotovitsia priniat' rezoliutsiiu s zhestkim osuzhdeniem Rossii", *Kommersant* (17 February 2011), available at <http://www.kommersant.ru/doc/1586895>.

22 Elena Chernenko, Vladislav Trifonov, "Rossiiu osudiat po 115-i stat'e", *Kommersant* (16 February 2010), available at <http://www.kommersant.ru/doc/1558213>.

23 For a detailed history of human rights and human-rights-related ideas in Russia, see Svetlana Glushkova, *Prava cheloveka v Rossii* (Iurist, Moscow, 2006).

24 A.N. Saidov, "Tsivilizatsionnaia teoriia prav cheloveka", in A.G. Svetlanov, *Prava cheloveka i sovremennoe gosudarstvenno-pravovoe razvitie* (Institut gosudarstva i prava RAN, Moscow, 2007), 112-130, at 113. See, also, Elena Lukasheva (ed.), *Prava cheloveka i protsessy globalizatsii sovremennogo mira* (Norma, Moscow, 2007) and *id.* (ed.), *Prava cheloveka i pravovoe sotsial'noe gosudarstvo* (Norma, Moscow, 2011).

25 Lukasheva, *op.cit.* note 2, 18. See, also, *id. Chelovek, pravo, tsivilizatsii: normativno-tsennostnoe izmerenie* (Norma, Moscow, 2009), 211.

26 Lukasheva, *Chelovek, pravo, tsivilizatsii*, *ibid.*, 367.

27 *Ibid.*, 313 and 367.

Lukasheva specifies:

> "In the public consciousness, in the culture of the country—both before and after the 1917 revolution—human rights did not take any kind of important place.[...] Not even among the intelligentsia were ideas about them spread widely. [...] All the following history of the Soviet state was characterized by grave mass violations of human rights. [...] Today in Russia, there is still no full respect towards the human being and his rights. [...] Human rights have not yet occupied a worthy place in our life; their violation takes a mass character. This is determined by the bureaucratization and dehumanization of the apparatus of state servants, corruption, lack of respect for the human being, law, and legal acts that has deep roots in our history."[28]

Lukasheva continues in the same highly critical spirit:

> "Russia today is not a rule of law country because human rights and freedoms have not become the highest value. [...] Let us pause on the reasons why it has been difficult to establish a state based on rule of law in Russia. One of the main reasons is the historical traditions of Russia, which were non-compatible with democracy and freedom. [...] The regime that was established after the October revolution constituted a step back because it rejected the main democratic values—freedom, supremacy of law, human rights, *Rechtsstaat*. Authoritarianism, full leveling down of the individuality and autonomy of the human being, rejection of his right to freedom of choice and self-determination became universal norms of new life. [...] Processes that occurred after the October victory were not accidental deviations in the development of the country. They were historically determined for Russia with its collectiveness, anti-individualist ideology, blindly succumbing to power [...]."[29]

These are very harsh and self-critically honest words. It is not typical for Russian authors to argue that violations of human rights during the Soviet period *were historically determined* by certain continuities in Russian history/civilization. (The current tendency is to cut out the Soviet period mentally as an anomaly and make a link back to the Tsarist Empire's glory, achievements, and traditions.)

At the same time, while Lukasheva criticizes the anti-human-rights legacy of Russian civilization, she is still critical of the Eurocentrism of universal human-rights discourse, arguing, for instance, that the Universal Declaration of Human Rights reflects European rather than universal values.[30] It is not at all clear that Lukasheva achieves what she normatively looks for when she reaches out to the concept of 'civilization'. The problem is that usually the concept of 'civilization' is used in order to defend cultural exceptionalism, not to undermine it. For example in 2010, Nikita Mikhalkov, a leading Russian filmmaker published his *Manifest Prosveshchennogo Konservatizma* ("Manifesto of Enlightened Conservativism") in which he defended 'Orthodox' civilization and, at the same time, rejected "pseudoscientific references to universal laws of history".[31]

28 Lukasheva, *op.cit.* note 2, 18-21.

29 *Ibid.*, 205-206.

30 See Elena Lukasheva, "Prava cheloveka: konflikt kul'tur", in V.G. Grafskii (ed.), *Nash trudnyi put' k pravu. Materialy filosofsko-pravovykh chtenii pamiati akademika V.S. Nersesiantsa* (Norma, Moscow, 2006), 241-255, at 248.

31 Afanasii Sborov, "Pridvornaia propoved'", *Kommersant Vlast'* (1 November 2010), available

Some of the Russian scholarly literature on human rights, indeed, gives the impression that Russia operates as an autonomous civilization where the leading figures prefer to stay only partially integrated with, and dependent on, the rest of the world. For example, a recent (otherwise very erudite) monograph by a former justice of the Russian Constitutional Court, Nikolai V. Vitruk, on legal theory and human rights, contains many interesting references to other authors but no references whatsoever (except to Marx and Engels, translated into Russian) to non-Russian authors.[32] The book is dialogical only with respect to other authors who have written in the Russian language. This kind of egocentrism is characteristic of autonomous civilizations.

In reality, today's European system of human-rights protection is a 'melting pot' of different legal cultures and, as has been suggested by Elena Lukasheva—perhaps even civilizations. It is natural that differences create tensions. One technique for dealing with differences within the European system of human-rights protection has been the use of the margin-of-appreciation doctrine. As a (former) Great Power, newcomer to the Strasbourg system and a country historically apart from the West, Russia could be a logical candidate for the application of this doctrine. Yet the ECtHR has been quite reluctant to apply the margin-of-appreciation doctrine *vis-à-vis* Russia (except, perhaps, in the Yukos case—although this was, of course, not expressed explicitly). Perhaps the margins of the margin-of-appreciation doctrine in Strasbourg are determined by the necessity not to undermine the system as such—which would happen if the understanding emerged that Strasbourg was not bold and 'tough' on a country such as Russia.

It is important to make sure that tensions created by different legal practices should not break the European system of human-rights protection. Many hold it essential that major countries—such as Russia, with unique traditions, perhaps even constituting a unique Eurasian civilization—should stay in the system. Yet, they should not stay in at the cost of breaking the system from within.

III

What prospects does Russia's interaction with Strasbourg have when we consider the existing tensions outlined above?

European human-rights law is a striking example of regional international law. How far this regional international law reaches, geographically and mentally, is important. The question of whether such unique countries as Russia and Turkey constitute part of Europe is already historically a contested one; today, both are members of the Council of Europe's system of human-rights protection. When the Russian Federation ratified the ECHR in 1998, optimists wanted to believe

at <http://www.kommersant.ru/doc/1530192>. The Manifesto is available in Russiain on the *Ekho Moskvy* website at <http://www.echo.msk.ru/blog/echomsk/721541-echo/>.

32 Nikolai Vitruk, *Obshchaia teoriia pravovogo polozheniia lichnosti* (Norma, Moscow, 2008).

that this would slowly but surely enable the resocializing of Russia in Europe's individualist value system. In practice, socialization and dialogic relationships can go both ways. Russia's resistance to some elements of the Strasbourg system can create additional difficulties within the system and put strains on it.[33] In the worst case, 'fighting the system from within' can paralyze and demoralize the system or even bring it to collapse. There is the saying that the strength of a chain is determined by the strength of its weakest link. If much of the energy in the Council of Europe is spent on keeping the weakest member(s) in line, this may lower the overall orientation to 'progressiveness' in the system. Some of the strongest members—countries historically strong in terms of the judiciary and protection of human rights—may distance themselves from a system that is mostly preoccupied with weaker members that are, in their turn, preoccupied with resisting the system or its outcomes.

Russia's membership in the ECtHR may be a model for other international legal regimes where Russia is still seeking membership. In December 2011, it was announced that, in 2012, Russia would become a member of the World Trade Organization. Although, of course, while the field of regulation of the WTO differs from the European human-rights regime, some lessons can be learned from Russia's membership in the Council of Europe. For example, when diplomats are unable to regulate a contested issue before the country's accession, it will be much harder to regulate it after the country has already become a member in the system. Moreover, different traditions of rule of law and different philosophical approaches to the question of what is legal and what is political will create additional frictions in the legal regime. This is not to say that the task is impossible; the role of international law in a time of globalization may well be to help bridge the gaps of differences between different legitimate interests, traditions, and actors. It is widely accepted that international law should no longer be imposed from above (from the civilized to the uncivilized; from the stronger to the weaker) but, instead, should be a result of compromises by all participants.

The tense relationship between the European system of human-rights protection and the Russian Federation, its biggest member, is a story to be continued. It is, on the one hand, an example of the enormous success of a regime set up by regional international law; on the other hand, it is an example that extending regional human-rights regimes to new horizons is a challenging historical task.

33 Anna Pushkarskaia and Ol'ga Pleshanova, "Evropa ustala ot Rossiiskikh del. Dmitriu Medvedevu rekomendovano reformirovat' sudebnuiu sistemu", *Kommersant* (21 May 2011), available at <http://www.kommersant.ru/doc/1645305>.

List of Contributors

Dara Hallinan is a researcher at Fraunhofer ISI, working in the ICT research group in the Emerging Technologies Department. His work at Fraunhofer focuses on understanding the legal and social significance of Information and Communication Technologies, in particular surveillance and security technologies. He has worked predominantly on the FP 7 project SAPIENT (PrIvacy and Ethics in surveillaNce Technologies), but has also contributed to a number of other FP7 projects including PRESCIENT (Privacy and Emerging Sciences and Technologies) and IRISS (Increasing Resilience in Surveillance Societies). He holds a batchelor's degree in law from the University of Birmingham and a Master's in Human Rights and Democratisation from the European Inter-University Centre in Venice. He is currently working towards his doctorate at the Vrije Universiteit Brussel on the regulation of genetic data in research biobanking. He is on the programming committee of the annual Computers Privacy and Data Protection conference.

He has had a long-running fascination with Russia, which culminated in his move to the Siberian city of Novosibirsk, where he lived for over a year in 2008-2009. This experience immersed him in Russian society and gave him an extended and in-depth understanding of the reality of life in Russia and Russian culture. The experience also opened his eyes to the complexity of the relationship between Russia and Europe and to the difference between Russian and European conceptions of social organization and law.

Lauri Mälksoo was educated at the University of Tartu in Estonia (LL.B. in 1998) and received an LL.M. at Georgetown University Law Center in Washington, DC (1999) and a PhD at Humboldt University Berlin (2002). Before his appointment as Professor of International Law at the University of Tartu Faculty of Law in 2009, he was a post-doc research fellow at New York University School of Law (2004-2005) and Tokyo University (2006-2007). He also was Emile Noël Fellow at NYU School of Law during the academic year 2013-2014. Professor Mälksoo was the founding director of the University of Tartu's Institute of Constitutional and International Law and currently is director of the Estonian Foreign Policy Institute, a think tank in Tallinn. In 2013, he was elected member of the Estonian Academy of Sciences. In 2009, he was awarded a five-year grant from the European Commission's European Research Council (Brussels) to study the contemporary Russian understanding of public international law and human-rights law. He is a member of the executive board of the European Society of International Law and was the main organizer of the Society's 2011 research forum held in Tallinn. He is also a member of the Council of the Centre for EU-Russia Studies (CEURUS) at the University of Tartu, an interdisciplinary center. A list of his recent publications—a number of them on Russian approaches to international law—can be found in the database <www.etis.ee>.

Lauri Mälksoo, ed.
Russia and European Human-Rights Law: The Rise of the Civilizational Argument 229-231

Angelika Nussberger graduated with a degree in Slavonics (1987) and in Law (1989) from the University of Munich. Her first state exam in law (*Staatsexamen*) was in Munich (1989); the second one in Heidelberg (1993); in that same year, she was awarded a doctorate degree by the University of Würzburg. Her doctoral dissertation was devoted to Soviet constitutional law during the transition period and her *Habilitation* to public international law (2002).

She was elected by the Council of Europe's Parliamentary Assembly as the judge from the Federal Republic of Germany to the European Court of Human Rights (in office since 1 January 2011) and she is also Professor of Law at the University of Cologne in Germany.

Since 2002, Judge Nussberger has been director of the Institute of East European Law (*Institut für Ostrecht der Universität zu Köln*) (currently on leave). The Institute was founded in 1964 by the late Boris Meissner, who was a graduate of the University of Tartu before it was Sovietized.

Judge Nussberger is a specialist in international human-rights law, Eastern European, particularly Russian, constitutional law and has authored a number of academic and popular publications on Russian law and government. A list of her publications can be found at <http://www.ostrecht.uni-koeln.de/fileadmin/dateien/institut/leitung/Veroeffentlichungen_Stand_August_2011.pdf>. She has also been a member of the International Labour Organisation's Committee of Experts on the Application of Conventions and Recommendations (2004-2010), a deputy-member of the Council of Europe's Venice Commission (2006-2010), Pro-rector of the University of Cologne and is the recipient of an honorary doctorate from Tbilisi State University (2010).

Petr Preclik graduated from Masaryk University in Brno (Czech Republic, 2010) and the European Inter-University Centre for Human Rights and Democratisation in Venice (Italy, 2008). In 2009, he was awarded an EU-UN fellowship and worked as a human-rights advisor with the Permanent Mission of the Czech Republic in Geneva and the Delegation of the European Union in New York. During the period 2010-2013, he was deployed as election observer throughout Africa, Caucasus, and Eastern Europe. Currently, Mr. Preclik serves in the foreign service of the Czech Republic. Throughout his research, Mr. Preclik has focused on the roles played by powerful states within international regimes—especially in those reinforced by judicial mechanisms. The main question remains whether strict judicialized regimes, indeed, possess the power to influence the behavior of their members. The Russian Federation, in this sense, represents the strongest border case in studying such impact.

Dorothea Schönfeld has an academic background in Philosophy, History and Theology. As Research Assistant at Ludwig-Maximilians-University in Munich (Germany), she pursued all-encompassing studies on inter-subjectivity and ethics. Later, she concentrated on the issue of human rights within the framework of the European Master's Programme in Human Rights and Democratisation in Venice (Italy) and Tartu (Estonia) in 2007-2008. Her preoccupation with the state of human rights in Russia prompted her to combine her interest in historical influences and philosophical preconditions, on the one hand, and in current political debates on the other hand. A research trip to St. Petersburg and Moscow provided an excellent opportunity to come into close contact with Russian NGOs and journalists' trade unions and to empathize with their difficult political situation. Her commitment to human rights is reflected in her professional activities for diverse human-rights organizations such as Index on Censorship and the International Rehabilitation Council for Torture Victims. Currently, she is employed as an Advocacy Officer with *Kindernothilfe*, a German child-rights organization running projects in 29 countries worldwide.

Vladislav V. Starzhenetskii graduated in 2000 from the Moscow Institute of International Relations (Russia) and specializes in International Law, Human Rights and Intellectual Property Law. In 2003, he received his PhD for his dissertation dedicated to comparative analyses of property-rights concepts under the ECHR and Russian law, which resulted in the publication of *Rossiia i Sovet Evropy. Pravo Sobstvennosti* (Gorodets, Moscow, 2004). He has also been a visiting scholar at Harvard University (2005). At present, Dr. Starzhenetskii lectures on International Law and the European Convention of Human Rights at the Russian *Akademiia Pravosudiia* (Academy of Justice) in Moscow. Furthermore, he is head of the Directorate of International Law and Cooperation of the Russian Federation's Higher Arbitrazh Court and has been with the Court since 1998; this has afforded him a fine opportunity to trace the evolution of the Russian legal and judicial systems.

Dr. Starzhenetskii has authored a number of articles that have appeared in leading Russian law journals dedicated to implementing ECHR standards in the Russian legal system, including "Mezhdunarodnye sudi i transformatsiia natsional'nikh pravovykh system", *Mezhdunarodnoe pravosudie* (2013) No.3, "Neispolnenie sudebnykh aktov. Narushenie Rossiei svoikh mezhdunarodnykh obiazatel'stv", *Vestnik Vysshego Arbitrazhnogo Suda Rossiiskoi Federatsii* (2006) No.1 and "Ogranichenie svobody vyrazheniia mneniia v interesakh pravosudiia: usloviia i predely", in the monograph edited by Professor T.N. Neshataeva, *Modernizatsiia statusa sud'i: sovremennye mezhdunarodnye podkhody* (Norma, Moscow, 2011).

Index

V

W

www.ingramcontent.com/pod-product-compliance
Lightning Source LLC
LaVergne TN
LVHW020635300926
849161LV00004B/716